Seeking God in Science

Seeking God in Science

An Atheist Defends Intelligent Design

Bradley Monton

broadview press

LIBRARY AND ARCHIVES CANADA CATALOGUING IN PUBLICATION

Monton, Bradley John, 1972-
     Seeking God in science : an athiest defends intelligent
design / Bradley Monton.

Includes bibliographical references and index.
ISBN 978-1-55111-863-5

1. Intelligent design (Teleology). 2. Religion and science. I. Title.

BL262.M65 2009   231.7'652   C2009-901799-7

BROADVIEW PRESS is an independent, international publishing house, incorporated in 1985. Broadview believes in shared ownership, both with its employees and with the general public; since the year 2000 Broadview shares have traded publicly on the Toronto Venture Exchange under the symbol BDP.

We welcome comments and suggestions regarding any aspect of our publications—please feel free to contact us at the addresses below or at
broadview@broadviewpress.com / www.broadviewpress.com.

NORTH AMERICA
Post Office Box 1243,
Peterborough, Ontario,
Canada K9J 7H5

2215 Kenmore Ave.,
Buffalo, New York, USA 14207
TEL: (705) 743-8990
FAX: (705) 743-8353

customerservice@broadviewpress.com

UK, IRELAND, & CONTINENTAL EUROPE
NBN International, Estover Road, Plymouth, UK
PL6 7PY
TEL: 44 (0) 1752 202300
FAX: 44 (0) 1752 202330
enquiries@nbninternational.com

AUSTRALIA & NEW ZEALAND
NewSouth Books
c/o TL Distribution
15-23 Helles Avenue, Moorebank, NSW, 2170
TEL: (02) 8778 9999
FAX: (02) 8778 9944
orders@tldistribution.com.au

Edited by John W. Burbidge

Designed and typeset by Em Dash Design

 This book is printed on paper
containing 100% post-consumer fibre.

Printed in Canada

TABLE OF CONTENTS

PREFACE

This book is not providing a full-fledged endorsement of intelligent design. But intelligent design needs to be taken more seriously than a lot of its opponents are willing to. Thoughtful people perceive the world as an amazing and mysterious place, and this has led to two sorts of reactions. One is to postulate that this world is the product of an all-powerful being, while the other is to investigate the details of how the world works, to dispel mystery with scientific understanding. While these two reactions are sometimes presented as divergent, they need not be. In principle, while investigating the details of how the world works, we could find evidence for the existence of its creator.

While the intelligent design proponents typically don't put it quite that way, that's how I understand their ultimate motivation: to find scientific evidence for the existence of God. This is a worthwhile project, not to be dismissed out of hand. Ultimately, I don't think very much evidence is there, but that conclusion can only be reached after careful evaluation of the arguments, evaluation of the sort I engage in in Chapter 3. This, by the way, is why I'm an atheist—I just don't see very much evidence for the existence of God, and I'm not going to believe that God exists in the absence of good evidence.

Philosophers are trained to be dispassionate evaluators of arguments, so it's especially unfortunate that so many of the objections that so many philosophers give against intelligent design arguments are unfair, emotionally driven, or not that well thought out. My goal is to do my best to look at matters more objectively. Ultimately, I hold that the intelligent design arguments do not provide that much evidence for the existence of God (or similar designer), but the arguments do have *some* force—they make me less certain of my atheism than I would be had I not heard the arguments. One can be an atheist without being *certain* that there is no God—just as one can be a theist (like Mother Teresa) while nevertheless harboring doubts.[1]

There are some people who aren't even willing to take seriously the arguments that science provides evidence for the existence of God, because they hold that, in principle, science can't consider supernatural hypotheses. I'll consider arguments for the position that intelligent design is not science in Chapter 2. One set of arguments I'll take issue with are the arguments given by Judge Jones in the famous 2005 Dover, Pennsylvania case, where Jones ruled that intelligent design is religion, not science, and hence can't be brought up in public school science classes.

But before doing that, one may already be wondering: what exactly is the doctrine of intelligent design, anyway? This question doesn't have an obvious answer, but I'll do my best to answer it in Chapter 1. One key issue I'll take up here is whether the doctrine of intelligent design is inherently theistic—I'll argue that it's not.

Chapter 3, the core chapter of this book, is the chapter where I consider what I take to be the ultimate motivation of intelligent design proponents: to find scientific evidence for the existence of God. Nevertheless, some commentators hold that that's not the ultimate motivation; some hold that the real goal of intelligent design proponents is to get religion taught in public school science classes. With some hesitation, I take up the issue of whether intelligent design should be taught in school in the final chapter, Chapter 4. The issue of what children should be taught raises quite different issues from the core philosophical issues I've discussed in the other chapters. Nevertheless, much of the intelligent design debate is related, either explicitly or implicitly, to the pedagogical debate. Given that that's the case, it does not seem imprudent for me to weigh in, given that I think I have something insightful to say.

In getting to the stage where I could write this book, I've been helped by numerous people, too numerous to list here. My interest in intelligent design emerged out of my years of work in philosophy of physics and probability theory. For example, the fine-tuning argument, which I'll discuss in Chapter 3, is a probabilistic physics-based argument for the existence of God. Many of those who have supported me in my work in philosophy of physics and probability theory probably won't be happy with the uses to which I've put that work here, and this includes my graduate advisor and friend Bas van Fraassen, who has a very different attitude toward the science/religion debates than I do (a difference far more fundamental than the fact that he's a theist and I'm an atheist). Nevertheless I thank Bas and all the others who have contributed to my intellectual development.

The people who have especially helped with this book include David Boonin, Branden Fitelson, Sandy Goldberg, Alan Hájek, Dien Ho, Brian Kierland, Jon Kvanvig, Jay Lynch, Chad Mohler, Wes Morriston, Al Plantinga, Dan Singleton, Katie Spence, Melissa Thompson, and Mike Zerella. I especially thank David

Boonin, Al Plantinga, and Mike Zerella for giving me detailed comments on the whole manuscript.

Also, for more helpful feedback, I thank audiences at Baylor University, University of Colorado at Boulder, Florida Institute of Technology, University of Maryland at College Park, University of Missouri at Columbia, University of Notre Dame, University of Toledo, a Society of Christian Philosophers conference at Asbury College, and a Society of Christian Philosophers conference at Cumberland College.

I've been told that the battle over intelligent design is like a war between two camps, but one of the purposes of my book is to transcend that. For some, this is unacceptable. For example, a prominent intelligent design opponent to whom I sent an early draft of this book responded as follows:

> Unfortunately in this debate a position between two sides, which you seem to adopt, is hardly tenable. It is a cultural war whose outcome will have immense consequences, so a book, to be useful, must unequivocally take a side and defend it vigorously. A position of supposed impartiality (which is hardly possible) necessarily serves one side despite the author's intention to remain unbiased.

But my goal isn't to serve one side or the other side, and in fact my goal isn't even to be useful. My goal is simply to evaluate the arguments on both sides as carefully and objectively as I can. If this ends up serving one side more than the other, I don't care; my goal is to do the best I can to get at the truth. (Moreover, I think part of the truth is that it's overly simplistic to think that there are just two sides to the intelligent design debate; there are many different positions that one can take, and I'm taking one position out of the many.)

When I think about what's influenced me to take a fair-minded, even if unpopular, approach to these questions, an early source has to be the positive influence of my mother, Celia Monton, who unfortunately passed away a few years ago. She wouldn't want me to unequivocally take one side in a culture war and defend it vigorously, come what may; she taught me to do my best to be fair-minded and sympathetic, and to do my best to understand where other people are coming from. For that reason and so many more, this book is dedicated to her.

Finally, I'm required to provide this information and disclaimer. This material is based upon work supported by the National Science Foundation under Grant No. 0346934. Any opinions, findings, and conclusions or recommendations expressed in this material are those of the author and do not necessarily reflect the views of the National Science Foundation.

CHAPTER 1

What Is Intelligent Design,
and Why Might
an Atheist Believe in It?

The End of Secular Society?

In atheist circles, intelligent design is typically associated with evangelical Christians who want to get religion taught in public school science classrooms. American courts ruled that creationism was fundamentally religious, and hence that teaching it in public school science classrooms violated the separation of church and state. The solution, as typically portrayed in atheist circles, was for creationists to hide the religious elements of their doctrine by talking about "intelligent design" instead of "creationism." Proponents of intelligent design just say that there's a designer, but they don't say that that designer is God. Many atheists think this is nefarious. As prominent intelligent design (ID) critic Barbara Forrest writes:

> the ID movement is the most recent version of American creationism. In
> promoting "intelligent design theory"—a term that is essentially code for the
> religious belief in a supernatural creator—as a purported scientific alternative
> to evolutionary theory, the ID movement continues the decades-long attempt
> by creationists either to minimize the teaching of evolution or to gain equal
> time for yet another form of creationism in American public schools.[2]

So the intelligent design proponents, according to people like Forrest, want to get creationism in the public schools, but that's not all:

ID creationists continue their campaign to de-secularize public education and, ultimately, American culture and government, thereby undermining foundational elements of secular, constitutional democracy.[3]

Well, I like secular, constitutional democracy as much as the next atheist. If the intelligent design proponents want to get rid of it, then I disagree with them. But is Forrest right? Do the intelligent design proponents want to get rid of secular, constitutional democracy? And if so, does this mean that we should reject intelligent design?

My personal opinion is that Forrest is making this into too much of a culture war. The evidence that people like Forrest cite for their claim that intelligent design proponents want to destroy secular democracy is, in my opinion, tenuous.[4] Moreover, the leading intelligent design think tank, the Discovery Institute, says that

As a matter of public policy, the Discovery Institute *opposes* any effort to require the teaching of intelligent design by school districts or state boards of education.[5]

Moreover, they explicitly say that the Discovery Institute "does not support theocracy."[6] Of course, Forrest would say that they're hiding their true cultural agenda.

One of the ideas that motivates this book is that, for the purposes of evaluating the doctrine of intelligent design, the cultural agenda of intelligent design proponents doesn't matter. Even if all intelligent design proponents are fighting a culture war against secular society, it doesn't at all follow that we should reject intelligent design, when intelligent design is understood as (roughly) the claim that we can find scientific evidence for the existence of a cosmic designer. Instead, we need to look at intelligent design on its merits. And even though I'm an atheist, I think that some arguments for intelligent design are worth taking seriously.

Bad People vs. Bad Arguments

Imagine two meteorologists looking at the weather data and having a disagreement about how to interpret that data. Alice says that the data suggests that it is probably not going to rain tomorrow, while Bob says that the data suggests that it is probably going to rain tomorrow. Looking in on this situation, and not having more evidence beyond what we've seen, we (not being expert meteorologists) might decide to be agnostic about whether it's going to rain tomorrow—after all, these two seemingly equally competent meteorologists disagree.

But now suppose we learn that Bob is a hard-core theist, and that Bob wants to de-secularize American culture, and American culture will get de-secularized much more quickly if it rains tomorrow. (For example, the rain could cause a levee to break, and that could lead to a flood which would wipe out a convention of all the prominent atheists in American society.) Should this lead us to think that Alice is more likely to be right? Should this lead us to think that it's probably not going to rain tomorrow?

My response is that we shouldn't discount Bob's opinion that it's probably going to rain just because he wants it to rain tomorrow. Bob is giving reasons based on the data for thinking that it's probably going to rain tomorrow, and his interpretation of the data could very well be correct, just as Alice's interpretation of the data could very well be wrong. We shouldn't reject Bob's interpretation of the data, just because we know that he wants his interpretation to be correct.

Of course, we might wonder: is this wishful thinking on the part of Bob, for him to think it's going to rain tomorrow? It would be perfectly reasonable for us to evaluate whether his desire for rain is coloring his interpretation of the data. But note that it is perfectly reasonable for us to do that for Alice too—she, being a nice person, doesn't want the atheists to be killed, so she doesn't want it to rain tomorrow. Her desire for clear skies might also be coloring her interpretation of the data.

Hopefully you see how this carries over to the intelligent design discussion. Let's suppose that Forrest is right, and proponents of intelligent design want to de-secularize American culture. In fact, let's suppose that Forrest is right about the ethical consequences of this; let's suppose that the proponents of intelligent design are bad people. But it doesn't at all follow that they're giving bad arguments. *Bad people are capable of giving good arguments.* I know some atheists with whom, to put it mildly, I wouldn't want to be friends. These atheists are bad people. Nevertheless, I endorse many of the arguments that they give for atheism. Similarly, if Forrest is right, the proponents of intelligent design are bad people too. But it doesn't follow that they're giving bad arguments for intelligent design.

Just as bad people are capable of giving good arguments, so good people are capable of giving bad arguments. For example, I agree with Forrest that American society shouldn't be de-secularized. For all I know, she's a wonderful person overall. But I think that her arguments against intelligent design are misguided. She focuses too much on attacking the proponents of intelligent design for the supposed cultural beliefs they have, instead of attacking the arguments for intelligent design that the proponents of intelligent design give.

In sum: if you want to know whether intelligent design is true or not, you have to look at the strengths of the arguments for and against intelligent design. Whether the people who happen to be giving the arguments are good people or bad people is irrelevant.[7]

SEEKING GOD IN SCIENCE

If you have trouble with this, imagine that the bad people who are giving the arguments in question suddenly all die out, and then some good people start promoting the same arguments. Would your evaluation of the arguments themselves change? It shouldn't—the arguments are what they are, regardless of who is promulgating them. Intelligent design is either true or false, regardless of whether the proponents of intelligent design are rabid proponents of theocracy in America, or the kindest most considerate freedom-loving people you've ever met. Similarly atheists who argue against the doctrine of intelligent design are either right or not, regardless of whether the proponents of such arguments are vitriolically fighting Potemkin culture wars, or defending American freedom from the darkness of theocracy, or ignoring cultural issues altogether.

For the purposes of the book, I'm happy to assume that the proponents of intelligent design are bad people and the opponents are good people, but I'm also happy to assume that the proponents of intelligent design are good people and the opponents are bad people. It doesn't matter—what matters are the strengths of the arguments for and against intelligent design, and that's independent of who is putting forth the arguments.

Here's a different way of putting my point. I would take issue with what prominent intelligent design opponent Eugenie Scott says here:

> "Intelligent design" has both a scientific/scholarly focus and a "cultural renewal" focus—viewed by both its proponents and its critics as complementary.[8]

While some intelligent design proponents may have linked together their cultural ideas and their scientific ideas, this is not a link that all intelligent design proponents would endorse nowadays—and even if they did, the ideas can conceptually be separated. For the purposes of this book, I am setting aside the "cultural renewal" focus of intelligent design (to the extent that there is one), and I'm just focusing on the scientific/scholarly side.

The Public Schools Issue

Much of the controversy surrounding intelligent design relates to what should get taught in American public schools. We can count on Forrest to make this explicit:

> In promoting "intelligent design theory" … the ID movement continues the decades-long attempt by creationists either to minimize the teaching of evolution or to gain equal time for yet another form of creationism in American public schools.

It is probably true that the people who believe intelligent design theory are more likely to think that it should be taught in public school than those people who don't believe intelligent design theory. But I want to make clear that one could be a proponent of intelligent design, and yet think that it should *not* be taught in public schools. It would be perfectly reasonable for someone to be a proponent of intelligent design, to think that intelligent design is a fundamentally religious doctrine, and to think that religious doctrines shouldn't be taught in public schools. There may also be more pragmatic reasons intelligent design proponents could think that intelligent design shouldn't be taught in public school. They could think that intelligent design is too difficult for youngsters to understand, or they could think that teaching intelligent design in public school would create a cultural backlash that would lead people to unreasonably reject intelligent design, or they could think that most teachers don't understand intelligent design and hence would do a bad job teaching it, or so on.

Even if the intelligent design movement is now focused on getting intelligent design taught in public schools, this isn't an essential component of the intelligent design movement. It could well turn out that, in the future, the new generation of intelligent design proponents will just focus on getting intelligent design taught to home-schooled children, or in private schools, or in universities, or what have you. Or, it could turn out that, in the future, the new generation of intelligent design proponents will just focus on arguing for the truth of intelligent design, without worrying about whether it gets taught in public schools.

What I want to do for most of this book is to set aside the issue of what should be taught in our public schools, and just focus on the issue of whether intelligent design is plausible. I will take up the public schools issue in the last chapter. As we'll see there, the issue of whether intelligent design should be taught in our public schools depends in part on whether intelligent design is true, but it depends in part on various other public policy issues, such as what the aim of a public education should be, and on how science can most effectively be taught to children. I'll argue that, even if intelligent design is false, it would be reasonable for it to be discussed and evaluated in public school science classes, as long as that discussion and evaluation happens in a non-proselytizing way.

What is Intelligent Design, Anyway?

The term "intelligent design" means different things to different people; there's no univocally agreed-upon account of what the doctrine of intelligent design actually is. There's nothing wrong with this; this is how terminology often works in our language. It would be a bit silly to argue that there is a single correct definition of "intelligent design"—who would have the authority to determine what that definition is? (You might say: the person who first coined the term has that authority. But, until recently, I didn't know who first coined the term, or what definition that person gave. Does this mean that, until recently, I couldn't talk about the doctrine of intelligent design?)

In fact, there are a cluster of ideas associated with the term "intelligent design," and there's pretty broad agreement—amongst intelligent design proponents, at least—about what those ideas are. Intelligent design opponents sometimes try to say that intelligent design is no different from creationism, but intelligent design proponents resist that. I think that it's legitimate for the intelligent design proponents to resist that—after all, they should be allowed to specify what doctrine it is that they're endorsing. (I'll discuss this in more detail in the next section.)

Whether I, as an atheist, actually want to endorse intelligent design depends on what exactly the doctrine of intelligent design is taken to be. There are some statements of the intelligent design doctrine which I think are true, and other statements of the intelligent design doctrine which I think are false. Examining these various doctrines will allow me to lay out to what extent I defend intelligent design. (Even for those intelligent design doctrines I think are false, I still want to offer a partial defense: I'll argue through the course of this book that the doctrines are scientific, they're worth taking seriously, and it's legitimate to consider them in public school.)

Let's start with the definition of intelligent design as given by the leading think tank associated with the intelligent design movement, the Discovery Institute:

> The theory of intelligent design holds that certain features of the universe and
> of living things are best explained by an intelligent cause, not an undirected
> process such as natural selection.[9]

Well, if this is really the statement of intelligent design, then I endorse it—and other atheists should too. There *are* certain features of living things that are best explained by an intelligent cause. For example, professional rock climber Sarah Watson's muscular arms are not best explained by an undirected process—they're best explained by her intelligent conscious choice to do lots of training and climbing. Similarly, there are certain features of the universe that are best explained by an intelligent cause. It's a feature of the universe that it contains the Petronas Towers in Kuala Lumpur. The existence of the Petronas Towers is not best explained by an undirected process; it's best explained by the intelligent purposeful activity of designing agents—the humans who built the towers.

Of course, the proponents of intelligent design are presumably trying to make a stronger claim than the one I'm wholeheartedly endorsing. But it's not trivial to figure out exactly what that claim is—I'm going to spend the rest of this chapter trying to work this out.

The rest of this chapter may sometimes look like just a terminological debate, but it's really not. The extant statements of intelligent design are defective, in the sense that they don't adequately capture what proponents of intelligent design are trying to endorse. So I'm not engaging in a debate about exactly how much should be built into the doctrine of intelligent design; I'm trying to figure how to formulate the doctrine of intelligent design so that I can more accurately represent what ID proponents are trying to say.

In doing so, I'll be talking a lot about what intelligent design proponents "should" or "could" say. A prominent intelligent design opponent who read this part of my manuscript was unhappy with this approach, saying that I was "remarkably unconcerned about the actual views and actions of the real group that he claims to be defending," and that my arguments "about what a hypothetical ID proponent 'could' believe or what they 'should' believe [pay] little regard to what they actually believe and advocate." But that is part of the whole point of this book. Intelligent design proponents have sometimes done a bad job promulgating their view, so I'm going to spell out how they can do it better. There's little point for intelligent design opponents to spend their time criticizing problematic statements of intelligent design, or weak arguments for intelligent design, if there are better statements and stronger arguments waiting in the wings. On the flip side, intelligent design opponents have sometimes given questionable arguments against intelligent design, and part of the point of this book is to make clear where their arguments should be focused. By elevating both sides of the debate, I'm fulfilling my ultimate goal, which is to promote the cause of reason.

So, intelligent design proponents have done a bad job of stating the doctrine of intelligent design. What should the doctrine of intelligent design be, ideally? To make the discussion simpler, let's separate the discussion about features of the universe from the discussion about features of living things, and let's start by talking about features of the universe.

What is Intelligent Design? Part I—Features of the Universe

There are some features of the universe that we all agree are a result of purposeful action by an intelligent agent, not an undirected process: it's a feature of the universe that it contains skyscrapers; it's a feature of the universe that it contains squirrel nests; it's a feature of the universe that it contains beehives.[10] These features of the universe indisputably exist as a result of an intelligent cause, even if that intelligent cause only came into existence as a result of an undirected process such as natural selection.

Why don't the intelligent design proponents simply state that the features of the universe they're talking about aren't features of the universe created by the Earthbound agents we're familiar with, but instead are created by God? They don't do this because one of the motivating ideas behind the intelligent design movement is that the proponents don't want their doctrine to be inherently theistic; they want their doctrine to be able to be true in non-supernatural ways. (This is part of how they want to achieve scientific legitimacy for intelligent design, as I'll discuss in more detail in Chapter 2.)

So the intelligent design proponents would want to make the intelligent design thesis stronger, so that they can rule out Sarah Watson's muscular arms and the Petronas Towers from providing evidence for their thesis, but they wouldn't want to make it so strong that they specify that the designer in question is God. How should they do this?

Maybe the intelligent design proponents should specify that they're not talking about features of the universe that are produced by intelligent activity of the sort of agents we're familiar with on Earth. They could then say:

> The theory of intelligent design holds that certain features of the universe are best explained by an intelligent cause, *where this intelligent cause is something other than the intelligent causes produced by the agents we're familiar with on Earth*.

This doctrine is stronger than the one we started with, but it's still too weak to capture what the intelligent design proponents are trying to claim. Suppose that there exists some alien civilization in a distant galaxy, with agents very different from the agents we're familiar with on earth. These alien agents could intelligently cause their versions of skyscrapers to exist, and hence the best explanation of the fact that the universe has these skyscrapers would be the intelligent causes produced by these alien agents. We wouldn't want the definition of intelligent design to be such that the doctrine comes out true simply because there exists an alien civilization that has created alien skyscrapers.

So that modification to the definition of intelligent design doesn't work so well. Let's consider a different modification. We can motivate this modification by pointing out that there is perhaps a similarity between life on Earth and any forms of alien life that exist. If atheism is true, then we would expect that all these forms of life arose via an undirected process such as natural selection. So perhaps, to properly formulate the doctrine of intelligent design, we simply need to make the claim that there exist features of the universe that result from an intelligent cause, but not the sort of intelligent cause that came to exist via an undirected process such as natural selection. Here's how that version would go:

> The theory of intelligent design holds that certain features of the universe are best explained by an intelligent cause, *where this intelligent cause did not come to exist via an undirected process such as natural selection*.

This is certainly more promising in its attempt to capture what intelligent design proponents are really trying to get at. In fact, maybe this is what they're trying to get at, but I'm not inclined to think so. The reason I'm inclined not to think so is that there's a somewhat unexpected way in which this doctrine could come out true, and I don't think intelligent design proponents would celebrate the truth of intelligent design if this doctrine came out true in that unexpected way.

The scenario I'm about to describe is not a scenario I believe, nor is it even a scenario I find at all plausible. But that doesn't matter—the scenario makes sense, it isn't self-contradictory, and (as far as I can tell) it's not completely impossible that this is a way our universe could be.

Imagine that the universe has been in existence forever, and moreover imagine that there are beings a lot like us who have been in existence forever. (You could imagine that the individual beings don't die, or you could imagine that they undergo the birth-death cycle like we do, but the species has always been in existence.) These beings did not come to exist via an undirected process like natural selection—they've been in existence forever. Moreover, these beings cause certain things to exist (just like we do), and hence they cause certain features of the universe to be what they are. It follows that, if such beings exist, the doctrine of intelligent design as stated just above is true: there are certain features of the universe that are best explained by an intelligent cause, where this intelligent cause did not come to exist via an undirected process such as natural selection.

Let's suppose that we actually discovered that the universe has been in existence forever, and that such beings have been in existence forever. Would the proponents of intelligent design claim victory? Perhaps, but it seems that this isn't really what they have in mind when they argue for a designer. These beings have been in existence forever, but they don't have any special powers to create that we don't have; they design features of the universe in the same way that we do. While we as a society would certainly be surprised if we discovered such beings, I can't picture the people who care about such things saying "ah, now I see that the doctrine of intelligent design is true." It seems that the designer that the intelligent design proponents believe in is supposed to have more control over the nature of the universe than the beings I've described would.[11]

Let's shift gears. Instead of focusing on the nature of the intelligent cause, let's focus on the features of the universe themselves. Which features of the universe do the intelligent design proponents think are designed, where most atheists would disagree?

So far, the features I've been talking about are *local* features of the universe— the fact that the universe contains the Petronas Towers, for example. But the sort of designer that proponents of intelligent design are interested in is a designer of the universe as a whole. This suggests that, when trying to state the doctrine of intelligent design, the focus should be on global features of the universe. So let's consider this formulation:

> The theory of intelligent design holds that certain *global* features of the universe are best explained by an intelligent cause.

I think that this formulation basically gets it right—this is what intelligent design proponents have (or should have) in mind. But what exactly is it getting at, with reference to "global features"? By "global features," I have in mind, for example, the values of the fundamental constants, and the overall structure of the universe. These are aspects of the universe that, prima facie at least, agents like us within the universe don't have any control over. So if these global features of the universe are designed, they're designed by some sort of cosmic designer outside our universe—this is the sort of designer that intelligent design proponents believe in.

Let's look in more detail at a particular global feature of the universe: the values of the fundamental constants. The fundamental constants I have in mind are fundamental constants of physics, such as the constant that determines the strength of the gravitational force, the constant that determines the ratio of the mass of the electron to the mass of the proton, and the cosmological constant (the constant in general relativity that helps determine the rate of the universe's expansion). (In the intelligent design literature, the values of the constants are treated as separate from the laws of physics themselves—the laws have free parameters, and the values of the parameters are set when the values of the fundamental constants are specified.)

In Chapter 3, I will take up some arguments for intelligent design that I find somewhat plausible. I don't find them plausible enough to make me stop being an atheist, but I do think that they have some merit—they make me less certain of my atheism than I would have been had I never heard of (or thought of) the arguments. One of the arguments I'll take up is the *fine-tuning argument*. The fine-tuning argument starts by pointing out that some of the fundamental constants are fine-tuned for life, in the sense that if the value of the fundamental constant were outside some narrow range, life couldn't exist. It would be unlikely for the value of the constant to be in the narrow range if the universe were undesigned, but it would be expected if there were a designer. Hence, the fact that the universe is life-permitting provides evidence for the existence of a designer. In Chapter 3, I'll point out that some of the key objections that intelligent design opponents give in response to the fine-tuning argument are flawed.

Now, let's look at another global feature of the universe, the overall structure of the universe. Here I have in mind two main issues. First, did the universe have a beginning, or has it been in existence forever? Second, is the universe spatially finite or spatially infinite?

Both these issues are related to arguments for intelligent design that I find somewhat plausible. First, if the universe had a beginning, then that lends support to what's called the *kalam cosmological argument*. The kalam cosmological argument holds that the universe began to exist, and everything that begins to exist has a cause of its existence, and hence the universe had a cause of its existence, and this cause is an intelligent designer. (I'll discuss this argument in Chapter 3.)

Second, if the universe is spatially finite, that lends support to an intelligent design argument based on the origin of life. I'll explain this in more detail in Chapter 3, but the basic idea is that if the origin of life from non-life on any particular planet is a very improbable event, assuming that there's no designer, then it would be improbable that that event would occur somewhere in a small, spatially finite universe, but it would be highly probable for that event to occur somewhere in a spatially infinite universe. So, if it really is highly improbable for life to arise from non-life on any particular planet, assuming that there's no designer, then if the universe is spatially finite, the fact that there is life provides some evidence for a designer.

Let's take stock of where we are. We've been considering the following statement of intelligent design:

> The theory of intelligent design holds that certain global features of the universe are best explained by an intelligent cause.

We've seen some ways in which this plays into intelligent design arguments—if the global features of the universe are designed, they're not designed by agents like us; they're designed by the sorts of God-like cosmic designers the proponents of intelligent design want to believe in. But we need to consider: are there ways that that statement of intelligent design could come out true, as the result of actions of agents like us? If so, then that statement of intelligent design wouldn't really capture what proponents of intelligent design are trying to get at; instead it would be the sort of claim that everyone could believe in.

Well, I don't see how agents like us could be the cause of the laws of physics, or of the values of the fundamental constants. But I do see one—admittedly far-fetched—way that perhaps agents like us could be the cause of the beginning of the universe. I'll describe this scenario now. Suppose there is some time at which the universe branches into multiple parts. Suppose further that one of the branches loops around in such a way that it forms the original, pre-branching universe. On one way of describing this scenario, the universe caused itself to exist; the universe is the cause of its own existence. What I've said so far sounds quite speculative, but in fact Princeton astrophysicist J. Richard Gott has shown that such a universe is allowed by general relativity (the best theory we have of the large-scale structure of the universe).[12] Now, let's suppose (and I recognize that this is getting more far-fetched) that tomorrow a scientist discovers how to time travel. She decides to travel back in time to the period just before the branching occurred. Suppose that her presence there ends up causing the branching to occur. There is a sense in which one could say that she is a cause of the beginning of the universe, in that she helped the universe to be a cause of its own existence.

So if the scenario I just described is true, would we say that the statement of intelligent design I've been considering is true, because we have a global feature of the universe that's best explained by an intelligent cause (where the global feature is the beginning of the universe, and the intelligent cause is the time-travelling scientist)? I'm really not sure—I could see different people giving different reasonable answers here. Those people who would say that the statement of intelligent design I've been considering does come out true on this scenario would then have legitimate grounds to say that my statement of intelligent design isn't really capturing what intelligent design proponents are trying to get at. Intelligent design proponents probably wouldn't celebrate the victory of intelligent design if time-travelling scientists were discovered, even if those time-travelling scientists had influence over the beginning of the universe. Or maybe the intelligent design proponents would celebrate? Most physicists would be very doubtful if you told them (without further elaboration) that an intelligent cause was involved in the beginning of the universe. Intelligent design proponents are trying to get scientists to take intelligent cause hypotheses seriously, and I've described one (far-fetched) way in which the scientists might be drawn to do that.

My take-away lesson from this discussion is that it's not completely obvious what exactly the doctrine of intelligent design amounts to. The best statement I've come up with is the following:

> The theory of intelligent design holds that certain global features of the universe are best explained by an intelligent cause.

It's not completely obvious that that statement exactly captures what intelligent design proponents are trying to get at. But at least it's an improvement over the Discovery Institute's statement.

What is Intelligent Design? Part II—Features of Living Things

Let's go back to the Discovery Institute's statement of intelligent design:

> The theory of intelligent design holds that certain features of the universe and of living things are best explained by an intelligent cause, not an undirected process such as natural selection.

To keep the discussion manageable, I had just been focusing on the "features of the universe" clause. Let's set that clause aside for now, and let's take up the "features of living things" clause.

As I discussed above, we all agree that certain features of living things (like Sarah Watson's muscular arms) are best explained by an intelligent cause, not an undirected process such as natural selection. (Of course, natural selection had a role in causing Sarah Watson to have muscles at all, but as for why her arms have the particular muscular structure that they do, an intelligent cause—Sarah Watson herself—clearly played a role.) But the statement of intelligent design isn't meant to be a banal truth that we all can endorse, simply by reflecting on muscle training, ear piercings, and hair cuts. So how can we modify the statement of intelligent design so that it actually captures the distinctive claim that proponents of intelligent design are trying to make?

It's worth making clear why the intelligent design proponents want to talk about an intelligent cause. The following won't do as a statement of intelligent design:

> The Darwinian theory of evolution is false.

The reason it won't do is that the Darwinian theory of evolution could turn out to be false in such a way that lends no support to the existence of a designer of life and the universe. For example, it could turn out that Lamarckism is true—that acquired traits are inherited.[13] (I would be highly surprised if Lamarckism turned out to be true, but it's at least logically possible.) The Darwinian theory would then be false, but not false in a way that gives any support for the existence of the sort of designer intelligent design proponents believe in.

So let's take the Discovery Institute's statement of intelligent design as our starting point, and see if we can put in extra clauses to make it more restrictive. Here's one attempt:

> The theory of intelligent design holds that certain features that living things have *at birth* are best explained by an intelligent cause, not by an undirected process such as natural selection.

This manages to rule out muscle training and ear piercings and hair cuts, but it doesn't rule out things that can be done by an intelligent cause to a fetus in utero. For example, some people think that reading to your fetus can give it certain features that unread-to fetuses don't have; if so then there would be features that the read-to fetuses have at birth that are best explained by an intelligent cause. But we don't want the statement of intelligent design to come out true just because some fetuses have been read to.

Perhaps we could change "at birth" to "at conception"? This doesn't work either. When doing in vitro fertilization, one can in principle look at the properties of lots of sperm and eggs, and pick which sperm and egg to fuse. In that scenario, there would be features of a living thing (the living thing that the fused sperm and egg eventually becomes) which are best explained by an intelligent cause—namely, the intelligent cause who chose that sperm and that egg to fuse.

Note that the same sort of objection can be raised to the following statement of intelligent design:

> The theory of intelligent design holds that certain *biologically innate* features of living things are best explained by an intelligent cause, not by an undirected process such as natural selection.

The biologically innate features that a living thing has are features that can be manipulated by humans during the process of in vitro fertilization.

Let's take a different tack. The proponents of intelligent design think that the intelligent cause is an intelligent cause that's somehow outside the realm of creatures on Earth that we're familiar with. Perhaps this is what needs to be built into the statement of intelligent design:

> The theory of intelligent design holds that certain features of living things are best explained by an intelligent cause *which is not biologically related to the living things*, not by an undirected process such as natural selection.

This statement of intelligent design looks more promising, but unfortunately it doesn't work either. Currently, almost all biologists believe in common descent: they believe that all living things on Earth evolved from the same source. But in principle, it could turn out that some animals on earth evolved from a different source than other animals. For example, perhaps most animals evolved from life that originated in a prebiotic swamp, while dogs evolved from life that originated in a volcano. If that's the case, then when I was bitten by a dog last year, I had certain features that were best explained by an intelligent cause that's not biologically related to me. But we wouldn't want the doctrine of intelligent design to come out true just because of a dog bite.

Let's try an even more restrictive statement. Let's combine the "not biologically related" clause with the "biologically innate" clause:

> The theory of intelligent design holds that certain *biologically innate* features of living things are best explained by an intelligent cause *which is not biologically related to the living things*, not by an undirected process such as natural selection.

This will rule out dog bite situations. But this still doesn't capture what we're trying to capture. The statement of intelligent design would come out true if the non-biologically-related dog is the one who chooses which biologically innate features a fetus has, by for example pushing a lever that determines which egg and sperm fuse. But we wouldn't want intelligent design to be true just because it happened to be the case that this (admittedly far-fetched) scenario took place.[14]

We are close to a promising statement of intelligent design though. While the dog that pushes the lever is intelligent, the dog would not be intelligently choosing which egg and sperm fuse—the dog would just be pushing the lever that it felt like pushing, not recognizing the consequences. So let's put in the further requirement that the actions of the intelligent cause have to be intended to bring about the biologically innate features in question. This is, in my opinion, the right statement of intelligent design (as it applies to features of living things):

> The theory of intelligent design holds that certain *biologically innate* features of living things are best explained by *the intentional actions of* an intelligent cause *which is not biologically related to the living things*, not by an undirected process such as natural selection.

What I'm trying to say is that the actions of the intelligent cause in question must be intended to produce the biologically innate features of the living things. The biologically innate features can't be an unintended byproduct of the action of the intelligent cause; the intelligent cause must be intelligently selecting the biologically innate features of the living things.

I'm going to stop giving different versions of the statement of intelligent design (as it applies to living things) now, but I want to register that I'm not completely happy with the version I've settled on. The reason is as follows. Some Mormons believe that God was once human—and they don't just have in mind the Incarnation of Christ; they mean that claim to apply to the God the Father part of the Trinity as well.

> God himself was once as we are now, and is an exalted man, and sits enthroned in yonder heavens! That is the great secret.... I am going to tell you how God came to be God. We have imagined and supposed that God was God from all eternity. I will refute that idea....[15]

If that's right, then God is presumably biologically related to humans. If this God were to intentionally and intelligently cause a biologically innate feature of a human, that wouldn't count as support for the intelligent design doctrine, according to my statement of intelligent design. But perhaps that's an acceptable result—perhaps that shouldn't count as support of intelligent design. After all, this God that was once a man didn't produce the origin of life on Earth—this God only arose after life and humans already existed. (As far as I can tell, these Mormons don't believe in time travel.) So where did life come from to begin with? Well, if I understand the view correctly, there have been gods forever.

If I go any further, I will be straying too far into controversies surrounding Mormon theology (if I haven't already). My point is simply that there are religious people who believe that God is biologically related to us, and they might balk at my statement of intelligent design. If their God were to intentionally and intelligently cause a biologically innate feature of a human, or any animal biologically related to a human, that wouldn't count as support for my statement of intelligent design, and they might say that that's a flaw in my statement. But perhaps they wouldn't; perhaps they would see it as a benefit that they can believe in their God, and believe that their God intentionally and intelligently causes biologically innate features, without having to believe in the maligned theory of intelligent design. I'm not sure.

In sum, it's not completely obvious that the statement I've come up with exactly captures what intelligent design proponents are trying to get at. But (to repeat what I said at the end of the previous section) at least it's an improvement over the Discovery Institute's statement.[16]

What is Intelligent Design? Part III—Combining the Features

Let's go back once more to the Discovery Institute's statement of intelligent design:

> The theory of intelligent design holds that certain features of the universe and of living things are best explained by an intelligent cause, not an undirected process such as natural selection.

To review: I divided my discussion up into two parts. In the part that focused on features of the universe, this was the best statement I could come up with:

> The theory of intelligent design holds that certain global features of the universe are best explained by an intelligent cause.

And in the part that focused on features of living things, this was the best statement I could come up with:

> The theory of intelligent design holds that certain biologically innate features of living things are best explained by the intentional actions of an intelligent

cause which is not biologically related to the living things, not by an undirected process such as natural selection.

But now we're faced with a question: how should these two statements be combined, into one overall statement of intelligent design? Well, the Discovery Institute statement has an "and" between the "features of the universe" clause and the "features of living things," so perhaps that's how it should be done:

> The theory of intelligent design holds that certain global features of the universe are best explained by an intelligent cause, *and* that certain biologically innate features of living things are best explained by the intentional actions of an intelligent cause which is not biologically related to the living things, not by an undirected process such as natural selection.

There's a problem though in joining the clauses with an "and." For an "and" statement to be true, both clauses joined by the "and" have to be true. (For example, if I say: "Grass is sometimes green, and the moon is made of cheese," I've said something false, because one of the clauses joined by the "and" is false.) So suppose that it turns out that the first clause—the "universe" clause—is true, but the second clause—the "living things" clause—is false. In that situation, the intelligent design statement I've given just above would turn out to be false. Similarly, if the first clause were false but the second clause were true, the intelligent design statement I've given just above would be false. But you would think that intelligent design proponents would be claiming victory if we all came to agree that a non-biologically related designer intentionally and intelligently caused biologically innate features of living things, even if there was no evidence that this designer caused global features of the universe. Similarly, you would think intelligent design proponents would be claiming victory if we all came to agree that global features of the universe were designed by an intelligent cause, even if there was no evidence that this intelligent cause designed features of living things. So I suggest that we should instead join the clauses with an "or":

> The theory of intelligent design holds that certain global features of the universe are best explained by an intelligent cause, *or* that certain biologically innate features of living things are best explained by the intentional actions of an intelligent cause which is not biologically related to the living things, not by an undirected process such as natural selection.

Here I mean the "or" to be read inclusively, so that if both clauses come out true, the statement as a whole comes out true. (Sometimes "and/or" is used to signify this.) In my opinion, there's no definitively right answer as to whether the "and" connective or the "or" connective is preferable; it's up to the individual proponents of intelligent design to decide which statement of intelligent design they take to capture the doctrine they're endorsing. But if they asked for my advice, my advice would be to go with the "or" connective, because the truth of either clause is enough to yield the result that a God-like intelligent designer exists. If scientists came to agree that a God-like intelligent designer exists, that would be a major revolution in the scientific worldview, and surely the intelligent design proponents would take some credit for that development.

Much of the literature on intelligent design, both for and against, focuses on Darwinian evolution. In my opinion, the arguments against evolution are among the weaker arguments that proponents of intelligent design give.[17] But there are many other pro-intelligent design arguments in the literature. I already described three of them above—an argument that starts from the fine-tuning of the fundamental constants, an argument based on the fact that the universe began to exist, and an argument based on the improbability of the naturalistic origin of life from non-life, and in Chapter 3 I'll explain why these (and other) pro-intelligent design arguments are somewhat plausible. (I'm not going to delve into why the evolution-based arguments for intelligent design are implausible; that's been covered to death by the anti-intelligent design literature.) If a proponent of intelligent design asked me for advice, I wouldn't tell them to completely stop promoting such evolution-based arguments, but I would tell them to avoid a myopic focus on those arguments. By not following my advice, they're making the case for intelligent design look weaker than it actually is.

CONFUSION IN THE LITERATURE

To give an example of the confusion that intelligent design proponents sometimes create when they discuss intelligent design as if it is solely focused on evolution, let's look at a 2005 paper by Stephen Meyer, "Not by Chance: From Bacterial Propulsion Systems to Human DNA, Evidence of Intelligent Design is Everywhere." Meyer is a Senior Fellow of the Discovery Institute, and the Director of the Center for Science and Culture program at the Discovery Institute. (The Center for Science and Culture is the part of the Discovery Institute that focuses on intelligent design issues.) The link to this paper by Meyer is prominently displayed on the Discovery Institute's web site: in the "Frequently Asked Questions" section, just after they give the statement of intelligent design that I've been critiquing above, they say: "For more information see Center Director Stephen Meyer's article 'Not By Chance'," and they hyperlink to Meyer's paper.

In the paper, Meyer writes:

> intelligent design is … an evidence-based scientific theory about life's origins—
> one that challenges strictly materialistic views of evolution.[18]

Here Meyer treats intelligent design as if it is essentially a challenge to materialistic evolution. Based on what he says, one would think that, if an argument doesn't challenge materialistic evolution, then it's not an intelligent design argument. But in fact, the very example that he uses—an argument for intelligent design on the basis of life's origins—has nothing to do with evolution. Evolution is not a theory about the origin of life from non-life. Mainstream biologists agree that, however life arose from non-life, it didn't happen via the Darwinian mechanism of natural selection. Darwinian evolution only comes into play once life already exists—it explains how, for example, simple forms of life evolve into more complex forms. Darwinian evolution doesn't explain (or even purport to explain) how life came to arise in the first place. So given that Meyer wants intelligent design to be at least in part about life's origins, he should not set up intelligent design as solely providing a challenge to the theory of evolution.

This leads to a question: does Meyer want intelligent design to be *solely* about life's origins, or *in part* about life's origins? In the quotation above, Meyer makes it sound like the sole topic of intelligent design is the origin of life. But in other places Meyer seems to treat intelligent design as being about more than life's origins. In fact, just three sentences before the passage I quoted above, Meyer talks about physics-based design arguments:

> Even as early as the 1960s and 70s, physicists had begun to reconsider the design
> hypothesis. Many were impressed by the discovery that the laws and constants
> of physics are improbably "finely-tuned" to make life possible.

Moreover, he talks about these physics-based design arguments in a section of his paper where he is laying out "the modern theory of intelligent design." Meyer seems somewhat confused about what exactly the doctrine of intelligent design amounts to, but he also seems happy to consider physics-based design arguments as providing support for the theory of intelligent design.

Perhaps some readers will insist that the intelligent design movement is essentially about challenging evolution, and that I'm being too charitable to intelligent design proponents by counting non-evolution-based arguments for a designer as intelligent design arguments. To those who are resolved in thinking that's the case, I won't protest—I'll simply say that I was confused, and it turns out that I'm not interested in their reading of intelligent design. What I'm interested in are the non-evolution-based arguments for a designer—there are smart people giving such arguments, and such arguments are somewhat plausible. I've tried to give a definition of intelligent design in such a way that it includes those arguments, and while my exact definition hasn't been given before, I don't think it's anomalous—I think it captures what the intelligent design proponents are trying to say.

To provide a bit more evidence that it is not anomalous for my reading of intelligent design to include arguments not focused on evolution, I'll cite some other people who also seem to treat intelligent design that way. Casey Luskin, the program officer for public policy and legal affairs at the Discovery Institute, says:

> Scientists who support intelligent design seek evidence of design in nature, and argue that such evidence points to intelligent design, based on our historical knowledge of cause and effect.[19]

I'm not sure what he's getting at with the appeal to our historical knowledge of cause and effect, but let's set that aside. The important thing to note for our purposes is that Luskin is not saying that intelligent design scientists are just looking for evidence of design in biology; he's saying that they are looking for evidence of design in *nature*—where nature would presumably include biological processes, but would also include a lot more (such as the values of the fundamental constants of physics, the overall structure of the universe, and so on).

Here is another relevant quotation. Intelligent design proponent Logan Paul Gage, in the course of discussing intelligent design issues, writes:

> the materialist story is false and, further, is contradicted by mounting physical evidence in physics, chemistry, and biology.[20]

Gage is not just appealing to evidence from evolutionary biology; he's including physics-based arguments as providing evidence against the doctrine that all there is in the world is material stuff.

As a final bit of evidence that people treat intelligent design as including physics-based arguments, I'd like to point to the introductory essay by intelligent design opponents Matt Young and Taner Edis in their edited collection *Why Intelligent Design Fails*. After a section entitled "Intelligent Design in Biology," they have another, even longer, section entitled "Intelligent Design in Physics and Information Theory."[21] Here they treat physics-based design arguments as intelligent design arguments:

> In cosmology, intelligent-design advocates point to the supposed fine tuning of the physical constants....

I could go on giving many more quotations, but really a simple perusal of the intelligent design literature shows that it's often the case that non-evolution-based arguments are treated as intelligent design arguments.

If one does this, though, one will also see that much of the intelligent design literature focuses on evolution issues, and as a result sometimes intelligent design is treated as being just about evolution. It is especially strange when those who do this elsewhere acknowledge that there are physics-based intelligent design arguments. For example, Young and Edis are guilty of this—just a few pages before their section on "Intelligent Design in Physics and Information Theory," they say that intelligent design is

a new and comparatively sophisticated form of creationism,

and that it's

A conservative religious agenda masquerading as a scientific alternative to evolution.[22]

I assume that Young and Edis are being sloppy, and what they really mean is that intelligent design is *in part* providing an ostensibly scientific alternative to evolution, but that it also involves other, non-biology-related, arguments. But why are they not clear about this? Perhaps part of what's going on is that it's rhetorically easy to criticize intelligent design by linking it to the highly questionable theory of creationism, while in fact some of the intelligent design arguments are not related to creationism, and those arguments have more intellectual force. That can't be the only explanation of what's going on, though, because as we've seen, intelligent design proponent Meyers shows a similar lack of clarity regarding whether the doctrine of intelligent design includes non-biology-based arguments. It is clear that there is confusion in the literature regarding what the doctrine of intelligent design actually amounts to; one goal of this chapter is to help clarify the issue.

This confusion comes out in a fascinating way in the introduction by biologist and intelligent design opponent Massimo Pigliucci to the 2007 edited collection *Scientists Confront Intelligent Design and Creationism*. Pigliucci writes:

Scientifically, … creationists and ID supporters don't have a leg to stand on, but they nevertheless manage to make a lot of noise. One of the recurring tricks I have experienced when talking with creationists is that they like to portray the debate as one concerning the "science of origins." Don't waste time looking up any "Origins Science" Department at the local college or university; like much else associated with creationism, it is a pure rhetorical device. The "origins" (plural) to which creationists refer are three: the origin of humans (sometimes extended to the origin of any species …), the origin of life, and the origin of the universe.

Even a superficial acquaintance with science reveals that these three subjects actually belong to three very distinct disciplines (evolutionary biology, biophysics, and cosmology), and that only the first one has anything to do with the theory of evolution proper. Darwinian mechanisms cannot get going until after life originates on a planet, and, last time I checked, planets and galaxies were not making babies that could be subjected to natural selection. In other words, to put it in terms of "origins" is misleading at best, which once again clearly reveals the thin veneer of science thrown over the creationist Trojan horse.[23]

My guess is that the people Pigliucci is talking about when he refers to "creationists" actually consider themselves intelligent design proponents, but I'll stick with his terminology. It is interesting that Pigliucci portrays the people he calls creationists as engaging in "tricks" when they portray the debate as being about the origin of humans, the origin of life, and the origin of the universe. Now, Pigliucci is surely right that the controversies over Darwinian evolution only come into play in the origin of humans case, but I would simply take this to show that the people he calls creationists are concerned about more than just the controversies over Darwinian evolution. The creationists aren't engaging in "tricks" when they talk about the origin of life and the origin of the universe; they're just expressing their opinions regarding issues beyond the issue of whether the theory of Darwinian evolution is true. Pigliucci seems to be making fun of the people he calls creationists for foolishly thinking that Darwinian evolution had something to do with cosmology, with his line "last I checked, planets and galaxies were not making babies." But there's no evidence that the people he calls creationists actually think that Darwinian evolution has something to do with cosmology. In fact, it's Pigliucci, not the people he calls creationists, who's confused—he doesn't recognize that, when the people he calls creationists talk about cosmological issues, they are concerned with issues that don't have anything to do with Darwinian evolution.

Setting aside the confusion, what this discussion shows is that one can't dismiss creationists (or intelligent design proponents) just on the basis of what they say about evolution. Even if they are wrong about that topic, there are other, non-evolution-based, arguments that they give.

It is the case, though, that most of the intelligent design discussion is on biological issues. For example, consider this passage from leading intelligent design proponent William Dembski:

Although design remains an important issue in cosmology, the focus of the intelligent design movement is on biology. That's where the action is. ... it will be intelligent design's reinstatement of design within biology that will be the undoing of naturalism in Western culture.[24]

That passage is from a book published back in 1999, and so far, Dembski's prediction hasn't come true: the intelligent design arguments haven't led to the undoing of naturalism. This should perhaps lead intelligent design proponents to contemplate whether the focus on the particular biological arguments they're giving is misplaced. In my opinion, there are some arguments for intelligent design that are stronger than the standard biological arguments that intelligent design proponents focus on. I'll be talking about those stronger arguments in Chapter 3 of this book.

LOGICAL DEPENDENCE

There's one final point I'd like to bring up in this section. (This point is somewhat complicated, and not relevant to the rest of the book, so feel free to simply move on to the next section.) Some intelligent design proponents think that Darwinian evolution is incompatible with theism, and this may lead them to consider the anti-Darwinian claims of intelligent design to be the key claims. Consider for example this quotation from Logan Paul Gage:

> Guided evolution is certainly compatible with a robust theism, but the blind, unguided Darwinian mechanism is not.[25]

I'm not completely sure what Gage means by "robust theism," but I could see Gage holding that, if God exists, then God designed the universe, and in such a God-designed universe, unguided Darwinian evolution didn't take place. In other words, I could see Gage holding that, if there's a designer of the universe, then there's a designer of living things.[26] Gage would then hold that, if the first clause (the "features of the universe" clause) in the intelligent design doctrine is true, then the second clause (the "features of living things" clause) is automatically true as well. In other words, the first clause entails the second. Gage could also hold that, in contrast, the second clause could be true while the first clause is false—in other words, the second clause does not entail the first. People like Gage could thus maintain that the second clause is the key one: if there is a designer of features of the universe, or features of living things, then the second clause will be true. Since the second clause is the key one, these people could say that the statement of intelligent design need only focus on the second clause; it need only focus on the features of living things.

My response to this is simply that one *could* say this, but one need not. Just because one holds that, if there's a designer of the universe, then there's also a designer of living things, it doesn't follow that one needs to build that into the statement of intelligent design that one endorses. For someone who holds that, if there's a designer of the universe, then there's a designer of living things, it is at most redundant to put in the "features of the universe" clause, so it doesn't hurt to include it.

But perhaps Gage would be unhappy with my line of response here. There are some people who believe in some sort of deistic designer of the universe, but who don't believe that that designer actively intervenes in the world; Gage might say that these people are not robust theists. Gage might then say that we wouldn't want intelligent design to be defined in such a way that it comes out true just because a deistic designer of the universe exists; we would only want intelligent design to come out true if there's a designer involved in causing the features of living things too.

I don't have any definitive reply to this imagined objection from Gage here; he is free to endorse whatever doctrine of intelligent design he wants. As a pragmatic matter, it would behoove intelligent design proponents to make the intelligent design doctrine as weak as possible, while still capturing the distinctive claims that intelligent design proponents want to make.[27] My sense is that Gage, as I'm portraying him here, is going beyond that desideratum, and building more into the doctrine of intelligent design than is needed. But he is certainly welcome to do that; to argue with him at this point would enter us into a purely terminological debate about how much should be built into the doctrine called "intelligent design."

Just to be clear, what I've been doing so far in this chapter isn't engaging in a purely terminological debate. As I mentioned above, the extant statements of intelligent design don't adequately capture what proponents of intelligent design are trying to endorse, and hence I'm trying to figure how to formulate the doctrine of intelligent design in such a way that it can accurately represent what intelligent design proponents are trying to say. While I have come up with a statement of intelligent design that is an improvement over the standard statement intelligent design proponents give, there are still controversial issues, as we'll see in the next section.

What is Intelligent Design? Part IV—The Explanation Issue

Let's go back (one last time) to the Discovery Institute's statement of intelligent design:

> The theory of intelligent design holds that certain features of the universe and of living things are best explained by an intelligent cause, not an undirected process such as natural selection.

There's a key part of that statement I haven't yet discussed: the "best explained" part. I have a lot to say about that part, so I'll do so now.

In trying to come up with a better formulation of the intelligent design doctrine, I kept the reference to explanation:

> The theory of intelligent design holds that certain global features of the universe are *best explained* by an intelligent cause, or that certain biologically innate features of living things are *best explained* by the intentional actions of an intelligent cause which is not biologically related to the living things, not by an undirected process such as natural selection.

But as long as that reference to explanation stays in there, intelligent design is a doctrine that I, as an atheist, would want to wholeheartedly endorse.

The basic reason is that I think there are some features of the universe that cannot be explained at all by an atheist; that is to say, as an atheist, I want to say that some things happen without a reason. The intelligent design proponent, on the other hand, can appeal to a designer to explain these features of the universe; the intelligent design proponent can say that the reason things happen the way they do is that the designer wanted it that way. Thus, I'm willing to grant that the intelligent design proponent has the best explanation of certain features of the universe—as an atheist, I don't think there's *any* explanation. But since the intelligent design doctrine, as I've portrayed it so far, just says that the best explanation is that there is an intelligent cause, then I'm willing to endorse that statement of intelligent design. The intelligent design proponents do have the best explanation of these features of the universe in question, it's just that their explanation—like all explanations of these features—is most likely false.

Perhaps this needs to be explained in more detail. It will help if we step back from the intelligent design debate, and consider a more neutral issue—the uranium atom in the box in my office, for example. Quantum theory will tell us what the probability is that this atom will decay in some time interval, but quantum theory doesn't tell us any more than that—it doesn't tell us when the uranium atom will actually decay. So let's wait for a while … ah, just now the atom decayed. What is the best explanation for why it decayed at that particular time?

Note that this request for the "best" explanation implies that there are multiple competing explanations. For example, just before the atom decayed, someone outside my office sneezed. So one explanation is that nearby sneezes cause uranium atom decay. Another explanation adopts the hypothesis that Bohm's theory—a deterministic variant of quantum mechanics—is true. According to Bohm's theory, particles always have definite positions, and it is the positions of these particles that deterministically establish what happens. So this explanation of the uranium atom decay holds that the particles in the atom were in just the positions they needed to be in for the decay to happen. I'll leave it to your imagination to come up with more explanations. The final explanation I want to put on the table is that an intelligent cause chose to make the uranium atom decay when it did.

Now, which of these explanations is the best one? Well, the sneezing explanation is a bit silly. Bohm's theory, according to Einstein at least, is "too cheap." We haven't (let's suppose) been imaginative enough to come up with other competing explanations. So it could be reasonable to hold that the best explanation for why the atom decayed when it did is that an intelligent cause willed it to decay then.

But even though an appeal to an intelligent cause is (let's suppose) the best explanation of the decay, does that mean that we should believe that that explanation is the true one? The answer is *no*. It could be that *all* the explanations of the decay are false; it could be that the right account of the decay is that there's no explanation for why the atom decayed when it did: the decay was just a spontaneous event, with no cause. Thus, we can believe that an intelligent cause is the best explanation for the decay, while also believing that an intelligent cause had nothing to do with the decay.

We can carry this line of reasoning back to the intelligent design debate. Consider some feature of the universe, such as its beginning to exist (assuming that it did begin to exist). There are various competing explanations we can consider for such a feature, and one of those explanations will be that the feature was due to an intelligent cause. We may judge this explanation to be the best one, but it doesn't follow that the explanation is true. The right account could be that there's no explanation at all for why the universe has the feature that it does.

Thus, if the doctrine of intelligent design is as I've stated above, with the claim that the best explanation for the features is an intelligent cause, then I endorse intelligent design. I can do this, as an atheist, because I reject the inference that the best explanation is true, or even likely to be true. My opinion is that it's probably the case that the true account is that there's no explanation at all.

I recognize that not all atheists will be happy with the move I'm making here. There are two types of objections I'd like to consider.

First, one could hold that, in fact, there does have to be an explanation for everything. This gets to a much-discussed issue in the history of philosophy, whether the *principle of sufficient reason* is true. This principle basically holds that, for every event that occurs, there has to be a reason that's sufficient to account for why that event occurs. If you believe that the principle of sufficient reason is true, and you have philosophical arguments to support your belief, I'm probably not going to be able to say anything here to convince you otherwise—this is one of those fundamental philosophical issues where it's hard to come up with convincing arguments on either side; as a result the two camps are pretty entrenched. In the interest of not getting bogged down, I'll simply state one of my reasons for rejecting the principle of sufficient reason. My reason is that it seems possible that the laws of physics could be indeterministic. Given the complete history of the world up to some time, and the indeterministic laws, it is not established how the future will turn out. In other words, there are events in the future that will happen, when there is no sufficient reason for why they happened. In fact, quantum theory is standardly understood as indeterministic—and that's why events like the radioactive decay of a uranium atom are standardly understood as events that happen without a sufficient reason.

Here's a second objection one could have to my claim that the best explanation need not be true because the truth of the matter is that there's no explanation at all. I find this objection to be a non-starter, but I've heard it enough in conversation that I feel the need to bring it up. What some people have said to me is that my claim that there is no explanation is itself an explanation—so the best explanation is always the true one; it's just that in cases like radioactive decay the best explanation is that there's no explanation.

Here's why this is confused. To say that the best explanation for some event is that there's no explanation is incoherent. In case you're not convinced, here's my argument. If "no explanation" is the best explanation for the event, then "no explanation" is an explanation. But if "no explanation" is an explanation, then it follows that there is an explanation for the event. But if there is an explanation for the event, then the claim that there's no explanation is false.

I conclude that if the statement of intelligent design says that an intelligent cause is the best explanation of some features of the universe and of living things, then it's plausible that intelligent design is true (even if we modify the doctrine to make clear which features of the universe and of living things we're talking about). As an atheist, I'm willing to admit that perhaps there's no explanation for why our universe has the laws that it does, or why the fundamental constants have the values that they do. Theists, on the other hand, have an explanation: God wanted things that way. I'm willing to grant that this appeal to God is the best explanation, and hence I'm willing to grant that the best explanation is the appeal to an intelligent cause—and thus the intelligent design doctrine, as I've stated it above, comes out true. The intelligent design doctrine as I've stated it above says that a designer counts as the best explanation of certain features of the universe, and I agree that a designer counts as the best explanation. The key point though is that *all* the explanations are false, including the explanation that appeals to a designer. The truth of the matter is that there's no explanation at all.

Perhaps this means that we need to modify the intelligent design doctrine as stated above. The intelligent design proponents wouldn't take that much solace in the knowledge that their appeal to an intelligent cause is the best explanation, if we've established that their explanation is a false one. So let's consider a further modification to the intelligent design doctrine, in an attempt to better capture what the intelligent design proponents are trying to assert. To keep things simple,

I'll focus on modifying the original Discovery Institute statement. So, instead of saying

> The theory of intelligent design holds that certain features of the universe and of living things are best explained by an intelligent cause, not an undirected process such as natural selection.

let's consider this statement:

> The theory of intelligent design holds that certain features of the universe and of living things *are the result of* an intelligent cause, not an undirected process such as natural selection.

That's an easy enough fix. Instead of going through the "best explanation" detour, the intelligent design proponents can just come out and directly say that the intelligent cause is what did it.

But even though there's nothing wrong with intelligent design proponents endorsing that doctrine, I think there's a reason that they originally had the "best explanation" detour, and we're missing that reason in the new doctrine. (I don't have any definitive evidence from intelligent design proponents on this matter, so I'm doing a bit of charitable speculation.) The reason intelligent design proponents want the detour is that they're not just trying to say that there is the intelligent cause in question; they're trying to say that there's *scientific evidence* for the intelligent cause. One of the key ideas behind intelligent design is that their theory is scientific, and one can get scientific evidence for the existence of the intelligent designer. While they would be happy to know that features of the universe and of living things are the result of an intelligent cause, this wouldn't really be a full vindication of intelligent design. To get a full vindication, it would have to be the case that the actions of the intelligent cause aren't completely hidden from us; it would have to be the case there are features of the universe and of living things that provide evidence for the existence of this intelligent cause.

So let's build this evidence claim into the statement of intelligent design. Here's how we can modify the Discovery Institute statement:

> The theory of intelligent design holds that certain features of the universe and of living things *provide evidence for the existence of* an intelligent cause, *and provide evidence against the doctrine that the features are the result of* an undirected process such as natural selection.

This is a doctrine that I endorse. But just as the original Discovery Institute statement was trivially true, so this statement is too. The doctrine that I really what to endorse is the doctrine that one obtains by modifying the best statement of intelligent design I came up with above to get rid of the appeals to explanation. Here for reference is the statement that I came up with above:

> The theory of intelligent design holds that certain global features of the universe are best explained by an intelligent cause, or that certain biologically innate features of living things are best explained by the intentional actions of an intelligent cause which is not biologically related to the living things, not by an undirected process such as natural selection.

And here is the suitably modified statement:

> The theory of intelligent design holds that certain global features of the universe *provide evidence for the existence of* an intelligent cause, or that certain biologically innate features of living things *provide evidence for the doctrine that the features are the result of* the intentional actions of an intelligent cause which is not biologically related to the living things, *and provide evidence against the doctrine that the features are the result of* an undirected process such as natural selection.

This is a doctrine that I endorse, though I recognize that not all atheists will endorse it. The reason I endorse the doctrine is that (as I'll explain in Chapter 3) I think that there is *some* evidence for an intelligent designer, and in fact, I think that there is some evidence that that intelligent designer is God. The arguments I'll consider in Chapter 3 make me less certain of my atheism than I would be had I never heard the arguments. The evidence isn't enough to make me stop being an atheist, though. Many—perhaps most—atheists wouldn't be happy with this; they would hold that the evidence simply isn't there. I'll take issue with these atheists in Chapter 3.

One could argue that the above statement of intelligent design isn't strong enough, since it doesn't specify *how much evidence* there is for an intelligent cause. There are many possible clauses we could add to the end of that statement, to specify how much evidence there is. For example, we could add:

> … where the evidence is strong enough that it's more likely than not that the intelligent cause exists.

Alternatively, we could add:

> … where the evidence is strong enough that it's at least twice as likely than not that the intelligent cause exists.

Alternatively, we could add:

> ... where the evidence is strong enough that it's beyond a reasonable doubt that the intelligent cause exists.

I'll leave it to the reader to generate other possibilities. Each of the additions I've proposed would lead to a statement of intelligent design that I would not endorse—I don't think that much evidence is there. But should the correct statement of intelligent design include such a clause? I can see good arguments on both sides. One could maintain that the clause is needed, so as to rule out the possibility that the intelligent design doctrine is true on the basis of weak evidence. Alternatively, one could maintain that the cause is not needed, since the doctrine is already controversial enough without the clause—many atheists say that there is *no* good evidence for the intelligent design claims.

At this point, the debate is just terminological—there are various plausible statements of intelligent design, and different intelligent design proponents would differ on which statement best captures the doctrine they endorse. Some statements of intelligent design are ones that I as an atheist would endorse. (I'd endorse the ones that say that the intelligent cause is the "best explanation," and the one that says that there's evidence for an intelligent cause, without specifying how much evidence.) But even for the statements I don't endorse, I still think that there are intellectually respectable arguments for those statements.

But a standard way of dismissing the intelligent design claims as not intellectually respectable is to say that they are inherently theistic. I'll take issue with this claim that intelligent design is inherently theistic now.

Theistic vs. Non-Theistic Intelligent Design

Let's start by going back to the Stephen Meyer quotation I gave a while back:

> intelligent design is ... an evidence-based scientific theory about life's origins—one that challenges strictly materialistic views of evolution.

You may have wondered what I replaced with the ellipsis. Here is the full quotation:

> intelligent design is *not a religious-based idea, but instead* an evidence-based scientific theory about life's origins—one that challenges strictly materialistic views of evolution.[28]

Many intelligent design opponents scoff at the claim that intelligent design is not religious-based. Barbara Forrest captured this sentiment well in the quotation I began this book with: she asserts that "intelligent design theory" is "a term that is essentially code for the religious belief in a supernatural creator."[29] So who is right, Forrest or Meyer?

I am on Meyer's side. It is true that almost all proponents of intelligent design believe in a supernatural creator, but it doesn't follow that the thesis that there is a supernatural creator is part of the intelligent design doctrine itself. (Similarly, almost all proponents of intelligent design believe that Abraham Lincoln was assassinated, but we don't take the Lincoln assassination thesis to be a part of the intelligent design doctrine either.) The intelligent design proponents are free to put forth a doctrine that doesn't include all the beliefs they endorse, and they have chosen to put forth their doctrine in such a way that it involves some sort of commitment to an intelligent cause, without specifying whether that intelligent cause is supernatural.

We could speculate on why intelligent design proponents want it to be the case that their doctrine isn't inherently theistic, but it's important to keep in mind that these speculations have nothing to do with whether intelligent design is true. Perhaps intelligent design proponents would not be happy if intelligent design turned out to be true in a non-theistic way, but nevertheless the doctrine of intelligent design has been stated in such a way that it could turn out to be true in that way.

Let's think about this in more detail. How could non-theistic intelligent design turn out to be true? Here are two scenarios.

First, the Raelians could turn out to be right. Raelians believe in *directed pansper-mia*, the doctrine that life on Earth was intentionally started by an intelligent alien civilization. If that's right, then certain features of living things would be the result of an intelligent cause, and hence the doctrine of intelligent design would turn out to be true. Raelians recognize this, and they market themselves as endorsing "intelligent design for atheists."[30] (Perhaps I should make explicit that I am not a Raelian.)

Second, it could turn out that we're living in a computer simulation. I'll actually give an argument for this in Chapter 3, but for now I'll just explain what the doctrine is. It could turn out that in the future, computers will be powerful enough that they will be able to run simulations of universes. The part of the computer that simulates someone's brain will be detailed enough that consciousness will be associated with the computer processes, just as consciousness is associated with the actual physical processes in someone's brain. (I use the "association" terminology so that I can avoid taking a stand on how consciousness actually arises.) But once we recognize that possibility, we recognize that we could be living in a computer simulation. In this scenario, features of the universe and of us would be the result of an intelligent cause: the intelligent alien kid playing his PlayStation 17 universe simulation game, for example. In this scenario, the intelligent design doctrine would be true.

Thus, intelligent design could turn out to be true in a non-theistic way. But I can imagine someone objecting: Meyer is nevertheless wrong to claim that intelligent design isn't religious-based, since the proponents of intelligent design had religious reasons for putting forth the doctrine in the first place.

Here we have to distinguish between a religious-*based* doctrine and a religious-*inspired* doctrine. To see this distinction clearly, it will help to consider an analogous (possibly apocryphal) story. In 1865, German chemist Friedrich Kekulé had a dream about a snake biting its tail, and that inspired him to realize that the molecular structure of benzene was circular. This model of benzene was *inspired* by the dream, but the model is not *based* on the dream. People believe the model, not because of the dream, but because of the scientific evidence in favor of the model. Similarly, intelligent design may be inspired by religion, in the sense that the original proponents of intelligent design came up with the doctrine in part because of the religious views that they had. But it doesn't follow that intelligent design is *based* on religion. When intelligent design proponents say that they have scientific evidence for their doctrine, their focus is not on any religious evidence they might have. If that scientific evidence exists, then that makes intelligent design a legitimate doctrine, regardless of whether there were non-scientific motivations for originally proposing the doctrine.

This leads to the question of whether it really is legitimate to treat intelligent design as a scientific doctrine. This is the issue we'll take up in the next chapter.

An Argument that Intelligent Design is After All Inherently Supernatural

But first, I want to look at one intriguing argument for the thesis that intelligent design is after all inherently supernatural. (If you're impatient you can just move on to the next chapter.) Anti-intelligent design philosopher Elliott Sober has written a paper admitting that the bare statement of intelligent design is compatible with there being no supernatural designer, but he nevertheless argues that "ID theory … has implications concerning the existence of supernatural designers."[31] Sober thinks that intelligent design theory has these implications because he thinks that, to understand the content of intelligent design theory, one has to take into account "independently plausible further assumptions."[32] Sober gives four independently plausible further assumptions, and he says that:

(a) these four assumptions are true,
(b) we are justified in believing these four assumptions, and

(c) when these four assumptions are coupled with the bare statement of intelligent design, it logically follows that there is a supernatural designer.

This leads Sober to reject the bare statement of intelligent design.

So what are the four assumptions? Here they are (preserving Sober's
numbering):

2. Some of the minds found in nature are irreducibly complex.
4. Any mind in nature that designs and builds an irreducibly complex system
   is itself irreducibly complex.
6. The universe is finitely old.
7. In nature, causes precede their effects.

Sober thinks that the bare statement of intelligent design, plus these four assumptions, entails the existence of a supernatural designer. Why does he think that?
Here's the argument:

1. If a system found in nature is irreducibly complex, then it was caused to
   exist by an intelligent designer.
2. Some of the minds found in nature are irreducibly complex.
3. Therefore some of the minds found in nature were caused to exist by an
   intelligent designer.
4. Any mind in nature that designs and builds an irreducibly complex system
   is itself irreducibly complex.
5. If the universe is finitely old and if cause precedes effect, then at least one of
   the minds found in nature was not created by any mind found in nature.
6. The universe is finitely old.
7. In nature, causes precede their effects.
8. Therefore, there exists a supernatural intelligent designer.[33]

I'm not convinced that the conclusion of this argument actually follows from
the premises, but I'm not going to push that point here. Instead I will explain
why I'm not convinced that any of the four assumptions is true.[34] This matters
because, as long as at least one of the four assumptions is false, Sober's argument
doesn't go through. In fact, even if all four assumptions are true, as long as we
aren't justified in believing at least one of the four assumptions, Sober's argument
doesn't go through.

Let's start with the first assumption, that "Some of the minds found in nature are
irreducibly complex." By calling a mind "irreducibly complex," Sober means that
the mind requires all its parts in order to function at all. Michael Behe has argued
that irreducibly complex biological systems would be unlikely to arise via naturalistic

Darwinian means, and hence the existence of irreducibly complex biological systems provides evidence for intelligent design.[35] I worry that, in calling a mind irreducibly complex, Sober is making a category mistake.[36] Behe's notion of irreducible complexity applies to physical biological systems that have parts, but it's not clear to me that a mind is a physical biological system that has parts. A brain certainly is, but Sober isn't talking about a brain, he's talking about a mind. Sober's argument that a mind is irreducibly complex involves representing the structure of the mind via a picture with six boxes labeled "Sensory Perception," "Memory," "Beliefs," "Desires," "Decision Rule," and "Intention." But "Decision Rule," for example, is not a biological subsystem that forms a part of a larger biological system.

Even if minds do count as the sorts of things that can be irreducibly complex, I'm not at all convinced by Sober's argument that they are irreducibly complex. It's true that if you divide up the parts of the mind as Sober has, into "Memory," "Beliefs," and so on, then the mind does look irreducibly complex, but perhaps one could divide the mind up differently, so that it does not. Sober himself points out this problem: he gives the example of a wine bottle, where if one imagined each tiny sliver of glass being a part, the bottle wouldn't be irreducibly complex, whereas if one imagined each donut-shaped slice of the bottle being a part, the bottle would be irreducibly complex. All Sober has to say about this is the following:

> I don't know how Behe's concept should be clarified, but it does seem that those who hold that the bacterial flagellum and the biochemistry of blood coagulation are irreducibly complex should also hold that the human mind is irreducibly complex.[37]

Since there's not much of an argument here, I'll simply report that I find this line of reasoning unconvincing.

Let's turn to the second assumption that Sober thinks is true, and that Sober thinks we are justified in believing. This is the assumption that "Any mind in nature that designs and builds an irreducibly complex system is itself irreducibly complex." Again, we have the problem that it may be a category mistake to apply the concept of irreducible complexity to minds. But setting that aside, it's not at all obvious that that claim is true. Imagine for the moment that our minds are irreducibly complex, and imagine that we have some evidence that intelligent life on Earth was created by aliens living on another planet. Why should we think that those aliens also have minds that are irreducibly complex? Sober's only argument for that thought is that the division into parts that he gives for human minds also holds for alien minds.[38] But I can think of multiple ways that the division into parts that Sober gives for human minds might not hold for hypothetical alien minds. I'll give a couple now.

First, it could be the case that the alien minds are so different from ours that they don't even function using the parts that Sober attributes to our minds. After all, some philosophers argue that the categories of "beliefs," "desires," and so on do not actually hold for human minds—those categories are just part of a superficial folk-psychological theory of minds that we have, a theory that will eventually be replaced by a more sophisticated theory informed by cognitive neuroscience.[39] Once one starts thinking about that possibility, it's easier to contemplate how alien minds might function without those categories (even if our minds do).

Here's a second way that the division into parts that Sober gives for human minds might not hold for alien minds. It could be the categories of "beliefs," "desires," and so on hold for alien minds, just as they hold for human minds, but in the alien minds they exist in a massively redundant way. For example, instead of having one part of the mind dedicated to "beliefs," there could be three parts of the mind, each dedicated to beliefs, with significant overlap between the beliefs in each of the three parts. If there was this sort of redundancy for each of the six categories that Sober attributes to a mind, then the alien minds would not be irreducibly complex. The reason they wouldn't be irreducibly complex is that the alien mind wouldn't need all its parts in order to function at all. For example, if the Belief_1 part was removed, there would still be the Belief_2 part and the Belief_3 part, and as a result the alien could function perfectly well.

Thus, I'm not at all convinced that Sober's second assumption is true. Let's turn to the third assumption, that "The universe is finitely old." Sober says that this is what "physics tells us."[40] But in fact, as I'll discuss in more detail when I discuss the kalam cosmological argument in Chapter 3, it's not completely evident that the universe is finitely old. That's the best picture one gets when one applies the theory of general relativity to the data that we have, but general relativity doesn't take into account quantum effects, and we don't yet have an agreed-upon theory that unifies quantum theory and general relativity. There are models of the universe, informed by quantum theory and general relativity, that are compatible with the universe having been in existence forever. Princeton astrophysicist Paul Steinhardt has such a model, the cyclic model.[41] While the big bang is typically presented as the beginning of the universe, the cyclic model holds that the big bang is just the beginning of this cycle of the universe, but this cycle has been preceded by previous cycles. Each cycle ends in a "big crunch," which provides the conditions for a new big bang.

These considerations suggest a way of improving Sober's argument. Sober doesn't need the claim that the universe began a finite amount of time ago, he just needs a weaker claim: "the causal chain of mind-creation in nature couldn't have gone on for more than a finite amount of time in the past." And indeed, even on the cyclic model, this weaker claim is true: living things (or at least, the sorts of living things we're familiar with) couldn't survive through the big crunch/big bang transition.

But, given what we actually know about the world, it's not obvious whether or not the weaker claim is true. Since we don't have a fully worked-out theory that builds on both quantum theory and general relativity, we have to be cautious in reading off lessons about the fundamental structure of the universe from current physics, and Sober is not being sufficiently cautious.[42]

Let's turn to the fourth and final assumption that Sober thinks is true, and that Sober thinks we're justified in believing. This assumption holds that "In nature, causes precede their effects." Sober's full justification for this is that "it seems entirely plausible," and that "physics tells us" that it is true. But in fact, physics does not tell us that. There are models of general relativity which could well apply to our universe which allow for time travel. For example, Princeton astrophysicist J. Richard Gott describes a situation where time travel can occur as a result of two cosmic strings getting close together.[43] A traveller could travel around the cosmic strings and visit her younger self, about to embark on the journey around the cosmic strings. In this situation, some causes would not be preceding their effects.

But as with the previous assumption, Sober is overreaching. He doesn't need the assumption that in nature causes precede their effects; instead he just needs the assumption that in nature, in situations relevant to the chain of mind-creation, causes precede their effects. My sense is that this is probably true, though I'm not as confident about it as Sober is. I'm not completely sure whether we're justified in believing it.

Let's step back. Recall that Sober is trying to argue that, while the bare statement of intelligent design isn't inherently supernatural, when the bare statement is coupled with four assumptions that are all true and that we're justified in believing, the bare statement has supernatural consequences. And remember, all four assumptions are needed for Sober's argument to work. In that sense, my critique of Sober is massively redundant—as long as you are convinced that at least one of the four assumptions is questionable, then Sober's argument fails.

Moreover, even if you do believe all four assumptions that Sober makes, it still doesn't follow that Sober's argument is successful. You could hold that, from your perspective, intelligent design theory has implications concerning the existence of supernatural designers, but you could also recognize that we aren't mandated by the constraints of rationality to believe the four assumptions. Hence, you could recognize that, while intelligent design theory has supernatural consequences by your lights, it would be reasonable for someone to endorse intelligent design theory and yet not hold that it has supernatural consequences, by rejecting one of Sober's four assumptions. In sum: for all the reasons I've given, I conclude that Sober has failed to show that intelligent design theory is inherently supernatural.

CHAPTER 2

Why It Is Legitimate to Treat Intelligent Design as Science

The first few sections of this chapter comprise a paper that I posted online in January 2006, entitled "Is Intelligent Design Science? Dissecting the Dover Decision."[44] As you'll see, the paper criticizes a judge's decision that intelligent design is not science. The judge was led to make this decision because the Dover, Pennsylvania school board decided that the following disclaimer had to be read to ninth-grade biology students prior to studying evolution:

> The Pennsylvania Academic Standards require students to learn about Darwin's Theory of Evolution and eventually to take a standardized test of which evolution is a part.
>
> Because Darwin's Theory is a theory, it continues to be tested as new evidence is discovered. The Theory is not a fact. Gaps in the Theory exist for which there is no evidence. A theory is defined as a well-tested explanation that unifies a broad range of observations.
>
> Intelligent Design is an explanation of the origin of life that differs from Darwin's view. The reference book, Of Pandas and People, is available for students who might be interested in gaining an understanding of what Intelligent Design actually involves.
>
> With respect to any theory, students are encouraged to keep an open mind. The school leaves the discussion of the Origins of Life to individual students and their families. As a Standards-driven district, class instruction focuses upon preparing students to achieve proficiency on Standards-based assessments.[45]

The school district was sued by the ACLU for violating the separation of church and state establishment clause of the Constitution, and the ACLU won.

The paper that I posted online generated a fair amount of discussion and achieved some notoriety.[46] Because of this, and because it's never appeared in print before, I'm including the paper as it was originally written. I flagged the paper "Draft—comments welcome!", and I received a fair number of comments. The most vitriolic comments I received were from philosopher Robert Pennock, who testified on behalf of the ACLU at the trial. After presenting my paper I'll elaborate on my disagreements with Pennock.

Introduction

In December 2005, US federal judge John E. Jones III handed down his decision in the much-publicized case of *Kitzmiller et al. v. Dover Area School District, et al.* The ruling holds that it is unconstitutional for the Dover Area School District to require that a pro-intelligent design disclaimer be read to public school students during the course of teaching them evolutionary theory. Intelligent design isn't really explained in the disclaimer: all it says is that "Intelligent Design is an explanation of the origin of life that differs from Darwin's view." For a more careful definition, consider this statement from the Discovery Institute:

> The theory of intelligent design holds that certain features of the universe and of living things are best explained by an intelligent cause, not an undirected process such as natural selection.[47]

(I will have more to say about the exact content of the theory of intelligent design below.)

Jones's ruling holds that intelligent design counts as religion, not science, and hence the teaching of intelligent design in public school is unconstitutional. In Jones's 139 page decision, he gives an answer to the contentious demarcation question—what criteria can we use to demarcate science from non-science? I will argue that Jones's proposed demarcation criteria are fundamentally flawed. Most of my discussion will focus on the issue of methodological naturalism—I will argue that rejection of the supernatural should not be a part of scientific methodology.

The reason this matters is that it's a dangerous practice to try to impose rigid boundaries on what counts as science. For example, as I will show, a consequence of Jones's criteria is that the aim of science is not truth. While this may be the case, one would expect this to be established by philosophical argumentation about the aim of science,[48] not by a specification of demarcation criteria to distinguish science from pseudoscience. My position is that scientists should be free to pursue hypotheses as they see fit, without being constrained by a particular philosophical account of what science is.

For the purposes of this essay, I'm not really interested in whether it's constitutionally permissible for the Dover Area School District to read the disclaimer to their students. My personal opinion is that it shouldn't be done—not because it's constitutionally impermissible, not because intelligent design isn't science, but simply because reading such a disclaimer is bad pedagogy. But I am trained as a philosopher; I have no special insight as to whether intelligent design should be taught in science class. More precisely, I have no specialized training which would help me to answer the following two questions: supposing intelligent design counts as science, should it be taught in science class? Supposing intelligent design does not count as science, should it be taught in science class? I do, however, have specialized training which will help me to answer the question of whether intelligent design counts as science.

So does intelligent design count as science? I maintain that it is a mistake to put too much weight on that question. Larry Laudan got the answer right:

> If we would stand up and be counted on the side of reason, we ought to drop terms like "pseudo-science" and "unscientific" from our vocabulary; they are just hollow phrases which do only emotive work for us.[49]

If our goal is to believe truth and avoid falsehood, and if we are rational people who take into account evidence in deciding what to believe, then we need to focus on the question of what evidence there is for and against intelligent design. The issue of whether intelligent design counts as "science" according to some contentious answer to the demarcation question is unimportant. Of course, on this approach it would be much harder to get a federal judge to rule that intelligent design can't be taught in public school. But sometimes it is more important to be intellectually honest than to do what it takes to stop people from doing something you don't like.

Jones's Demarcation Criteria

In Jones's decision, he implicitly gives three necessary criteria for something to count as science. He maintains that intelligent design fails all three:

> We find that ID fails on three different levels, any one of which is sufficient to preclude a determination that ID is science. They are: (1) ID violates the centuries-old ground rules of science by invoking and permitting supernatural causation; (2) the argument of irreducible complexity, central to ID, employs the same flawed and illogical contrived dualism that doomed creation science

in the 1980's; and (3) ID's negative attacks on evolution have been refuted by the scientific community.[50]

I find all three criteria unconvincing. The first criterion is the most promising one, so I'll have most to say about it. But I will start by taking issue with the third and second criteria.

THE SCIENTIFIC COMMUNITY

Let's start with the third criterion, that intelligent design's negative attacks on evolution have been refuted by the scientific community. There are two problems with this criterion.[51]

Even if it is true that intelligent design's negative attacks are wrong, that doesn't necessarily impugn intelligent design's positive doctrines. Suppose that Theory A is in competition with Theory B, and suppose that the proponents of Theory A have given bad arguments against Theory B, arguments which have been refuted by the scientific community. This is compatible with Theory A being true, and moreover, this is compatible with there being good scientific evidence for Theory A. This is also compatible with there being good scientific evidence against Theory B—it could simply be that the proponents of Theory A picked the wrong arguments to give against Theory B.

Now, suppose that it's not only the case that intelligent design's negative attacks have been refuted, but also that intelligent design itself has been refuted. Even so, this doesn't make intelligent design unscientific. Consider Newtonian physics—this is uncontroversially a scientific theory. Note that it counts as a scientific theory even though it has been refuted. (For example, Newtonian physics predicts that clocks in differing gravitational fields will run at the same rate, while it has been empirically shown that clocks in stronger gravitational fields run slower.)

One might be tempted to say that under the supposition that intelligent design is false, we can at least conclude that it shouldn't be taught in public school. But even that doesn't follow: Newtonian physics is false, and yet that is the theory that everyone is taught in high school physics classes.[52] I conclude that even if intelligent design's negative attacks on evolution have been refuted by the scientific community, it doesn't follow that intelligent design is not science.

IRREDUCIBLE COMPLEXITY

Jones's second criterion is that the argument of irreducible complexity is flawed. Here Jones has in mind the arguments given by Michael Behe.[53] Behe argues that some biochemical systems are irreducibly complex: they have multiple parts, and they need all their parts to do anything. Behe claims that we wouldn't expect such systems to arise via evolutionary means, since random chance would have to bring all the parts together at once for the system to be functional; the existence of the system can't be accounted for via a step-wise evolutionary process.

This demarcation criterion is no good, and one way we can see that is by going back to the second point made just above. Just because an argument is flawed, it doesn't follow that the argument is unscientific. Scientists sometimes give flawed arguments, but they are still doing science when they do so.

This demarcation criterion is mistaken in other ways too. Intelligent design consists of more than Behe's argument from irreducible complexity. For example, there are physics-based arguments for intelligent design, such as the fine-tuning argument, which have nothing to do with irreducible complexity. (According to the fine-tuning argument, some of the values of the fundamental constants in physics are fine-tuned for life, in the sense that if the values were slightly different life couldn't exist. This arguably provides evidence for the existence of God.)[54] In addition to physics-based arguments for intelligent design, there are also biology-based arguments for intelligent design that have nothing to do with irreducible complexity. For example, one popular pro-intelligent design argument is to claim that the origin of life from non-life is so improbable, it would take a miracle for it to occur.[55] Thus, even if Behe's irreducible complexity argument is unscientific, it doesn't follow that intelligent design is unscientific.

METHODOLOGICAL NATURALISM

We come now to the most promising of Jones's three criteria, the criterion of methodological naturalism. In this section I will grant that intelligent design does postulate supernatural causation, and I will argue that that is compatible with it being scientific. In the next section I will argue that in fact intelligent design is not inherently supernatural, and hence intelligent design can count as science even if the restriction to naturalism is part of the scientific methodology.

I will now argue that it is counterproductive to restrict scientific activity in such a way that hypotheses that invoke the supernatural are ruled out. Specifically, I will argue that it is possible to get scientific evidence for the existence of God. The scenario I am about to describe is implausible, but there is nothing logically inconsistent about it. The point of the scenario is that in the described situation, it would be reasonable for scientists to postulate and test the hypothesis that there is supernatural causation occurring.[56]

Imagine that some astronomers discover a pulsar that is pulsing out Morse code. The message says that it's from God, and that God is causing the pulsar to pulse in this unusual way. The astronomers are initially skeptical, but they find that when they formulate questions in their head, the questions are correctly answered by the message. The astronomers bring in other people to examine this, and the questions are consistently answered. The message goes on to suggest certain experiments that scientists should perform in particle accelerators—the message says that if the experiments are set up in a specified precise way, then God will cause a miracle to occur. The experiments are done, and the resulting cloud chamber tracks spell out Biblical verses. Then the message explains to the scientists how to form a proper quantum theory of gravity....

I could go on, but you get the picture. The evidence doesn't *prove* that God exists—maybe some advanced alien civilization is playing a trick on us; maybe the scientists are undergoing some sort of mass hallucination; maybe all this is happening due to some incredibly improbable quantum fluctuation. But the evidence does provide some support for the hypothesis that God exists. It would be silly for the scientists to refuse to countenance the hypothesis that God exists, due to some commitment to methodological naturalism. Of course, it is important to consider the naturalistic hypotheses, but one has to consider the theistic hypothesis as well.

Note that the theistic hypothesis here is testable. For example, when the message tells the scientists that they will get a miraculous result from certain experimental setups, the scientists are testing the hypothesis the pulsar message is from God. If the experiments had not resulted in any unusual data, this would provide disconfirming evidence for the hypothesis that the message is from God. Hence, the fact that the experiments do result in unusual data provides some confirming evidence for the hypothesis that the message is from God. (The probability shift in favor of the hypothesis that the message is from God may be small, but the point is just that the unusual data does count as confirming evidence.)

The fact that the theistic hypothesis here is testable shows that some of the expert testimony that Jones relied on in formulating his decision is flawed. Specifically, philosopher of science Robert Pennock claims, in his expert report, that "Supernaturalism is not allowed" in science, "because it is not testable."[57] I have given a counterexample to that line of reasoning, by presenting a situation where a supernatural hypothesis is testable.

Jones, in support of his demarcation criterion of methodological naturalism, cites the definition of science from the prestigious National Academy of Sciences:

> Science is a particular way of knowing about the world. In science, explanations are restricted to those that can be inferred from the confirmable data—the results obtained through observations and experiments that can be substantiated by other scientists. Anything that can be observed or measured is amenable to scientific investigation. Explanations that cannot be based upon empirical evidence are not part of science.[58]

Just after this quote, Jones says that "This rigorous attachment to 'natural' explanations is an essential attribute to science by definition and by convention." But in fact the NAS definition never makes reference to "natural" explanations—there is no restriction to naturalism at all in their definition. In my hypothetical scenario described above, the supernatural explanation is based on empirical evidence, evidence that is obtained through observations and experiments that can be substantiated by other scientists. It follows that, on the NAS definition of science, supernatural explanations are in principle allowed, and hence it is illegitimate for Jones to appeal to their definition to support his demarcation criterion of methodological naturalism.

I don't know how Jones would respond to my argument against methodological naturalism based on the pulsar example, but I do have evidence for how Pennock (also a supporter of methodological naturalism) would respond. At the end of Pennock's expert report, he writes: "if someone were to find a way to empirically confirm the existence of an immaterial designer or any other supernatural being, science should change its methodology."[59] Pennock might then say that my pulsar example is one where the existence of a supernatural being has been empirically confirmed, and that in that situation science should change its methodology.

There is a problem with this idea that science should change its methodology in light of empirical confirmation of the existence of a supernatural being. How does this empirical confirmation take place, if not scientifically? By Pennock's lights, there must be some other epistemic practice that one can engage in where one can get empirical evidence for some proposition. What epistemic practice is this, and why doesn't it count as science? Pennock doesn't say. Also, note that the scientific status of that epistemic practice will presumably shift: at a time before one gets the empirical evidence that a supernatural being exists, the epistemic practice is unscientific, but after one gets that empirical evidence, the methodology of science changes in such a way that the epistemic practice (presumably) counts as scientific.

By Pennock's lights, it is possible for intelligent design to count as science. All the intelligent design proponents need to do is to provide enough evidence to confirm that there is a supernatural being—then scientific methodology will no longer include methodological naturalism. Thus, given that scientific methodology can change in light of new evidence, the debate over whether intelligent design counts as science hinges on the debate over whether there is empirical evidence that confirms the existence of a supernatural being. I am happy with this result, because this latter debate is the one that is interesting and important. We shouldn't get caught up debating whether intelligent design counts as science; the focus should be on the empirical arguments for and against intelligent design.

To sum up, I reject Pennock's claim that science should change its methodology if the existence of a supernatural being is empirically confirmed—but even if Pennock's claim is correct, it is possible that intelligent design can still count as science.

Now, I will turn to the final issue of this section, the issue of whether there is a consensus in the scientific and philosophical communities that methodological naturalism is a constraint of science. Jones's judgment reads as if there is a consensus, while I maintain that there is not. I can understand why Jones would think that there is a consensus, since expert witnesses for the plaintiffs testified that there is, and the defense didn't do an adequate job refuting that.

First, I will examine whether there is a scientific consensus in favor of methodological naturalism. The most straightforward approach here would be to do an opinion poll of scientists, but (as far as I can tell) no one has done that. Pennock[60] argues that there is such a scientific consensus by citing a literature search—nowhere in the contemporary scientific literature could he find scientists appealing to the supernatural. After he describes this literature search during his direct examination, this exchange follows:

> Q: So methodological naturalism is basic to the nature of science today?
> A: As I said, I could not find an exception to that.
> Q: And the rule is well accepted in the scientific community?
> A: That's right.[61]

There is a problem with the line of reasoning that goes from the results of the literature search to a conclusion about accepted scientific methodology. From the fact that there are no appeals to the supernatural in current scientific literature, it in no way follows that such appeals are excluded on methodological grounds. Consider the following parallel situation: a literature search will show that there is no postulation of the existence of an elementary particle with mass 1.73615 times that of the electron. But it in no way follows that the postulation of such a particle is excluded on methodological grounds. The reason that such a postulation doesn't appear in a literature search is that there's no evidence for such a particle. I maintain that one can find no postulation of the supernatural for the same reason.

Since I don't have the resources to do an opinion poll, I will simply cite some counterexamples to the proposition that all scientists endorse methodological naturalism. Of course, some scientists who are proponents of intelligent design, like biochemist Michael Behe, reject methodological naturalism, but even some scientists who are opponents of intelligent design reject it as well. For example, anti-intelligent design physicist Mark Perakh writes:

> a definition of science should not put any limits on legitimate subjects for the scientific exploration of the world. Indeed, although science has so far had no need to attribute any observed phenomena to a supernatural cause, and in doing so has achieved staggering successes, there still remain unanswered many fundamental questions about nature.... Until such answers are found, nothing should be prohibited as a legitimate subject of science, and excluding the supernatural out of hand serves no useful purpose.[62]

I conclude that it is not evident that there is a consensus by scientists in favor of methodological naturalism.

Now, I will turn to the issue of whether there is a consensus by philosophers of science that methodological naturalism is a constraint of science. During Pennock's cross-examination, he was asked the following question:

> Q: Dr. Pennock, isn't it true that there's not agreement among philosophers of science concerning the validity of methodological naturalism?

Pennock implies that only philosophers of science who are sympathetic to intelligent design reject methodological naturalism:

> A: The term methodological naturalism is fairly straightforward in the litera-
> ture. There have been criticisms of it from people like Del Ratzsch from
> discussions specifically of this debate. So there's some who have taken up
> a sympathetic position to the intelligent design folks and tried to argue
> that we could dispense with this.[63]

Larry Laudan is a good counterexample to this: he is not sympathetic to intelligent design, yet he rejects methodological naturalism as a demarcation criterion for science. (This follows from the sentence from Laudan's paper I quoted on page 49, as well as from the rest of Laudan's paper.) Later in cross-examination, the defense asks Pennock about Laudan. After Pennock says that he is familiar with Laudan, he is asked:

> Q: And Larry Laudan said he believes that creationism is science, it's just bad
> science, correct?

Pennock's response to this question takes up three pages of the trial transcript. In my opinion, Pennock misleadingly implies that Laudan would endorse methodological naturalism. Pennock says that if creationism is understood as a naturalistic hypothesis (focusing on its naturalistic implications about the age of the Earth, for example), then it is bad science, but if it is understood supernaturalistically, then it is not science at all. Pennock doesn't explicitly attribute this view to Laudan, but someone who hadn't read Laudan would probably come away thinking that this is Laudan's view. For example, Pennock says:

> If you seriously take the supernatural possibility, then you can't disconfirm
> it. So that's the sense in which it's important to say under the assumption of
> methodological naturalism, we have disconfirmed it, it's bad science, that's what

Laudan is talking about, but if you were to take seriously the non-natural part, that's to say rejecting scientific method, then it's just not science....[64]

Now, what the defense should have done here is pushed Pennock to clarify, to make clear to Jones that Laudan does not endorse methodological naturalism. But in fact the defense responds to Pennock's three-page answer with the following:

Thank you, Your Honor. I have no further questions.[65]

The defense dropped the ball: it would be reasonable for Jones to conclude on the basis of this cross-examination that (except for a few supporters of intelligent design) philosophers of science agree that methodological naturalism is a constraint of science.

Of course, Laudan is not the only philosopher of science who rejects methodological naturalism. I'll cite just one more example, that of anti-intelligent design philosopher Niall Shanks. Shanks *says* that he endorses methodological naturalism, but he gives a nonstandard account of methodological naturalism, an account proponents of intelligent design would be pretty happy with:

The methodological naturalist will not simply rule hypotheses about supernatural causes out of court ... But the methodological naturalist will insist on examining the evidence presented to support the existence of supernatural causes carefully .... methodological naturalists do not rule out the supernatural absolutely. They have critical minds, not closed minds.[66]

I conclude that it's not the case that there's a clear consensus in favor of methodological naturalism (when understood to rule out appeals to the supernatural) in the scientific or philosophical communities.

Intelligent Design is Not Inherently Theistic

Let's suppose that the above arguments are incorrect, and that in fact methodological naturalism is a demarcation criterion for science. I will now argue that this does not entail that intelligent design is unscientific, since intelligent design is not inherently theistic.

It is true that most—perhaps all—proponents of intelligent design are theists, and it's true that they sometimes say things that imply that intelligent design has supernatural consequences. For example, Jones, in his decision, quotes defense witness Steve Fuller, who referred in his expert report to "ID's rejection of naturalism and commitment to supernaturalism."[67] Pennock emphasizes in his expert report that "ID is inherently theistic,"[68] and the bulk of Barbara Forrest's lengthy expert report is devoted to arguing that "Anti-naturalism is an integral part of ID."[69] Jones agrees with these assessments, and that is why he maintains that intelligent design fails the methodological naturalism demarcation criterion.

"Intelligent design" means different things to different people, and while some view it as essentially committed to supernaturalism, others do not. What this really boils down to is a terminological issue. In the official formulations of intelligent design that proponents give nowadays, they are careful to avoid any commitment to the supernatural. For example, the Discovery Institute definition simply says that "The theory of intelligent design holds that certain features of the universe and of living things are best explained by an intelligent cause,"[70] without specifying whether that intelligent cause is natural or supernatural. If opponents of intelligent design insist that that definition is a misrepresentation of intelligent design, since intelligent design is inherently theistic, then the natural response is to put a new doctrine on the table, *shintelligent shesign*: "The theory of shintelligent shesign holds that certain features of the universe and of living things are best explained by an intelligent cause."[71]

It should be clear that shintelligent shesign is not inherently theistic. The intelligent cause could be God, but it need not be. It may be that living things on Earth were created by a highly intelligent alien civilization, as Raelians believe.[72] It may be that the whole universe we experience is really just a computer simulation being run by highly intelligent non-supernatural beings, as Nick Bostrom argues is plausible.[73] It takes just a bit of creativity to come up with other possibilities as well.

Proponents of intelligent design (construed supernaturalistically) are also proponents of shintelligent shesign. It follows that the vast majority of proponents of shintelligent shesign are theistic—they maintain that the intelligent cause is a supernatural God. But it in no way follows that shintelligent shesign itself is committed to supernaturalism. Shintelligent shesign is a disjunctive theory[74]—one possibility is that the intelligent cause is supernatural, but the other possibility is that the intelligent cause is natural. Just because most proponents of shintelligent shesign endorse one of the disjuncts, it in no way follows that the theory itself is not disjunctive.

I have introduced this "shintelligent shesign" terminology to placate those who say that intelligent design is inherently theistic. But my definition of "shintelligent shesign" is the same as the definition of "intelligent design" that for example the Discovery Institute endorses. I recommend that, to avoid terminological messiness, we simply take proponents of intelligent design at their word that the doctrine they are endorsing is the doctrine that I've called "shintelligent shesign." It follows that intelligent design is not inherently theistic.

Science and the Pursuit of Truth

If science really is permanently committed to methodological naturalism, it follows that the aim of science is not generating true theories. Instead, the aim of science would be something like: generating the best theories that can be formulated subject to the restriction that the theories are naturalistic. More and more evidence could come in suggesting that a supernatural being exists, but scientific theories wouldn't be allowed to acknowledge that possibility. Imagine what might happen in my pulsar message scenario: long after overwhelming evidence has convinced everyone that supernatural causation is occurring, scientists would still be searching for naturalistic causes. The scientists themselves may agree that the causes are supernatural, but, because they are subject to the constraint of methodological naturalism, they are not allowed to postulate such causes while doing science. Science would rightfully be marginalized—what is the point of spending all these resources investigating naturalistic causes, long after it is evident that the causes are supernatural? I'm not saying that society would want to completely stop investigating the possibility of natural causes, but by failing to countenance the possibility of supernatural hypotheses in the pulsar scenario, scientists would be missing out on a potential revolution in our understanding of the world.

Jones seems aware of the fact that his demarcation criteria entail that the aim of science is not truth. He writes that "while ID arguments may be true, a proposition on which the Court takes no position, ID is not science."[75] But if science is not a pursuit of truth, science has the potential to be marginalized, as an irrelevant social practice. If lots of evidence comes in against naturalism, investigation of the world that assumes naturalism has the potential to become otiose. Given the commitment to methodological naturalism, the success of science hinges on the contingent fact that the evidence strongly suggests that naturalism is true.

I maintain that science is better off without being shackled by methodological naturalism. Our successful scientific theories are naturalistic simply because this is the way the evidence points; this leaves open the possibility that, on the basis of new evidence, there could be supernatural scientific theories. I conclude that intelligent design should not be dismissed on the grounds that it is unscientific; intelligent design should be dismissed on the grounds that the empirical evidence for its claims just isn't there.

Dembski's Blog Post

That concludes the paper that I posted online in January 2006. The paper was quickly approvingly cited by leading intelligent design proponent William Dembski on his blog. I'll quote his post in full, because it will be relevant for the discussion below.

> Bradley Monton, a Princeton-trained philosopher on the faculty at the University of Kentucky, has an important piece on Dover here. Though Monton is not an ID proponent (he is a philosopher of physics who in his professional work is quite critical of fine-tuning as evidence for God), he exhibits little patience for the reasoning in Judge Jones's decision. Note especially the following paragraph from his article:
>
>> There is a problem with this idea that science should change its methodology in light of empirical confirmation of the existence of a supernatural being [a point that Pennock had conceded in testimony]. How does this empirical confirmation take place, if not scientifically? By Pennock's lights, there must be some other epistemic practice that one can engage in where one can get empirical evidence for some proposition. What epistemic practice is this, and why doesn't it count as science? Pennock doesn't say. Also, note that the scientific status of that epistemic practice will presumably shift: at a time before one gets the empirical evidence that a supernatural being exists, the epistemic practice is unscientific, but after one gets that empirical evidence, the methodology of science changes in such a way that the epistemic practice (presumably) counts as scientific.
>
> The lesson, which should be obvious to Pennock and Forrest if only it didn't provide such a wide opening for ID, is that methodologies are tools for assisting inquiry but cannot define (or confine) inquiry.

Some philosophers would not be happy if they were approvingly cited by Dembski; to them he is on the wrong side of the culture war. But I don't mind; though I disagree with Dembski on a lot of issues, I also think that some of his philosophical views are correct. Dembski and I clearly agree on the methodological naturalism issue, and not only do I agree with his conclusion, I agree with many of the arguments he gives for his conclusion. I am simply concerned with philosophical truth; I'm not concerned with whether there's a culture war, and if there is a culture war I'm not concerned with which side I'm on.

To give an anecdotal example of how much anyone who talks about intelligent design issues is viewed as being in one of two opposing camps, one of my colleagues at University of Colorado (where I was hired in Spring 2006) was at a conference shortly after I was hired, and she was told something like "I can't believe you hired that creationist Bradley Monton." Of course, I'm not a creationist, but the fact that I had written this paper critiquing the Dover decision was enough to get me labeled as such.

Pennock's Email

Shortly after my paper was posted online, Pennock sent me an email expressing extreme unhappiness with my paper, saying that it was "defamatory," and telling me that I had to take it off the internet. (For more on this email, go to bradleymonton. org.) For the record, I left my paper online.

Sifting through the sound and fury, his main point was that I had misrepresented his philosophical views in my paper, and that his court testimony neither was nor purported to be a philosophical treatment of the subject. He said that the distinctions and detailed arguments supporting his views could be found in his published philosophical writings—the main one presumably being his voluminous 1999 book, *Tower of Babel: The Evidence Against the New Creationism*.

I agree that there's a sense in which court testimony is not a philosophical treatment of a subject; but nevertheless, one should accurately reflect one's philosophical views in such testimony, and to the extent that philosophical arguments are needed to defend one's position, one should give them. It turns out that the decision of the judge partly depended on a philosophical claim—a claim about the nature of science—and the judge gave implicit philosophical arguments for that claim. So in these senses, the judge's decision is a philosophical treatment. Moreover, Pennock's testimony is relevant, to the extent that the judge based his reasoning on Pennock's testimony.

Let me explain why Pennock says that I misconstrued his arguments. In his expert report—a written document submitted to the court in advance of the trial—Pennock says:

> if someone were to find a way to empirically confirm the existence of an
> immaterial designer or any other supernatural being, science should change
> its methodology.

I'll call this the doctrine of *weak methodological naturalism*. This doctrine holds that we should endorse methodological naturalism just because the evidence isn't there; if the evidence were to come in, then we should change the methodology of science by dropping the criterion of methodological naturalism. Contrast that with the doctrine I'll call *strong methodological naturalism*—the doctrine that science should not change its methodology, no matter what. In Pennock's book, he endorses strong methodological naturalism. I'll discuss the arguments from his book in more detail later in this chapter, but his basic argument is that it's not possible to get empirical evidence for the supernatural.

I was aware that there was a tension between what Pennock said in his book and what Pennock said in his expert report, but I decided to go with what Pennock said in the expert report, because my goal wasn't to critique Pennock; my goal was to critique the judge's decision. Jones based his decision on Pennock's expert report; he did not base his decision on Pennock's book. In fact, since the expert report came after the book, I thought that perhaps Pennock changed his mind. His email made clear to me that he didn't.

Because it turns out that Pennock didn't change his view, I was wrong to say the following:

> By Pennock's lights, it is possible for intelligent design to count as science. All the intelligent design proponents need to do is to provide enough evidence to confirm that there is a supernatural being—then scientific methodology will no longer include methodological naturalism.

What I was trying to do here is just elucidate the doctrine of weak methodological naturalism that Pennock endorsed in his expert report. But in fact, I made a logical error: one can endorse weak methodological naturalism, and nevertheless maintain that it is impossible for science to change its methodology. One can do this by maintaining that it is impossible to empirically confirm the existence of a supernatural being—and this is what Pennock maintains. So when Pennock says "if someone were to find a way to empirically confirm the existence of [a] supernatural being, science should change its methodology," for him that's a lot like saying "if someone were to find a way to show that $2+2=5$, science should change its methodology."

So in principle, one can consistently endorse both weak and strong methodological naturalism. But it is somewhat misleading to do so, because typically when someone makes a conditional claim like "if A were to happen, then B should happen," that person thinks that it is at least possible for A to happen. It's unfortunate that Pennock doesn't make clear that that's what he's doing in his expert report.[76]

In my opinion, the position that it's possible for intelligent design to count as science, which is the position I was attributing to Pennock, is a reasonable one.[77] It turns out that Pennock endorses what by my lights is a much less reasonable view, that it's impossible to empirically confirm the existence of a supernatural being. I'll look at Pennock's arguments for that view now, by looking at the discussion in his book. I'm focusing on Pennock in part because he's a leading intelligent design opponent, and in part because his arguments provide good examples of the sorts of arguments intelligent design opponents give to argue that intelligent design is not science.

Pennock's Book

Pennock was not happy that I focused on what he said in the trial about methodological naturalism; instead he wanted me to focus on what he said in his book, *Tower of Babel*. As I'll now explain, the arguments for methodological naturalism in Pennock's book are similarly flawed. I'll divide the discussion up into seven parts.

1. ALLOWING SUPERNATURALISM MAKES THE SCIENTIST'S TASK TOO EASY

Here's the first of Pennock's arguments against methodological naturalism that I'll consider:

> allowing appeal to supernatural powers in science would make the scientist's task too easy, because one would always be able to call upon the gods for quick theoretical assistance…. Indeed, all empirical investigation beyond the purely descriptive could cease, for scientists would have a ready-made answer for everything.[78]

This argument strikes me as unfair. Consider a particular empirical phenomenon, like a chemical reaction, and imagine that scientists are trying to figure out why the reaction happened. Pennock would say that scientists who allow appeal to supernatural powers would have a ready-made answer: God did it. While it may be that that's the only true explanation that can be given, a good scientist—including a good theistic scientist—would wonder whether there's more to be said. Even if God were ultimately the cause of the reaction, one would still wonder if the proximate cause is a result of the chemicals that went into the reaction, and a good scientist—even a good theistic scientist—would investigate whether such a naturalistic account could be given.

To drive the point home, an analogy might be helpful. With the advent of quantum mechanics, scientists have become comfortable with indeterministic events. For example, when asked why a particular radioactive atom decayed at the exact time that it did, most physicists would say that there's no reason it decayed at that particular time; it was just an indeterministic event.[79] One could imagine an opponent of indeterminism giving an argument that's analogous to Pennock's:

> allowing appeal to indeterministic processes in science would make the scientist's task too easy, because one would always be able to call upon chance for quick theoretical assistance…. Indeed, all empirical investigation beyond the purely descriptive could cease, for scientists would have a ready-made answer for everything.

It is certainly possible that, for every event that happens, scientists could simply say "that's the result of an indeterministic chancy process; there's no further explanation for why the event happened that way." But this would clearly be doing bad science: just because the option of appealing to indeterminism is there, it doesn't follow that the option should always be used. The same holds for the option of appealing to supernatural powers.

As further evidence against Pennock, it's worth pointing out that prominent scientists in the past have appealed to supernatural powers, without using them as a ready-made answer for everything. Newton is a good example of this—he is a devout theist, in addition to being a great scientist, and he thinks that God sometimes intervenes in the world. Pennock falsely implies that this is not the case:

> God may have underwritten the active principles that govern the world described in [Newton's] *Principia* and the *Opticks*, but He did not interrupt any of the equations or regularities therein. Johnson and other creationists who want to dismiss methodological naturalism would do well to consult Newton's own rules of reasoning....[80]

But in fact, Newton does not endorse methodological naturalism. In his *Opticks*, Newton claims that God sometimes intervenes in the world. Specifically, Newton thinks that, according to his laws of motion, the orbits of planets in our solar system are not stable over long periods of time, and his solution to this problem is to postulate that God occasionally adjusts the motions of the planets so as to ensure the continued stability of their orbits. Here's a relevant passage from Newton. (It's not completely obvious that Newton is saying that God will intervene but my interpretation is the standard one.)

> God in the Beginning form'd Matter in solid, massy, hard, impenetrable, moveable Particles ... it became him who created them to set them in order. And if he did so, it's unphilosophical to seek for any other Origin of the World, or to pretend that it might arise out of a Chaos by the mere Laws of Nature; though being once form'd, it may continue by those Laws for many Ages. For while Comets move in very excentrick Orbs in all manner of Positions, blind Fate could never make all the Planets move one and the same way in Orbs concentrick, some inconsiderable Irregularities excepted, which may have risen from the mutual Actions of Comets and Planets upon one another, and which will be apt to increase, till this System wants a Reformation.... [God is] able by his Will to move the Bodies within his boundless uniform Sensorium, and thereby to form and reform the Parts of the Universe....[81]

A scientist who writes this way does not sound like a scientist who is following methodological naturalism.

It's worth noting that some contemporaries of Newton took issue with his view of God occasionally intervening in the universe. For example, Leibniz writes:

> Sir Isaac Newton and his followers also have a very odd opinion concerning the work of God. According to them, God Almighty needs to wind up his watch from time to time; otherwise it would cease to move. He had not, it seems, sufficient foresight to make it a perpetual motion.[82]

Note, though, that Leibniz also thought that God intervened in the world:

> I hold that when God works miracles, he does not do it in order to supply the wants of nature, but those of grace.

Later investigation revealed that in fact planetary orbits are more stable than Newton thought, so Newton's appeal to supernatural powers wasn't needed. But the key point is that Newton is willing to appeal to supernatural powers, without using the appeal to supernatural powers as a ready-made answer for everything.

Pennock says that "Without the binding assumption of uninterruptible natural law there would be absolute chaos in the scientific worldview."[83] Newton's own approach to physics provides a good counterexample to this—Newton is a leading contributor to the scientific worldview, and yet he does not bind himself by the assumption of uninterruptible natural law.[84]

2. MERELY NATURALISTIC SCIENTIFIC TRUTH VS. ONTOLOGICAL (METAPHYSICAL) ABSOLUTE TRUTH

A powerful argument against strong methodological naturalism is that it is incompatible with the view that science is essentially a pursuit of truth. Naturalism could be false, and yet science (under the requirements of strong methodological naturalism) would not be allowed to consider supernatural hypotheses. Science wouldn't give us the truth, it would just tell us what *would be* true, under the (false) assumption that naturalism is true.

Pennock replies to this argument by making a distinction between two types of truth, "merely naturalistic scientific truth" and "ontological (metaphysical) absolute truth." Here is the relevant passage:

> Consider … the geneticist who, applying methodological naturalism, searches for a natural explanation for hypertrichosis. People with hypertrichosis grow hair all over their faces and upper bodies, and were once thought of as were-

wolves. Finding evidence for the X-linked gene and an evolutionary explanation of the trait, the geneticist might reassure a patient that his disorder is "the result of a purposeless and natural process that did not have him in mind," the phrase of G.G. Simpson that creationists find so offensive. Surely we may accept that statement as true, even though as a merely naturalistic scientific truth, it does not rule out the possibility of an intelligent supernatural cause—a "curse of the werewolf," say—so it cannot be said to be absolutely true in the ontological (metaphysical) sense.[85]

This distinction between these different types of truth is, as far as I know, original to Pennock. I am uncomfortable with the very notion that there are different types of truth. The only time I would want to use the term "truth" is when I am talking about what Pennock calls "ontological (metaphysical) truth"—this sort of truth describes the way the world actually is. What Pennock calls "a scientific truth" may actually be false, in the sense that the world actually is not that way.

I can't definitively show that Pennock is wrong to use his truth terminologies in the way that he does. I can simply register my discomfort with it, and also point out that I've never seen another philosopher doing this. What's important to keep in mind is that, if one uses Pennock's terminology, one can call a statement "true" even though the statement is actually false, because the concept of truth one is using when one calls the statement "true" is the concept of merely naturalistic scientific truth. Merely naturalistic scientific truths are the claims one would make about the world, under the assumption of methodological naturalism—but since naturalism might be false, the merely naturalistic scientific truths might be false too.

By Pennock's lights, science is not aiming at truth—science is not aiming to tell us the way the world actually is. Instead, science is aiming at something else—what Pennock calls "merely naturalistic scientific truth." It would be surprising to me if it were built into the very methodology of science that science ends up not aiming to provide a true account of the nature of the world. (And by "true account of the nature of the world," I mean an "ontological (metaphysical) absolutely true account of the nature of the world"—I will continue to use "true" in this way for the rest of the book.)

3. THE INHERENT MYSTERY OF THE SUPERNATURAL

According to Pennock, one reason we can't scientifically investigate the supernatural is that the supernatural "is inherently mysterious to us."[86] Here's one way he puts the point:

Scientific models must be judged on natural grounds of evidence, for we have no supernatural ground upon which we can stand since any such ground is necessarily a mystery to us.[87]

The claim that the supernatural is inherently mysterious is controversial. It is surely a claim that many Christians would disagree with. For example, consider those who take John 3:16 literally:

> For God so loved the world, that He gave His only begotten Son, that whosoever believeth in Him shall not perish, but have everlasting life.

Just this one sentence tells us a lot about the nature of God. For example, we learn that God loves us, that God gave his son to us, and that believing in God will give us everlasting life. If a being were inherently mysterious to us, we wouldn't be able to learn such things about it.

Pennock argues for his view that the supernatural is inherently mysterious to us by claiming that "As natural beings, all our knowledge comes via natural laws and processes." But think about what many Christians would say about John 3:16: they would say that this passage comes from the Bible, and that the Bible is the divinely inspired word of God. They would say that the knowledge of God that we get from the Bible is not via a purely naturalistic process, because the Bible itself has supernatural inspiration.

Of course, it may be that these Christians are wrong, and in fact all our knowledge does come from natural laws and processes. But my key point is that, on the basis of the relatively uncontroversial claim that we are natural beings, Pennock can't infer the controversial claim that all our knowledge comes via natural laws and processes. Just because we are not supernatural, it doesn't follow that we can't learn things about God via the divinely inspired word of God.

4. CONTROL OVER THE SUPERNATURAL

Another argument Pennock gives for methodological naturalism hinges on the claim that we cannot control the supernatural. Here is what Pennock says:

> Experimentation requires observation and *control* of the variables. We confirm causal laws by performing controlled experiments in which the hypothesized independent variable is made to vary while all the other factors are held constant so that we can observe the effect on the dependent variable. But we have no control over supernatural entities or forces; hence these cannot be scientifically studied.[88]

For the moment let's grant that experimentation requires observation and control of the variables. A problem arises when Pennock attempts to infer that, because we have no control over supernatural entities or forces, these supernatural entities or forces cannot be scientifically studied. What Pennock is ignoring is the distinction (standardly made in philosophy of science) between *experimental* science and *historical* science.[89] Consider paleontology: what scientists who are engaging in this practice are doing is making observations and drawing inferences based on those observations. We can't do a controlled experiment to determine whether the dinosaurs died out as the result of an asteroid impact—we can't vary an independent variable while holding all other factors constant. Nevertheless, we can make lots of observations in the world (of dinosaur bones, geological strata, asteroid craters, and so on) and we can make scientific inferences on the basis of these observations. Also, consider cosmology: we can't do a controlled experiment to find out whether the universe started with a big bang, but we can make astronomical observations and make scientific inferences on their basis. I conclude that we can scientifically study aspects of reality that we can't experimentally control. Thus, it doesn't follow from the claim that we have no control over supernatural entities that we can't study them.

Another problem with Pennock's argument is that *control* isn't actually needed to do experiments; instead *influence* is all that's needed. Consider the medical experiments that have been done on the intercessory effects of prayer.[90] The experimenters do not claim that these experiments are designed in such a way that the prayers are having *control* over the hypothesized supernatural prayer-granting entity. Instead, the experimenters just claim that the experiments are designed to test whether the prayers are having *influence* over the supernatural entity. And indeed, suppose it turned out that medical patients who were prayed over by Christians were healed, while those patients who were prayed over by members of other religious faiths were not. This would provide at least a small amount of experimental evidence that the Christian God exists.

5. THE REQUIREMENTS OF SCIENTIFIC EVIDENCE

Pennock claims that "There is a simple and sound rationale for the principle [of methodological naturalism] based upon the requirements of scientific evidence."[91] His argument is that the requirements of scientific evidence are such that any hypothesis must be *testable*, but supernatural hypotheses are not. Why aren't supernatural hypotheses testable, according to Pennock? Here's what he says:

> in any situation, any pattern (or lack of pattern) of data is compatible with the general hypothesis of the existence of a supernatural agent unconstrained by

natural law. Because of this feature, supernatural hypotheses remain immune from disconfirmation.[92]

Pennock's idea here is that, because a supernatural agent is free to do anything, then any observation one makes is compatible with the existence of a supernatural agent. Thus, one could never make an observation that disconfirms the hypothesis that a supernatural agent is responsible for what's observed.

There is a logical flaw in Pennock's argument. Let's suppose that Pennock is right to say that any pattern of data is compatible with the general hypothesis of the existence of a supernatural agent. What follows from that is that the general hypothesis of the existence of a supernatural agent is immune from disconfirmation. It does *not* follow that *any* supernatural hypothesis is immune from disconfirmation. A supernatural hypothesis can be specific about the nature of the supernatural being; a supernatural hypothesis need not be simply a general one that states that a supernatural agent exists. For example, the supernatural hypothesis could specify that God exists, and that God wants a universe with simple laws of nature. This supernatural hypothesis is subject to disconfirmation—we could discover that the laws are not simple.

6. A NATURALIZED GOD

Early in this chapter, I presented an example of a pulsar pulsing Morse code, and I suggested that this could provide some evidence for the existence of God. Pennock rejects this, saying that this is "naturalizing God."[93] He makes the point explicitly in the context of ghosts, but it is clear from his whole discussion that he would say the same thing about God:

> To conceive of ghosts as supernatural entities is to consider them to be outside the natural realm, outside the law-governed world of cause-and-effect physics. But to say that science could test and confirm their existence, as in our hypothetical case, is to reconceive them as natural entities. ... such "ghosts" are no longer supernatural—they have been naturalized.[94]

Here's a related point Pennock makes about God:

> In proposing a theistic science, Johnson claims to be expanding science to supernatural possibilities undreamed of in this philosophy, but what he and other Creation scientists are really doing is reducing God to a scientific object, placing God in the scientific box.[95]

Finally, here is how Pennock sums up his view:

if one naturalizes God to make the Creation hypothesis scientific, then we find ourselves faced with a God who is not very godly.[96]

I've given a number of quotations from Pennock because, despite the fact that he goes on for a few pages about this issue, I'm really not sure what the argument is. I simply don't see how God intervening in the world in such a way that we could get evidence of God's existence makes God natural as opposed to supernatural, and puts God in a scientific box, and makes God not very godly. It's a standard part of many religious doctrines that God does intervene in the world via, for example, miracles. Our witnessing these miracles is meant to provide confirming evidence of the existence of God. (Admittedly, we aren't *testing* the existence of God, we're just making observations that confirm the existence of God. But this relates back to the historical vs. experimental science issue we discussed above.) Just because God is intervening in the world in the form of miracles, I don't see how it follows that God is not supernatural, and has been put in the scientific box, and is not very godly. Perhaps Pennock's particular theistic views are such that he doesn't want to believe in that sort of intervening God, but he should recognize that there is a large historical tradition of theists believing in exactly that sort of God.

Here is another way to bring out the problem with Pennock's line of reasoning. Suppose that we do get scientific evidence for the existence of a being that is the creator and sustainer of the universe and everything in it, and that has created a heaven, and decides who goes there. Pennock would say that, since we're getting scientific evidence for such a being, the being is not supernatural, the being is a scientific object, and the being is not very godly. Pennock can say all that, but most theists would disagree. Most theists would consider such a being supernatural and godly, even if the being interacts with the world in such a way that we can get scientific evidence of the being's existence.

It would be interesting if Pennock were to argue that a being that we could get scientific evidence for could not be the sort of being that created and sustained the universe, or is all-powerful, or is all-knowing, and so on. If Pennock could establish this, then Pennock would have an effective argument that any being that we could get scientific evidence for is not very godly. But Pennock does not try to establish this point, and moreover I don't see any even prima facie plausible argument for such a thesis.

7. WORSHIP

Here's what Pennock says about the possibility of Christians coming to believe in a naturalized God:

Christians would be wise not to even start down the dead-end road of creation-science or theistic science, for it is unlikely that they would find a naturalized God to be worthy of worship.[97]

To be honest, this strikes me as demeaning to Christians. I would think the Christians would want to follow the evidence where it leads—if they have false beliefs about God, I would think they would want to know that. Granted, there are some Christians who might choose to willfully ignore evidence to delusionally maintain their false beliefs, but there are some non-Christians who do that too. Those people are beyond the scope of intellectual discourse, and for Pennock to imply that all Christians are like that is, quite simply, offensive.

The question of whether God is worthy of worship is a question that should only be considered once one evaluates the evidence for the existence and nature of God. It would be intellectually dishonest to let one's desire to worship God influence one's evaluation of the evidence for the existence and nature of God—unless, that is, one had independent evidence for the thesis that whatever God exists is a being that is worthy of worship. I haven't heard of any arguments for such independent evidence, so I think the best way for Christians—and for everyone else—to proceed is to decide whether God exists, and if so what God is like, and only then decide whether one wants to worship that God. In short, one should follow the evidence where it leads.

It's worth noting that this is what intelligent design proponents like Philip Johnson want, for Christians to follow the evidence where it leads:

> If Christian theists can summon the courage to argue that preexisting intelligence really was an essential element in biological creation and to insist that the evidence be evaluated by standards that do not assume the point in dispute, then they will make a great contribution to the search for truth, *whatever the outcome*.[98]

Johnson is not out to protect his religious beliefs come what may; he's out to find the truth. (Or at least, this is what he says, and I have no reason to think that he's being misleading here.) Johnson thinks that the truth is Christianity, but he recognizes the epistemic possibility that he's mistaken.

Here is how Pennock replies to this passage from Johnson:

> If we are to take him at his word, this means that he would then have to admit that the Creation hypothesis is false. This is just the line of reasoning that the atheists have already followed to its "natural" conclusion.[99]

Well, Pennock thinks that that's where the evidence leads, but Johnson disagrees. To determine who is right, one actually has to look at the evidence for a creator. We're going to look at some of that evidence in the next chapter. My own view is that the atheists are right, but it's not completely obvious that the atheists are right. The pro-intelligent design arguments are worth taking seriously, and in taking them seriously we will be making at least a modest contribution to the search for truth, whatever the outcome.

To finish up, I'd like to consider one more aspect of Pennock's claim that Christians shouldn't pursue arguments for a naturalized God because they would be unlikely to find it worthy of worship. Pennock's claim raises the following question: how does one determine what should be worshipped? This strikes me as a personal matter, not the sort of issue that philosophers and scientists should be adjudicating with evidence and argument. But that said, the naturalized God that Pennock talks about seems to me like it could be the God that a lot of Christians believe in and worship. The naturalized God that Pennock is talking about acts in the world in such a way that we can get evidence for the existence of this God. But a key part of Christian doctrine is that God became flesh in the form of Jesus Christ, and that Christ acted in the world in such a way that we can get evidence of his existence, and of his divinity. As a result, it would be perfectly reasonable for Christians to say to Pennock: "the God I believe in is a naturalized God in your sense, and verily, this God is worthy of worship."

Other Arguments that Intelligent Design Is Not Science

Pennock is not the only person who gives bad arguments for the thesis that intelligent design is not science. While the argument from methodological naturalism is certainly a popular one, other arguments have been given, and I'll look at some of those arguments now.

I'll focus on Matt Young and Taner Edis, two intelligent design opponents who hold that intelligent design is not science. Young and Edis summarize their arguments as follows:

> the advocates of intelligent design do not practice science, not because their ideas are religiously motivated but because they make no substantive predictions, do not respond to evidence, have an ax to grind, and appear to be oblivious to criticism.[100]

As the "not because they are religiously motivated" line suggests, Young and Edis reject the methodological naturalism argument for the claim that intelligent design is not science. Nevertheless they have four other reasons for thinking that intelligent design is not science. Let's separate out the first reason, the "make no substantive predictions" reason, from the other three, and let's take up the other three first.

The other three reasons—the "do not respond to evidence, have an ax to grind, and appear to be oblivious to criticism" reasons—are critiques of intelligent design proponents, not critiques of intelligent design theory itself. Let's suppose that Young and Edis are right, and that intelligent design proponents do all behave this way. This does nothing to show that intelligent design is not science; it just shows that intelligent design proponents are not behaving as good scientists should. Good scientists should not fail to respond to evidence, have an ax to grind, and appear to be oblivious to criticism. (Though, I hazard to guess that many scientists are guilty of having an ax to grind on some issue or another—to the extent that one can objectively characterize anyone as having an ax to grind.)

Perhaps Young and Edis think that, because all intelligent design proponents behave in the way that they describe, this is enough to show that intelligent design is not science. But if that's right, the conclusion is highly tenuous. All it would take is some future intelligent design proponent to be the sort of person who does respond to evidence, doesn't have an ax to grind, and isn't oblivious to criticism. Once someone like this becomes a proponent of intelligent design, the argument that holds that intelligent design isn't science on the basis of the characteristics of its proponents will lose force.

Let's turn to the other argument of Young and Edis, that intelligent design proponents are not practicing science because they make no substantive predictions. I would say that intelligent design proponents are making a prediction: they are claiming that, if one looks, one will find evidence that there is a designer (where this designer is the cause of some features of the universe or of living things, as described in the intelligent design doctrine discussed in Chapter 1). Perhaps Young and Edis would say that this prediction isn't a substantive one, and that's what makes it unscientific. But compare that doctrine to other big-picture claims, like the claim that there is matter in the universe. Is that claim a substantive claim, and if not does that make it unscientific? I would say that that claim is a substantive claim, because it suggests that, if one looks, one could find evidence that there is matter in the universe. But perhaps Young and Edis would say that the claim is not substantive, because it doesn't tell one any details about the nature and distribution of this matter. Even though it is true that the claim is not detailed in that sense, I wouldn't want to say that the claim that there's matter in the universe is unscientific. It seems much more reasonable to say that it's a big-picture scientific claim, a claim that can be supplemented by other more detailed claims about the nature of matter.

Similarly, I would want to say that the intelligent design claim is a big-picture claim, one that can be supplemented with more detailed claims about the nature of the designer. When we get to the specific arguments for intelligent design in the next chapter, we'll see the sorts of specific claims that are made to supplement the big-picture statement of intelligent design. These specific claims are always tied to specific predictions, and hence Young and Edis are wrong to claim that intelligent design proponents do not make substantive predictions. (For example, with the fine-tuning argument, we'll see the specific claim made that, if the values of the fundamental constants were outside some narrow range, life couldn't exist. We can make this a prediction by predicting that we won't discover that, if the values of the fundamental constants were outside the narrow range, life could exist.)

I conclude that, in the course of arguing for intelligent design, intelligent design proponents do make substantive predictions. The general statement of intelligent design is a big-picture claim that perhaps doesn't count as substantive, but big-picture claims are sometimes made in science.

So Is Intelligent Design Science?

After all the discussion of the last two chapters, one still may be left wondering: by my lights, is intelligent design science, or isn't it? Well, my view is that giving an answer to that question largely just does emotive work for us (as Laudan suggested in the passage I quoted on page 49). If you're an intelligent design proponent, you're inclined to say "yes"; if you're an intelligent design opponent, you're inclined to say "no."

I admit that there are ways in which discussing the issue of whether intelligent design is science is fruitful. It leads one to address helpful issues, like what the nature of science is, and how best to understand the claims of intelligent design proponents, and what the evidence for intelligent design is. But sometimes engaging in the debate distracts one from the important issues, and instead gets one bogged down in questions like whether individual claims or only whole theories are disconfirmable, and whether one should countenance different notions of truth, and what exactly counts as "supernatural." While these questions can be interesting to consider, and while answering them can be philosophically informative, they distract us from the central issue associated with intelligent design.

Ultimately, what we really want to know isn't whether intelligent design is science—what we really want to know is whether intelligent design is *true*. We could, if we wanted, agree with Pennock and Judge Jones that intelligent design is not science. But if it turns out that intelligent design is true, would the fact that it's not science really matter to us? This would certainly tell us something interesting about how "science" is understood in our society, but it wouldn't stop us from investigating the important questions regarding the nature of the intelligent designer and the scope of its design.

If it doesn't really matter whether intelligent design is science, then why did I engage in so much discussion of the issue? Well, as you've perhaps gathered by now, one of the main lines of attack that many atheists (and other intelligent design opponents) give against intelligent design is to argue that intelligent design isn't science. Even though I'm an atheist, I wanted to defend intelligent design by taking issue with this line of attack.

So the reason I focused on the issue of whether intelligent design is science is that so many of the anti-intelligent design arguments are based on that issue. But with that issue safely behind us, we can move on to the important issue: is intelligent design true?

Since this is a tough question to answer directly, let's look instead at a more nuanced question: how plausible are arguments for intelligent design? In the next chapter, I'll argue that the answer is: "somewhat."

CHAPTER 3

Some Somewhat Plausible Intelligent Design Arguments

After much seeking, you finally reach the Oracle. You've come equipped with a long list of questions, but when the Oracle sees you, she says: "Look, I'm busy, I only have time to answer one question. I know you've been thinking about intelligent design, and I'm glad you understand the doctrine now; Monton has given the right definition. I'll give you two options. Do you want to know whether intelligent design is science, or do you want to know whether intelligent design is true?"

Which would you pick?

For those who would pick the "Is intelligent design science?" question, feel free to go back and reread the previous chapter. Even though much of the philosophical discussion of intelligent design relates to that question, by my lights the important question is whether intelligent design is true. I'm going to consider four arguments for intelligent design that I find somewhat—but only somewhat—plausible. The four arguments I'll discuss are the fine-tuning argument, the kalam cosmological argument, the argument from the origin of life, and the simulation argument. (And if you don't know what these arguments are, don't worry, I'll explain them in due course.) I'll also have a section on the standard evolution-based intelligent design argument, though (as I'll explain) I find that argument less plausible than the other four I take up.

There's a lot one could say about each of the arguments, but I'm not going to try to be comprehensive. I'll follow some strands of reasoning associated with each argument that I find to be especially interesting, and my discussion will be such that even cognoscenti should find something new to think about.

The Fine-Tuning Argument

Here's the basic version of the fine-tuning argument. Consider the fundamental constants of physics, like the strength of the gravitational force, or the mass of the proton, or the strength of the strong force (the force that holds the nucleus of an atom together). These constants are *fine-tuned for life*: for each of those constants, if the value of the constant were more than slightly different than it actually is, life couldn't exist. Some people say that this provides evidence for the existence of God. The reasoning requires two parts. First, if God were to exist, God would want the values of the constants to be life-permitting. Second, if God weren't to exist, there is no reason to expect the values of the constants to be life-permitting—and given how narrow the life-permitting range is, there would be reason to expect the values of the constants to be *non*-life-permitting. So given that the values of the constants actually are life-permitting, this provides evidence for the existence of God.

Here's a bit more formal way of putting the argument:

Premise 1: The fundamental constants that are involved in the laws of physics which describe our universe are finely tuned for life, in the sense that if some of the constants had values outside some narrow range then life could not exist. (I will call this "the fine-tuning evidence"; I'll explain this evidence in more detail below.)

Intermediate Conclusion: It would be very unlikely for the universe to have life-permitting fundamental constants by chance. (This follows from Premise 1.)

Premise 2: If God created the universe, we would expect it to be life-permitting.

Premise 3: The universe is life-permitting.

Final Conclusion: Thus, given the fine-tuning evidence, the fact that the universe is life-permitting provides evidence for the existence of God. (This follows from the Intermediate Conclusion and Premises 2 and 3.)

Here's an analogy that will help you to see the reasoning behind the fine-tuning argument. Suppose you're in a bar with a dartboard on one wall, and a large box opposite the dartboard. You know that inside the box is either your friend Fred or a dart-throwing machine, but you don't know which one. Fred is an expert dart-thrower—whatever region of the dartboard Fred aims at, Fred hits. You're pretty sure that, if Fred were to throw a dart, he would aim for the bull's-eye. You're not completely sure that that's what Fred would do, but given your knowledge of Fred, you're pretty sure—in other words, you assign it a high probability. The dart-throwing machine, by contrast, doesn't aim for any particular region of the dartboard. It always manages to hit the dartboard, but other than that it has no aim. When it throws a bunch of darts, its darts are randomly distributed across the whole dartboard.

So, you think there's some chance that Fred is in the box, and some chance that the dart-throwing machine is in the box. It actually doesn't matter for the argument what probability you assign to each of those possibilities (as long as both probabilities are non-zero). The only constraint is that, since those are the only two possibilities allowed, your two probability assignments must sum to 1. You could think it equally likely that Fred is in the box as that the dart-throwing machine is in the box—you could assign probability 1/2 to each hypothesis. Or, you could think it more likely that Fred is in the box. Or, you could think it more likely that the dart-throwing machine is in the box. No matter what your starting probabilities are, as long as they're both non-zero, the argument I'm about to give will go through.

Here's the argument. Suppose that you see a dart emerge from the box, and hit the bull's-eye. I claim that this should lead you to increase your probability for the hypothesis that Fred is in the box. If Fred is in the box, you would predict that the dart probably would hit bull's-eye, since you think that Fred would probably aim for bull's-eye, and Fred's aim is impeccable. If the dart-throwing machine is in the box, though, you would predict that the dart probably *wouldn't* hit bull's-eye, since the machine doesn't aim at any particular region of the dartboard, and bull's-eye is a very small region of the dartboard. So, given that the dart does hit bull's-eye, this should lead you to increase your probability for the hypothesis that Fred is in the box. (Also, this should lead you to decrease by an equal amount your probability for the hypothesis that the dart-throwing machine is in the box.)

The probabilistic reasoning I've just presented is uncontroversial; that's what formal probability theory would tell you to do. What is controversial is whether that sort of dart-throwing case is a good analogy to the fine-tuning argument.

Here's how the analogy is meant to go. Each point on the dartboard represents a possible set of values of the fundamental constants that go into the laws of physics. One point on this dartboard represents our actual universe, while other points represent different possible universes, with different sets of values of the fundamental constants. The bull's-eye region of the dartboard represents the universes that are life-permitting. The fact that this region is small corresponds to the fact that the fundamental constants are finely tuned for life, in the sense that if some of the constants had values outside some narrow range then life could not exist.

So that's the dartboard; what about Fred and the machine? Fred being in the box corresponds to God existing (where God is understood as the creator of the universe). The dart-throwing machine being in the box corresponds to the non-existence of God. The fact that you think that Fred probably will aim at bull's-eye represents that you think that God would probably create a life-permitting universe. The fact that Fred's aim is impeccable corresponds to God being omnipotent. The dart-throwing machine not having any aim corresponds to the fact that, assuming there's no God, we wouldn't expect any particular set of values of the fundamental constants to be more likely than any other set of values.

The analogy continues with the starting probability assignments. For the dart story, you start out by assigning some probability to the hypothesis that Fred is in the box, and some probability to the hypothesis that the dart-throwing machine is in the box. Since you think these are the only two possibilities, your two probability assignments sum to 1. Similarly, for the fine-tuning argument, you start out by assigning some probability to the hypothesis that the universe was created by God, and some probability to the hypothesis that the universe not. Now, it doesn't matter whether your starting probability for Fred being in the box is low or high—the fact that the dart hits bull's-eye should lead you to increase your probability for the hypothesis that Fred is in the box. Similarly, it doesn't matter whether your starting probability for the hypothesis that God created the universe is low or high—the fact that the universe is life-permitting should lead you to increase your probability for the hypothesis that God created the universe.

Let's sum up. Given the dartboard/box setup, the fact that the dart hits the bull's-eye leads you to increase your probability for the hypothesis that Fred is in the box. So if the analogy goes through, then given the fine-tuning evidence, the fact that the universe is life-permitting should lead you to increase your probability for the hypothesis that God exists. I think the reasoning in the dart story is clearly successful, and I find the analogy plausible, at first glance at least. Thus, I find the fine-tuning argument plausible at first glance. How could one object to it?

I'll consider three objections. The first is somewhat abstract, and questions how non-experts come to believe that the fundamental constants are fine-tuned for life. The second questions whether the constants really are fine-tuned for life—perhaps life could exist if the values of the constants were quite different than they actually are. The third questions whether the existence of multiple universes preempts the fine-tuning argument for the existence of God. I'll hold that these objections have some weight, but they don't succeed in completely removing the force of the fine-tuning argument.

OBJECTION 1: EVALUATING THE FINE-TUNING EVIDENCE

Let's look carefully at Premise 1 of the fine-tuning argument. What is this "fine-tuning evidence"? I'll first present the evidence the way a proponent of the fine-tuning argument would, and then I'll raise some issues with such presentations of the evidence.

Let's start with the force of gravity. The idea is that if the gravitational force were a lot stronger or a lot weaker than it actually is, then life couldn't exist. The constant G is the constant that represents the strength of the gravitational force. If the gravitational constant were 0—that is, if there were no gravity—then stars couldn't form, since part of what brings the particles that make up a star together is the gravitational force. Similarly, if the gravitational constant were negative—that is, if the gravitational force was repulsive instead of attractive—then stars couldn't form, because the particles would be repulsed from each other. If stars couldn't form then there couldn't be life. All chemical elements heavier than hydrogen and helium (the two lightest elements) were made in stars. Since we're made of elements like carbon and oxygen, we (arguably) couldn't exist without stars having existed in the past. (We really are stardust.)

What if the gravitational constant were stronger than it actually is? Well, if the strength of gravity were increased by a factor of 3000, then stars couldn't last longer than one billion years—they would burn out a lot more quickly than they do now. This would inhibit the evolution of life—on Earth, for example, it took life well over one billion years to emerge. Also, the sort of life that could emerge probably couldn't be intelligent life. Animals couldn't have legs that were strong enough to support them; only animals the size of insects would be possible.

Now, you might think that an increase by a factor of 3000 is a rather large increase; this doesn't really seem like *fine*-tuning. But the gravitational force is weak, compared to the other forces in nature. The strongest force we know of—called, appropriately enough, "the strong force"—is 10^{40} times stronger than the force of gravity. (Recall, 10^{40} is the number that starts with 1 and has forty 0s after it.) So, compared with the total range of values—from 0 to $10^{40}G$—the range from 0 to $3000G$ seems rather small. In fact, the range of life-permitting gravitational forces is only about one part in 10^{36} of the total range of forces.[101]

To visualize this, imagine randomly throwing a dart at a line, and imagine that the dart is constrained to land somewhere on the line. (Yes, this is strange to imagine, but work with me here.) Imagine that the line is finite: one end of the line represents the gravitational force having strength 0, and the other end of the line represents the gravitational force having strength $10^{40}G$. Suppose that the dart has equal chance of landing anywhere on the line. Now, what are the chances that the dart will land somewhere in the range from 0 to $3000G$? The chances are only about 1 in 10^{36} that this will happen. This is incredibly unlikely. (By contrast, the odds of winning the multi-million dollar jackpot in a typical state lottery are around 1 in 10^{8}.) That's why the strength of the gravitational force is taken to be fine-tuned.

I started with the gravity example, because it doesn't take much knowledge of physics to see how it works. Most of the other examples of fine-tuning are more technically sophisticated. Let's look at a couple of these other examples.

In fact, let's look at the aforementioned strong force. The strong force is responsible for holding particles in the nucleus of the atom together. The strong force controls the fusion reaction that produces a helium atom from two hydrogen atoms. This fusion reaction goes on in the Sun, and explains why the Sun produces so much energy (in the form of heat and light). Where does the energy come from? Well, when two hydrogen atoms fuse to form a helium atom, 0.7 per cent of the mass of the hydrogen atoms is converted to energy (and the rest of the mass of the hydrogen atoms goes into the helium atom). But if the strong force were slightly weaker than it actually is, such that only 0.6 per cent of the mass of hydrogen atoms could be converted to energy, then it turns out (as a result of some complicated physics) that helium couldn't be formed at all. It also turns out that, not only could helium not be formed, no heavier elements could be formed either. The only atoms in the universe would be hydrogen atoms, and as a result there couldn't be life.

What about if the strong force were slightly stronger than it actually is? Well, if the strong force were stronger, then more of the mass of the hydrogen atoms could be converted to energy. If 0.8 per cent of the mass of the hydrogen atoms could be converted to energy, then it turns out (again, as a result of some complicated physics) that all the hydrogen in the universe would quickly be converted to heavier elements. It follows that there would be no hydrogen left to fuel stars, and there would be no hydrogen left to form organic molecules which are essential for life. So the strong force is also taken to be fine-tuned.

Let's look at one more example, the mass of the neutron. The actual mass of the neutron is 938 MeV. (For elementary particles, mass is often measured in units of energy, using Einstein's famous $E = mc^2$ equivalence between mass and energy.) If the mass of the neutron were increased by just 1.4 MeV, then (as a result of some complicated physics) hydrogen couldn't be converted to helium, and heavier elements couldn't come to exist either. The only atoms in the universe would be hydrogen atoms, and so life couldn't exist.

If, on the other hand, the mass of the neutron were decreased by 0.8 MeV, then (again, as a result of some complicated physics) protons would be converted into neutrons. Since these all-neutron objects wouldn't have electromagnetic repulsive forces, they would bond with other all-neutron objects and collapse, either into small incredibly dense neutron stars, or (if large enough) into black holes. Again, in such a universe, life (arguably) couldn't exist.

I've given just three examples, but I could go on and on and on. In fact, many proponents of the fine-tuning argument go into far more detail about how these various constants are fine-tuned. I understand why they're doing so—they're trying to convince the reader that the constants they're talking about really are fine-tuned for life. Stephen Barr, for example, spends about twenty pages of his book *Modern Physics and Ancient Faith* doing this sort of thing.[102] (Barr is a physicist who endorses the fine-tuning argument.) But there's something not quite right about these extensive discussions of the details of what the universe would be like given different values of the fundamental constants. The problem is that the vast majority of the readers of books like Barr's don't know enough physics to evaluate these claims. Authors like Barr realize this, and as a result they attempt to give a crash course in the physics to justify their claim that the fundamental constants are fine-tuned. For a book that's not about technical physics, twenty pages of technical physics is a lot to handle. But twenty pages isn't even *close* to enough for what it would take to learn enough high-level physics to actually *cogently evaluate* the fine-tuning claims that people like Barr are making. Moreover, these are the sorts of claims about which even competent physicists disagree. For example, Nobel-prize-winning physicist Steven Weinberg has said that he is "not impressed with these supposed instances of fine-tuning."[103] Weinberg takes issue with the technical details associated with some of the arguments for the fine-tuning evidence.

I'm not going to get into the details of these arguments for and against the fine-tuning evidence (at least, not any more than I already have). Most readers wouldn't be competent to cogently evaluate the arguments, and most of those that would would probably have a better understanding of the details of the physics than I do. But I raise this point because, as far as I can tell, it's a point that's rarely made when technical science is cited in the course of a philosophical argument. We have to think critically about what someone is doing when that person gives arguments in a situation where we know that almost everyone presented with the arguments won't be able to evaluate them cogently.

Just as the readers often lack the technical expertise to evaluate the arguments, the philosophers giving the arguments often lack the expertise too. It would be more intellectually honest for such philosophers to be up front about their lack of technical expertise, and to be up front about their sources. Instead of saying "we know from physics that...," they'd be better off saying "I read in multiple physics textbooks that...," or "my colleague in the physics department assures me that almost all physicists believe that...," or "I haven't carefully looked into this issue, but Robin Collins has, and he says that...."[104] And where there are controversies in physics, it's not clear that it's intellectually appropriate for philosophers even to have strong opinions, unless they have the technical expertise to evaluate the arguments, or unless they just decide to believe whatever the majority of experts believe.[105] I've read a lot of the literature on the fine-tuning argument, but I've never seen an opinion poll of experts, so it's not clear to me what the majority do believe regarding the fine-tuning evidence. However, it is clear to me that the promulgators of the fine-tuning argument aren't relying on such an opinion poll.

None of what I've said here is meant to show that the fine-tuning argument is definitively flawed. Instead I'm just raising some concerns about the level of expertise needed to evaluate some of the technical aspects of the fine-tuning argument cogently, and suggesting that this leaves many people in a position where it's not clear that they can cogently evaluate the argument.

OBJECTION 2: THE VARIETY OF LIFE

A lot more could be said about the issues I raised in the previous section, but instead let's move on to another criticism one could make of Premise 1 and the fine-tuning evidence. Let's suppose that the technical arguments are right, and that, for example, if the mass of the neutron were slightly larger than it actually is, no atoms bigger than hydrogen atoms could exist. The question I want to ask now is: is it really true that intelligent life couldn't exist in such a universe?

It's clear that life like us couldn't exist, since we are essentially composed of atoms bigger than hydrogen atoms—as well as molecules, which also couldn't exist in the large-neutron universe. If we know of a reason that, assuming God were to exist, God would want life *like us* to exist, then the fact that forms of life different from us could exist in a large-neutron universe wouldn't impact the fine-tuning argument. The relevant evidence wouldn't be that the universe is life-permitting; the relevant evidence would be that the universe is this-sort-of-life-permitting, and the fine-tuning argument would hold that to get a this-sort-of-life-permitting universe, the constants have to be finely tuned. But in fact, this isn't how the argument is standardly presented. The way the argument is standardly presented, God is understood as the sort of being that would want a universe with intelligent life, but God isn't understood as the sort of being that especially wants a universe with a particular sort of intelligent life. So, could intelligent life exist in a universe with no atoms larger than hydrogen atoms?

This isn't the sort of question that has received rigorous inquiry, in part because all the considerations are so speculative. At first glance, it seems that intelligent life couldn't exist in such a universe. But I'll consider some ways that perhaps it could.

I am of the opinion that, in our universe, minds exist as a result of brain activity. What the exact relationship is between minds and brains is, however, controversial, and I won't take a stand on that issue. My position is simply that, in our universe, without a functioning brain, there won't be a mind. Some philosophers, especially theists, might disagree with my claim that minds exist as a result of brain activity— they might hold that we have souls, and these souls are capable of being physically disembodied, so their mental activity isn't necessarily correlated with any brain activity. But if one takes that position, then there is a serious problem with the fine-tuning argument. Given that souls exist, then the values of the fundamental constants aren't fine-tuned for life—no matter what the values of the fundamental constants are, life could exist, it would just be physically disembodied souls that are alive. So, for those who believe in disembodied souls, it would be unproblematic to have life in a hydrogen-only universe, because it would be unproblematic to have life in a universe no matter what its physical configuration.

What about those people who believe in the possibility of disembodied souls and also endorse the fine-tuning argument? They would have to believe that there's some special reason God wanted *embodied* life, and that the fundamental constants aren't fine-tuned for life; they're fine-tuned for embodied life. In my opinion, the probability of a God existing who wants embodied life is lower than the probability of a God existing who wants life.[106] (The probability can't be higher, since a God who wants embodied life is a God who wants life.) So if the proponent of the fine-tuning argument is arguing for the existence of a God who wants embodied life, my starting probability for the existence of such a God is even lower than my starting probability would be if the proponent of the fine-tuning argument were just arguing for the existence of a God who wants life.

Let's focus on the argument that holds that God wants embodied life. Now the question we have to ask is: could embodied life exist in a universe where the values of the fundamental constants are very different? For example, could embodied life exist in a universe with no atoms larger than hydrogen atoms?

There is a commonly accepted position in philosophy of mind called *substrate independence*. This position holds that a mind doesn't actually have to exist with a brain. More specifically, the assumption holds that it doesn't take the particular physical stuff a brain is made of in order to produce a mind. As long as one has the right sorts of physical processes going on, it doesn't matter what is instantiating those processes; a mind will be associated with those processes.

This is a purposefully vague account, in large part because we don't know the details of what it actually takes to produce a mind. But given our lack of knowledge here, it seems possible (to me, at least) that a system of hydrogen atoms could do so. It is plausible to think that the particular physical actions of a brain that lead to a mind are the connections between neurons—when one neuron fires, with a particular strength, that (along with other neurons) can cause another neuron to fire at a certain strength. An analogue of this sort of system could be found in hydrogen atoms. When one hydrogen atom, with a particular velocity, impacts another hydrogen atom, that (along with other hydrogen atoms impacting) can cause the impacted hydrogen atom to move with a certain velocity. Just as the neurons fire in such a pattern that a mind is produced, so it seems possible that the hydrogen atoms could impact each other in such a pattern that a mind is produced.

To make this view somewhat more plausible, I will argue that the time scale for the interactions of the hydrogen atoms need not be the same as the time scale for the interactions of the neurons. I'll first give the argument for two brains—consider a normal brain, and then consider a brain just like the normal brain except that all the processes in the brain are slowed down. A pattern of neuron firing that takes the normal brain five seconds takes the slowed-down brain 50 years. Nevertheless,

I would hold that, just as the normal brain can have a conscious thought in those five seconds, so the slowed-down brain will have the same conscious thought, it's just that having that thought will take 50 years. We are used to conscious processes happening at a certain rate, but I see no reason in principle that they couldn't happen at a very different rate. Thus, for the hydrogen atom case, the hydrogen atoms could perhaps interact in such a way that there's a mind that takes ten years to have a single thought—or the hydrogen atoms could perhaps interact in such a way that there's a mind that can live a whole life in a fraction of a second. This line of reasoning makes it somewhat more plausible that interacting hydrogen atoms could produce a mind—the interactions need not happen on the time scales that we're familiar with.

So far I've just focused on the universe with no atoms larger than hydrogen atoms. But depending on how one varies the values of the fundamental constants, different sorts of universes would be produced, and I'd have to give a similar line of argument for many of the different types of universes, in order to argue that life could exist even if the values of the fundamental constants were very different than they actually are. This would be a long discussion, and I'm not going to give it here. But hopefully I've said enough to show how the discussion would go, and why I lend some credence to this objection to the fine-tuning argument. Ultimately, though, I don't think this objection is conclusive—despite my argument above, I wouldn't be surprised if it turns out that actually minds could not exist in a world with just hydrogen atoms.

OBJECTION 3: MANY UNIVERSES

Suppose there are many universes in existence—perhaps an infinite number. Further, suppose that the values of the fundamental constants differ in the different universes. (Perhaps there are universes where other features differ too, but at least suppose that there are lots of universes with the same laws of physics as our universe but different values of the fundamental constants. For simplicity I'll just assume that all the universes have the same laws of physics as the actual universe; nothing will hinge on that assumption.) In this scenario, assuming that the fine-tuning evidence is right, and assuming that the values of the fundamental constants vary randomly, it follows that most of the universes will not be life-permitting, because in most of the universes the values of the constants will fall outside the narrow life-permitting range. But it isn't surprising that some universes are life-permitting—given the existence of all these universes, we should expect that some happen to have the needed life-permitting values (just as when a machine randomly throws lots of darts, we would expect some to hit bull's-eye).

These sorts of considerations motivate a standard objection to the fine-tuning argument. For example, this objection is given by Richard Dawkins in his notorious book *The God Delusion*. After presenting the fine-tuning argument, Dawkins presents the multiple-universe hypothesis as a way of responding to it. He suggests that the fact that this universe is fine-tuned doesn't require an explanation in terms of God, because, given the existence of multiple universes, we'd expect some to have values of the fundamental constants that are fine-tuned for life. Given that we exist, we have to find ourselves in a life-permitting universe. Dawkins then writes:

> It is tempting to think (and many have succumbed) that to postulate a plethora of universes is a profligate luxury which should not be allowed.... The key difference between the genuinely extravagant God hypothesis and the apparently extravagant multiverse hypothesis is one of statistical improbability. The multiverse, for all that it is extravagant, is simple.... The very opposite has to be said of any kind of intelligence.[107]

Basically, Dawkins is saying that it is legitimate to postulate the existence of multiple universes in the face of the fine-tuning evidence, even though it is not legitimate to postulate the existence of God.

There are two problems with Dawkins' line of reasoning. First, it is not obvious that simplicity is linked to statistical probability in the way that Dawkins intends. That is an assumption that is sometimes made by metaphysically- and theologically-minded philosophers, but it's an assumption that's rejected by many other philosophers, especially those of an empiricist bent. For example, Bas van Fraassen, who is probably the most famous contemporary empiricist philosopher, writes:

> it is surely absurd to think that the world is more likely to be simple than complicated (unless one has certain metaphysical or theological views not usually accepted as legitimate factors in scientific inference).[108]

I am not saying that van Fraassen is definitively right here; to get into these arguments would take us too far away from the main line of discussion. But I do want to point out that Dawkins is taking a controversial philosophical stand, and he's arguably aligning himself with metaphysics or theology, not science, when he does so.

Here is the second problem with Dawkins' line of reasoning. Even supposing that the God hypothesis is much more improbable than the multiverse hypothesis, it doesn't follow that Dawkins has given a fully effective reply to the fine-tuning argument. The reason is that Dawkins is not *certain* that these other universes exist. If appealing to the existence of other universes is the only way Dawkins has of replying to the fine-tuning argument, then under the supposition that the other universes don't exist, the fine-tuning argument is successful. Thus, Dawkins has to assign a non-zero probability to the hypothesis that the fine-tuning argument is successful. This means that the fine-tuning argument would lead to *some* increase in the probability Dawkins assigns to the hypothesis that God exists (as long as Dawkins does not initially assign probability 0 to the God hypothesis). The increase may not be much, but it would be something.

To sum up: I haven't said anything definitive against the fine-tuning argument, but remember, that's my point. The argument doesn't stop me from being an atheist, but I don't have any completely definitive objections to it—and I have problems with all the objections that are presented as completely definitive. (There are many more objections than what I've presented above, but my opinion about those objections is the same—either the objections don't work, or they do work somewhat, but they aren't completely definitive.) This is why I consider the fine-tuning argument to be somewhat plausible.[109]

The Beginning of the Universe

In this section I want to take up another science-based argument for the existence of God, the kalam cosmological argument. (Cosmological arguments are arguments for the existence of God on the basis of basic features of the universe, like that all chains of causation (ostensibly) must be finite. The kalam cosmological argument is about the basic feature that the universe (ostensibly) began to exist.) The kalam cosmological argument is standardly formulated as follows:

Premise 1: Everything that begins to exist has a cause of its existence.

Premise 2: The universe began to exist.

Conclusion: Therefore the universe has a cause of its existence.

One can then argue that the cause of the universe's existence counts as God (or at least, some sort of intelligent designer). If you think of the universe as everything that physically exists, or as everything that exists in nature, then it makes sense that any cause of the universe is somehow supernatural (unless, that is, the universe caused itself to exist).[110] I won't press this issue here; instead I'll just focus on the argument for the conclusion that the universe has a cause of its existence.

There are other sorts of cosmological arguments besides the kalam cosmological argument, but I'm just going to focus on the kalam cosmological argument, because it's standard practice for proponents of the kalam cosmological argument to cite scientific evidence for Premise 2 as a key factor in their defense of the argument. (Scientific issues also importantly come up in the discussion of Premise 1, as we'll see.) For short, I'll sometimes use the term "cosmological argument" to refer to the kalam cosmological argument.

The cosmological argument is valid, in the sense that the conclusion does logically follow from the premises. But the crucial question is: are the premises true?

PREMISE 1

I'll start with Premise 1. William Lane Craig is probably the most prominent contemporary defender of the cosmological argument, but interestingly, Craig doesn't give a detailed defense of Premise 1. Craig thinks the cosmological argument all hinges on Premise 2. He says that Premise 1

> is so intuitively obvious, especially when applied to the universe, that probably no one is his right mind *really* believes it to be false.[111]

Well, I don't definitively believe Premise 1 to be false, but I am not at all sure that it's true. I'm going to present four reasons that one might reject Premise 1; I think that all four reasons have some merit, but none is completely convincing.

Reason 1: Uncaused Quantum Events

Traditionally, a vacuum is considered to be nothing; there is zero energy associated with such a vacuum. In quantum theory, though, the vacuum still has some energy, just the minimum amount of energy it is possible for a quantum field to have. According to quantum theory, pairs of particles sometimes pop into existence out of this quantum vacuum, via what's called a "vacuum fluctuation." Various opponents of the cosmological argument have cited this fact as providing an empirical refutation of Premise 1. They maintain that the pairs of particles begin to exist spontaneously; they do not have a cause for their existence.

This refutation of Premise 1 sounds plausible to me, but proponents of the cosmological argument don't concede defeat. Here is how Craig responds:

> In the case of quantum events, there are any number of physically necessary conditions that must obtain for such an event to occur, and yet these conditions are not jointly sufficient for the occurrence of the event.... The appearance of a particle in a quantum vacuum may thus be said to be spontaneous, but cannot properly be said to be absolutely uncaused, since it has many physically necessary conditions.

Basically, Craig is saying that events that appear to be spontaneous are actually caused, because such events have physically necessary conditions for occurring.

There's a problem here. Craig seems to be treating necessary conditions as causes, but that can't be right. A necessary condition for X is just a condition that has to hold in order for X to come about. For example, a necessary condition for my going clubbing tonight is that clubs exist. But the existence of clubs is in no way a *cause* of my going clubbing tonight. For the spontaneous particle creation case, the existence of a quantum vacuum is a physically necessary condition for the particle creation. But it seems strange to say that the existence of the quantum vacuum *caused* the particle creation—the standard account quantum theory gives is that the particle creation happened spontaneously. There's no particular event in the quantum vacuum that brings about the particle creation; the quantum vacuum is just there, and occasionally particle creation happens. In sum, Craig is mistaken to treat necessary conditions as causes.

But here is a way of perhaps charitably interpreting Craig's reply to this objection to Premise 1. We can see Craig as giving an implicit reformulation of the cosmological argument:

Premise 1 (revised): Everything that begins to exist has a necessary condition for its existence.

Premise 2: The universe began to exist.

Conclusion (revised): Therefore the universe has a necessary condition for its existence.

One could then conclude that this necessary condition is God.

I'm really not sure what to make of this argument. Premise 1 (revised) strikes me as more plausible than Premise 1. The reason it strikes me as more plausible is that the claim that something has a cause of its existence is a stronger claim than the claim that something has a necessary condition for its existence. But because of that, the modified conclusion is weaker than the original conclusion. It seems reasonable to equate the cause of the universe with God, because causation is an active notion; whatever caused the universe has to do something for the universe to exist. But it seems more questionable to equate the necessary condition for the existence of the universe with God; something can be a necessary condition for something else in a passive way. For example, the existence of carbon is a necessary condition for the existence of DNA, but carbon didn't *do* anything to bring about the existence of DNA. In the case of the universe, perhaps the necessary condition for the existence of the universe is just the prior non-existence of anything.

So perhaps the universe does have a necessary condition for its existence. It would require sophisticated further argumentation, however, to establish that that necessary condition is God.

Reason 2: Causation is a Temporal Notion

Here's another reason one might want to reject Premise 1 (the claim that everything that begins to exist has a cause of its existence). Arguably, the reason we believe that premise is that we've had lots of experiences of something beginning to exist, and every time we are able to identify the cause of that thing beginning to exist. The problem is that all these experiences of something beginning to exist are of something beginning to exist *at some time*. Moreover, the cause that we identify is some event that occurs in time. Typically, the cause temporally precedes the event of creation. Arguably, it doesn't have to be that way: in cases involving time travel, the cause could occur temporally later than the event of creation. But in all these cases, the cause and the event of creation both occur in time; the cause happens at some time and the event of creation happens at some time.

One may be tempted to conclude from this that causation is a fundamentally temporal notion: the cause and the effect are both events, and these events have to occur in time. If that's right, then the notion of causation doesn't apply to the beginning of the universe! The beginning of the universe is the beginning not only of the stuff in the universe, but of time (and space) itself. So if the universe comes into existence, it isn't via an event that occurs in time. But if causation is a fundamentally temporal notion, then the universe doesn't have a cause of its existence.

I'm going to look at two responses the proponent of the cosmological argument might want to give to the above objection to Premise 1.

1. First, proponents of the cosmological argument might argue that causation is *not* a fundamentally temporal notion. To defend this claim, they might appeal to the much-discussed (by academic philosophers, at least) *counterfactual analysis* of causation. The basic version of the analysis is as follows:

> Event A causes event B if and only if: if A had not occurred, B wouldn't have occurred.

To get the idea behind this analysis, consider the following example: a baseball is thrown at a window, and the window breaks. Did the baseball cause the window to break? Well, if the baseball hadn't been there, the window wouldn't have broken, so it follows from the counterfactual analysis that the baseball caused the window to break.

With respect to the issue of whether causation is a temporal notion, a potential virtue of the counterfactual analysis is that it doesn't explicitly utilize temporal notions: it doesn't say that A had to occur before B, or even that A and B have to occur in time. (There are other analyses of causation that *do* build in such temporal requirements.) So if it's correct to understand causation counterfactually, then it could be true that the universe has a cause of its existence, even though that cause didn't occur in time. The reasoning would go as follows: if God hadn't existed, the universe wouldn't have existed; it follows that God caused the universe to exist.

Now, it turns out that the simple counterfactual analysis I've given above doesn't work. It's subject to counterexamples, where intuitively we would say that A causes B, even though it's not the case that if A hadn't occurred, B wouldn't have occurred. For example, consider a baseball and a softball both heading toward a window: the baseball gets there first, so the baseball causes the breaking of the window, but if the baseball hadn't been there, the window still would have broken (because of the presence of the incoming softball). This has led some philosophers to come up with more sophisticated versions of the counterfactual analysis, and this has led other philosophers to come up with more sophisticated counterexamples. I took a whole graduate course on the counterfactual analysis of causation, and to be honest, it gets old fast.

Anyway, no one has come up with a version of the counterfactual analysis that isn't subject to counterexamples, though a lot of people are still trying. So if something like the counterfactual analysis is right, then causation isn't a fundamentally temporal notion. It's definitely an open question, though, whether the counterfactual analysis is right.

2. Here's the second response proponents of the cosmological argument might want to give to the above objection. (To refresh your memory: that's the objection that causation is a fundamentally temporal notion, and thus God couldn't cause the universe to exist, because there was no time before the existence of the universe.) Proponents of the cosmological argument could admit that causation is a fundamentally temporal notion, but they could claim that the event of God causing the universe to exist *did* occur in time. Specifically, they could claim that the event of God causing the universe happened at the first instant of time. In other words, the event of God causing the universe was *simultaneous* with the beginning of the universe.

Hopefully you see why this claim is controversial. The most natural way to build temporality into the notion of causation is to specify that the cause has to come *before* the effect. In the baseball/window example, the incoming baseball causes the window to be broken, and the baseball is incoming *before* the window breaks. Now, one might want to allow for time travel and backwards causation, where the time traveler pushing a button in his time machine in 2050, say, causes the appearance of the time traveler in 1980. In that sort of example, the cause comes after the effect—but the cause and the effect still happen at different times. But is it possible for the cause and effect to happen at the same time? Does the notion of simultaneous causation make sense?

There is a well-known defense of simultaneous causation, put forward by Immanuel Kant. Kant gives the example of a ball resting on a cushion, where the weight of the ball causes a depression in the cushion. Kant cites this as an example of the cause being simultaneous with the effect. What I want to point out is that this particular example, which purports to be an example of simultaneous causation, actually doesn't count. The ball resting on the cushion at time t actually causes the depression at some slightly later time t^*, and so the cause temporally precedes the effect. The reason this is the case is that, even though the ball and the cushion are in contact, on a microscopic level none of the particles of the ball is actually in contact with any of the particles of the cushion. Instead, the particles are just very close together, and there is electromagnetic repulsion between the particles, which results in the ball staying on top of the cushion (as opposed to, for example, sinking through the cushion). The effects of this electromagnetic force are transmitted at a finite speed—the speed of light, to be precise. So if the ball were to instantaneously disappear at time t, the cushion wouldn't react until some slightly later time. Kant's example isn't a good example of simultaneous causation.

My argument doesn't show, though, that simultaneous causation is impossible, just that a particular (famous) argument for simultaneous causation is a bad argument. To be honest, I don't know what to think regarding the issue of whether simultaneous causation is possible. So a simultaneous-causation-based reply to the objection that causation is a fundamentally temporal notion, and thus God couldn't cause the universe to exist, *might* be a good reply. I don't know of any good arguments for or against that reply, so I'll withhold judgment.

Reason 3: Causation is Just Folk Science

This sort of uncertainty I feel regarding simultaneous causation might be indicative of something important. (That is, my uncertainty might not just be due to lack of insight on my part.) What I have in mind is that the concept of causation might not even apply outside the familiar realms in which we're used to applying it. Since we're only used to cases where the cause temporally precedes the effect, then perhaps the concept of causation doesn't even apply in other cases.

This brings us to another reason one might want to reject Premise 1, the claim that everything that begins to exist has a cause of its existence. According to this reason, causal principles are not fundamental principles of nature; the world is not fundamentally causal. If this were right, then any sort of fundamental causal principle like "everything that begins to exist has a cause of its existence" would surely be false.

Various philosophers of science have argued for this sort of rejection of causation; the strongest argument I know of is due to philosopher John Norton.[112] The basic idea behind the argument is that, if causal principles were fundamental principles of nature, then you would expect physics to discover them. You would expect our best theories in physics to tell us, for any two events, whether one event is a cause of the other event. And if you look at our best physical theories, like quantum theory, general relativity, or M-theory, they don't talk about causes at all. They talk about energies, forces, and conservation laws, but not causes. Some theories give equations specifying that if the system is in a certain state at some time, then it will be in a different state (with some specified probability) at some specified later time. But the earlier state of the system isn't identified as a cause of the later state of the system; the equation just describes how the system evolves through time.

Now, you might think: "granted, the physical theories don't actually use the language of causation. But surely what they're talking about is causation, even if they're not using that sort of terminology. We just need to find a way to redescribe what the physical theories are telling us in causal terms."

If you think that, then you're thinking like a philosopher. And indeed, philosophers have tried to do this sort of thing, but so far they've failed. Either they come up with causal principles that turn out to be applicable only for certain theories, or they come up with causal principles that are so general as to be vacuous. This history of failure leads some people to conclude that causation isn't a fundamental part of nature at all.

This doesn't mean that we should stop using causal language though; we're still allowed to say that the incoming baseball caused the window to break. It's just that these sorts of causal claims can't be understood as claims of fundamental physics. Instead, they have to be understood as claims of "folk science." Folk science is not a fundamental physical science, but it does capture various regularities we perceive in the world at the level of our everyday interactions with the world. The domain of folk science includes everyday events like colliding billiard balls and boiling water and falling pianos. It doesn't include events like black hole formation, particle collisions, and the expansion of the universe. Causal principles are applicable in the domain of folk science, but not in general.

It would follow from all this that a principle like Premise 1, which says that everything that begins to exist has a cause of its existence, is only applicable in the limited domain of folk science. Since the beginning of the universe (assuming the universe has a beginning) is clearly outside the domain of folk science, then it is illegitimate to apply Premise 1 to the beginning of the universe.

I am of the opinion that this argument against Premise 1 is not conclusive. Just because causal language isn't found in our fundamental physics, it doesn't follow that causal language doesn't objectively and correctly describe the world; it may just be that it's not the role of fundamental physics to supply a causal account. Here's an alternative way of putting this sort of point: just because our current physical theories don't incorporate causal principles, it doesn't follow that future physical theories won't either. In general, one has to be wary of drawing philosophical conclusions from contemporary science, because contemporary science can change. So Reason 3 gives me some reason to reject Premise 1 of the cosmological argument, but it's not conclusive.

Reason 4: The Finitude of Time is Like the Finitude of Space
Here's the fourth and final reason I have for why one might want to reject Premise
1, the claim that everything that begins to exist has a cause of its existence. One
could argue that the motivation for Premise 1 comes from a mistaken understanding of the nature of time.

To understand how this argument goes, let's look at it in steps. Consider the
actual universe, and suppose that the dimensions of space are all infinite. That
is, if you go in any spatial direction, you'll keep going forever. Now suppose that
that's wrong, and one of the spatial dimensions is finite. (This is hard to picture for
three-dimensional space, but relatively easier to picture for two-dimensional space.
Consider a sheet of paper, where both spatial dimensions are finite, and imagine
taking two parallel edges and pulling them apart, lengthening the sheet of paper until
it is infinitely long in that direction. This sheet of paper now has one finite spatial
dimension and one infinite spatial dimension.) By calling the spatial dimension
finite, I mean that it has an edge—if you tried to go in that direction of space, you
would reach a point where you couldn't go any further. (I'm not saying that this
sort of space is allowed by current or true theories of physics; all that matters for
this argument is that this sort of space is logically possible.) The dimension that's
finite could be finite in one direction, or finite in both directions—you could hit
an edge going one way, but not going the opposite way, or you could hit an edge
going both ways.

Now, consider the question: does the fact that this spatial dimension is finite
make it any more likely for God to exist than if all the spatial dimensions were
infinite? The question seems ludicrous; in my opinion, at least, the answer is clearly
"no." Whether the spatial dimension is finite or infinite has nothing to do with
whether God exists.

The reason this is relevant to the issue of the universe having a beginning is
that many philosophers hold that time is a dimension just like the dimensions of
space. On this account, the universe consists of a four-dimensional space-time
manifold, with events scattered throughout this manifold. The event of Lincoln's
assassination, for example, is in one location of the manifold, the event of you
reading this now is in another location in the manifold, and the event of your first
great-great-grandchild being born (if there will be such an event) is at yet another
location in the manifold. There is nothing special about the present time, other
than that this part of you is located in that region of the manifold.

So, suppose that this theory of time (called *eternalism*) is true. What we have
then is a block four-dimensional universe, timelessly existing. The dimensions in
the block universe could all be infinite, or they could all be finite, or some could
be finite and some infinite. We already decided that, if one of the dimensions of
space is finite, that has no consequences for whether or not God exists. But since
time is a dimension just like the dimensions of space, then it plausibly follows

that if the time dimension is finite, that too has no consequences for whether or not God exists.

So what impact does this have on Premise 1, the claim that everything that begins to exist has a cause of its existence? Let's focus on Premise 1 as applied to the universe: it says that if the universe began to exist, then the universe has a cause of its existence. Let's grant for now that the universe began to exist, in the sense that the past of the universe is finite. It follows from eternalism that that dimension of time is finite (at least, it's finite going in one direction). So what the eternalist universe version of Premise 1 really amounts to is the following claim: if the temporal dimension of the universe is finite, then the universe has a cause of its existence.

So stated, Premise 1 doesn't look that plausible. According to eternalism, the dimension of time is like the dimensions of space, so the eternalist version of Premise 1 should have the same amount of plausibility as the following claim: if a *spatial* dimension of the universe is finite, then the universe has a cause of its existence. But whether space has an edge should have nothing to do with whether or not the universe has a cause of its existence! It would follow that whether time has an edge has nothing to do with whether the universe has a cause of its existence.

Now, let me be the first to point out that this eternalist-based argument against Premise 1 is by no means watertight. First of all, different eternalists differ on how exactly eternalism should go, and some of them hold that there are *some* differences between the dimension of time and the dimension of space. They might hold that these differences are relevant to the issue of whether a finite dimension means that the universe has a cause of its existence. Second, eternalism itself might be false. For what it's worth, I lean towards non-eternalism, and it's perhaps worth pointing out that Craig, the main contemporary proponent of the cosmological argument, is a committed non-eternalist. So Craig wouldn't be moved by this particular argument against Premise 1.

Moving Beyond the Four Reasons

So, I've looked at four reasons to reject Premise 1 of the cosmological argument, the claim that everything that begins to exist has a cause of its existence. While each reason strikes me as somewhat plausible, I haven't been convinced by any of them.

I'm also not convinced that Premise 1 is true, though. In contrast, consider this passage from philosopher C.D. Broad:

> I must confess that I have a very great difficulty in supposing that there was a first phase in the world's history ... I suspect that my difficulty about a first event or phase in the world's history is due to the fact that ... I cannot really *believe* in anything beginning to exist without being *caused* (in the old-fashioned

sense of *produced* or *generated*) by something else which existed before and up
to the moment when the entity in question began to exist.

Broad isn't endorsing the cosmological argument, because he's suggesting that the
universe *doesn't* have a beginning. But the reason he thinks that is that he finds
himself wedded to Premise 1: he holds that nothing can begin to exist without
there being a cause of its existence, and he doesn't want the universe to have a
cause of its existence.

Proponents of the cosmological argument like to cite the above passage from
Broad as part of their argument for why Premise 1 is indubitable. As we saw Craig
put it at the beginning of this discussion, Premise 1

is so intuitively obvious … that probably no one in his right mind *really*
believes it to be false.

Well, I'm not as moved as Craig and Broad are. The four reasons I've cited above
against Premise 1 all have some weight. On the other hand, I'm not willing to
definitively say that Premise 1 is false.

PREMISE 2

Premise 2 of the cosmological argument holds that the universe began to exist. Why
should we believe that? Well, there are two types of arguments standardly given in
the literature: philosophical arguments and empirical arguments. The philosophical
arguments argue that it's impossible for an actually infinite series of events to exist,
and hence the universe could not have been in existence forever. While I think that
these arguments are wrong, they've been much-discussed in the literature, and I
don't have anything new to say about them, so I won't discuss them here.

The empirical arguments appeal to the evidence from physics that the universe
began to exist. For example, atheist William Rowe writes:

it must be acknowledged that the emergence of the Big Bang theory of the
origin of the universe has given new weight to an argument for the existence
of some sort of creator.[113]

I am not that moved by these empirical considerations; I hold that, given the current state of play in physics, it is completely reasonable to hold that physics does
not provide evidence that the universe began to exist. I'll argue for this now.

As a preliminary point, I prefer to refer to "the big bang hypothesis" rather than
"the big bang theory." The big bang hypothesis holds that the universe, including
space and time itself, came into existence a finite amount of time ago, and shortly

after the universe came into existence it was in a state of large energy density, and the energy density in each region of the universe has overall been decreasing, due to the expansion of the universe (or, less tendentiously, due to the fact that at large scales almost everything in the universe is getting further apart from almost everything else). The overall theory within which the hypothesis has been formulated is general relativity, which is the best theory we have to describe the large-scale structure of spacetime. General relativity has an infinite number of models of spacetime, and in some of the models there is a big bang, while in others there isn't. Based on the empirical data we have about our universe, the models of general relativity that best describe our universe are models where there is a big bang.

Because there is frequent ignorance of this point, it's worth noting that the big bang hypothesis does not include the hypothesis that the universe started out very small, and has been expanding ever since. This is one possibility for how our universe has evolved, but another possibility is that the universe is spatially infinite, and has been spatially infinite ever since the big bang (assuming that the big bang hypothesis is true). In fact the latest empirical evidence suggests that the universe is spatially infinite.[114]

I maintain that if the big bang hypothesis is true, then the first premise of the cosmological argument is true. There is some controversy about this conditional, because some have maintained that for something to begin to exist, there must be a first moment of its existence.[115] But the big bang hypothesis is compatible with the universe being in existence a finite amount of time, without having a first moment of its existence. That is, it could be the case that the set of times at which the universe exists is open at the beginning. In other words, we could pick a coordinate system with the following result: the universe does not exist at time $t = 0$, but the universe exists at every time $t > 0$. I maintain that, if the big bang theory is true but the universe did not have a first moment of its existence, it nevertheless began to exist, because it has only been in existence a finite amount of time.

So if the big bang hypothesis is true, Premise 2 is true. This leads to the question: should we believe the big bang hypothesis?

William Lane Craig believes the big bang hypothesis. In his 1979 book, *The Kalam Cosmological Argument*, he writes:

> the scientific evidence related to the expansion of the universe points to an absolute beginning of the universe about fifteen billion years ago.[116]

As part of his justification for this claim, he cites a paper by four astrophysicists, with J. Richard Gott as the lead author. Gott and his co-authors write:

> the universe began from a state of infinite density about one Hubble time ago [i.e., about 15 billion years ago]. Space and time were created in that event and

so was all the matter in the universe. It is not meaningful to ask what happened before the big bang; it is like asking what is north of the North Pole.[117]

At first glance, this passage looks like it is supporting Craig's claim. But one has to be careful here. When physicists present a theory, they may be presenting it *as true*, or they may just be presenting it as a live option, putting it on the table for consideration. According to Bas van Fraassen's understanding of science, at least, physicists can *accept* a theory, and treat the theory as if it is true for the purposes of doing their science, without actually *believing* the theory.[118]

In this vein, it's worth noting that Gott and his co-authors put an important caveat in their paper, a caveat that Craig doesn't quote. Gott and his co-authors write:

> That the universe began with a big bang is an inevitable conclusion *if* the known laws of physics are assumed to be correct and in some sense complete. It is conceivable, however, that there are laws of nature whose effects are negligible on the scale of the physics laboratory, or even on the scale of the solar system, but that might predominate in determining the behavior of the universe as a whole.[119]

So this leads to the question: should we assume that the known laws of physics are correct and complete?

The answer is: we should not. There are currently two fundamental theories of physics on the table, general relativity and quantum theory. Both theories are strongly confirmed in their respective domains, but the problem is that the two theories contradict each other. Physicists are trying to come up with a new theory, a theory of quantum gravity, to replace both general relativity and quantum theory. So far, though, physicists have not been completely successful. The most promising candidate is string theory (or its possible replacement, M-theory), but this theory is not understood well enough to enable us to figure out what it says about whether the universe has a beginning. (And it may be that the theory fails to give a univocal answer; it may be that the theory has multiple models consistent with all the data we have, where in one model the universe has a beginning while in another model it doesn't.)[120]

In sum, the big bang theory doesn't take into account quantum theory, and that gives us reason not to believe the big bang theory.[121] In Craig's 1979 book, he doesn't seem aware of this potential problem regarding taking quantum effects into account, but by 1993, he shows more awareness of the potential problem. In 1993, Craig and Quentin Smith published a debate book, *Theism, Atheism, and Big Bang Cosmology*. The first chapter in the book consists of selections from Craig's

1979 book. At the end of the chapter Craig has a postscript, discussing our lack of knowledge of certain aspects of the big bang. He writes:

> During the 1980s, through the marriage of particle physics and cosmology, scientists have attempted to push back the frontiers of our knowledge of the early universe ever closer to the Big Bang.... Prior to 10^{-12} sec, however, the physics becomes speculative.... Prior to 10^{-35} sec the physics becomes extremely speculative and even unknown.[122]

I'll start with a couple preliminary points to elucidate what Craig is talking about here, and then I'll make my main critical point.

Preliminary point 1: When Craig talks about "Prior to 10^{-12} sec," he's talking about the time period between the big bang and 10^{-12} seconds after the big bang.

Preliminary point 2: Physicists tend to talk about stages in the development of the early universe, not in terms of the time period after the big bang, but in terms of the approximate amount of energy particles in the universe have at that time. So, 10^{-12} seconds corresponds to energies of 100 GeV (that is, 100 billion electron volts), while 10^{-35} seconds corresponds to energies of 10^{14} GeV.

Now, my main point: If one were to watch the history of the universe going backwards in time, one would see the energies increasing. Let me make the same point that Craig made about the physics getting speculative, but put in terms of energy. As the energy increases to 100 GeV, the physics becomes speculative—we're not really sure what happens at that point. As the energy increases to 10^{14} GeV (assuming it does increase to that point) the physics becomes extremely speculative, even unknown. In other words, we just don't know what happens once the energies get that high.

The way Craig puts the point, it sounds like we know that there's a big bang, and we know what happens in the history of the universe once 10^{-12} seconds have passed, but we don't know what happens between the big bang and 10^{-12} seconds after the big bang. But in fact our lack of knowledge is much more fundamental. Because the physics doesn't tell us what happens once we trace the history of the universe backwards in time to these high energies, we don't even know if there's a big bang at all.

So given that the physics is unknown, we ought to conclude that it's unknown whether there's a big bang, and hence (assuming that the philosophical defense of Premise 2 is flawed) we ought to conclude that it's unknown whether the universe began to exist. Hence, we are not warranted in believing that Premise 2 is true, and hence we are not warranted in believing that the cosmological argument is successful.

It doesn't follow though that the cosmological argument is definitively a failure; I have said nothing to definitively show that either one of the premises is false. Perhaps the universe did begin to exist, and perhaps this global feature of the universe provides scientific evidence for the existence of a cosmic designer. This is why I consider the cosmological argument a somewhat plausible intelligent design argument.[123]

The Origin of Life

So far, we've considered intelligent design arguments that have to do with global features of the universe; now let's turn to an intelligent design argument that has to do with features of living things. Specifically, what I want to focus on is the existence of life itself. How did life in the universe originate? Did God create life, or did life arise from non-life via chance naturalistic processes?

We do not know how life originated from non-life, and in fact it seems like the sort of process that would be very unlikely to happen naturalistically. Intelligent design proponents like to quote the following summary by biologist Francis Crick (the co-discoverer of the structure of DNA). He writes:

> An honest man, armed with all the knowledge available to us now, could only state that in some sense, the origin of life appears at the moment to be almost a miracle, so many are the conditions which would have had to have been satisfied to get it going.[124]

If Crick is right, it seems very improbable that life could have arisen from non-life via naturalistic means. Our knowledge is so limited that precise numerical estimates seem unreasonable, but they have been given. Robert Shapiro[125] cites Hoyle and Wickramasinghe's estimate of the chance of life naturalistically arising on a particular planet like ours as 1 in $10^{40,000}$, as well as Morowitz's estimate of 1 in $10^{100,000,000,000}$. (Actually, those odds are the odds for a particular trial—a particular physical process that could in principle form life from non-life. Shapiro estimates that on Earth there were 10^{51} trials available. But the difference between 1 in $10^{40,000}$ and 10^{51} in $10^{40,000}$ is well within the margin of error for these estimates.) Given these odds, this leads some to infer that the process of life arising from non-life happened via design.

How would this argument go? Well, suppose for the moment that there's just a single planet in the whole universe—there's just a single place where life could possibly originate. (Or at least, there's a single place where the sort of embodied life that's like us could originate—let's set aside the esoteric possibilities for life we discussed previously.) One hypothesis is that God exists, and God is the sort of being who wants life to exist. Supposing that such a God exists, it's very likely that life would exist on this one planet. Another hypothesis is that there is no God, or at least no God of the sort that would have any desire for life to exist. Under that hypothesis, it seems rather unlikely that the conditions on the planet just happened to be right for life to come to exist. Thus, in this hypothetical single-planet scenario, finding that there is life on the planet provides evidence for the hypothesis that God exists.

In my reasoning here, I'm appealing to a standard principle of scientific confirmation. Suppose we're about to do an experiment, and we are wondering whether some particular phenomenon is going to occur. (For example, we could be wondering whether the litmus paper will turn blue, or whether the ammeter will register current, or whether the laboratory will blow up.) Suppose that, according to Theory A, in this experimental setup the phenomenon is very unlikely to occur. Suppose that, according to Theory B, in this experimental setup the phenomenon is very likely to occur. Now, suppose that we do the experiment, and the phenomenon occurs. The fact that the phenomenon occurs provides evidence for Theory B. (This is how probability theory works; this is how science works.) Now, we may have initially thought that Theory B was very unlikely, and, even after observing the phenomenon in question, we could still think that Theory B is unlikely—we would just have to think that Theory B is less unlikely than we did before.

There is a potentially important difference between the Theory A/Theory B hypothetical scenario I just described, and the origin of life from non-life scenario that's our topic of discussion. By highlighting this difference, we'll get a better sense of how the origin of life argument for God works.

The key difference is that, in the origin of life case, the evidence in question is *old evidence*—we already knew about the evidence before we considered how the evidence impacted the hypotheses in question. In the Theory A/Theory B scenario, in contrast, we have the theories in advance, and then we do the experiment to get the evidence.

But does this really matter? Well, it raises some technical issues in confirmation theory that I won't get into here; there is a significant literature on "the problem of old evidence." The reason it's standardly taken to be a problem is that people think that at least sometimes evidence should be able to confirm a theory, even if the evidence is evidence we already have, and yet standard probabilistic confirmation theory doesn't yield that result, so people conclude that standard probabilistic confirmation theory needs to be modified.[126]

Let's set aside that technical issue—there is a more fundamental philosophical issue associated with old evidence. Suppose that one came up with a hypothesis while knowing that the evidence is there. Should we then be allowed to think that the evidence confirms the hypothesis?

At first glance, the answer seems to be "no." Suppose that Carl is familiar with some surprising experimental result, and so Carl goes home and writes up a theory that predicts exactly that experimental result. Carl then cites the experimental result in support of his theory. It seems that Carl is being unfair—after all, Carl designed his theory to correctly predict that very experimental result.

But now suppose that Deb has been ensconced in her office for a long time working on developing a theory, and she hasn't heard about the experimental result in question. Suppose that her theory turns out to be exactly the same as Carl's. It seems that in this situation, we should take the experiment to provide support for the theory. After all, it's just happenstance that the experiment was done before Deb came up with her theory—since her development of the theory had nothing to do with the experiment, it could have just as easily happened that the experiment was done after the theory was developed.

But should our assessment of the relationship between the theory and the experiment depend on who happened to come up with the theory? Suppose we are handed a theory but we don't know the origin—are we forced to say that we can't judge whether the experimental results provide support for the theory? Suppose it turns out that the theory was developed by someone like Carl. Does it matter that there just doesn't happen to be someone like Deb who came up with the theory independently?

These are contentious questions, but my inclination is to say that it doesn't matter who came up with the theory, and how they came up with it; the theory needs to be evaluated on its own merits. Even if the theory was generated by someone like Carl, who knew about the experimental results, it's just happenstance that the theory wasn't also developed by someone like Deb, who didn't know about the results. So I don't think that whether evidence is old evidence matters for the assessment of a theory—but I recognize that that claim is contentious.

How does this carry over to the argument from God based on the origin of life? Well, one could say that the theists who give that argument are being like Carl—they started out knowing that life exists, and then they formulated their hypothesis that God exists, and God would want there to be life, and then they cited the existence of life as evidence for the existence of God. My opinion is that the evidence for the hypothesis that this sort of God exists needs to be evaluated independently of how that hypothesis was generated, and hence even if supporters of that hypothesis knew that life exists when they formulated the hypothesis, it's still potentially legitimate to cite the existence of life as evidence for the hypothesis. But as I say, my claim here is contentious.

Above I made the unrealistic assumption that there is just one planet in the universe—there's just a single place where life could possibility originate. But in fact, we know that that's false—we have direct evidence for a few handfuls of planets now, and we surmise that there are lots more. How does the existence of many planets affect the argument that the existence of life provides evidence for the existence of God?

My short answer is: it depends on how many planets there are. One can see this intuitively by considering extreme cases.

Suppose that there are exactly two planets. The reasoning I went through above wouldn't be much different—under the hypothesis that there's no God, it would be very unlikely for life to arise on either planet, so finding life on a planet provides evidence for the existence of God.

But now consider the hypothesis that there are an infinite number of planets. Even though it is extremely improbable for life to arise on any particular planet, we would expect life to arise somewhere (as long as the probability of life arising on any particular planet is greater than 0). In fact, we would expect life to arise an infinite number of places. Thus, if there are an infinite number of planets, we would expect life to arise somewhere, regardless of whether or not there's a God. It follows that, if there are an infinite number of planets, the existence of life does not provide evidence for the existence of God.

I'll discuss this infinite universe possibility in more detail below.

LIFE IN AN INFINITE UNIVERSE

Current evidence from physics lends support to the hypothesis that there are an infinite number of planets. I'll explain why now.

General relativity is our best current theory for the large-scale structure of the universe. General relativity allows for two types of models of space—models where space is finite in extent, and models where space is infinite in extent. The mainstream view of contemporary cosmologists is that the evidence suggests that space is infinite. Specifically, the evidence suggests that on a large scale space is not curved. For example, the Wilkinson Microwave Anisotropy Probe (WMAP) was recently used to measure the Cosmic Microwave Background radiation. The temperature fluctuations in the radiation suggest that space is flat, and hence infinite. Before the WMAP results the universe was predicted to be spatially infinite with a 15 per cent margin of error; the WMAP results reduce that margin of error to 2 per cent.[127]

So what is the rest of the universe like, beyond the limited region that we can observe? We can't be certain about this, but it is reasonable to think that matter elsewhere in the universe is similar to matter here—just as there are stars and planets here, there are stars and planets elsewhere. Moreover, it's reasonable to think that there is some variability in what exists here as opposed to what exists elsewhere. It *could* be that there is no variability—for example, it could be that the universe is divided into an infinite number of 500 trillion-light-year-cubed cube-shaped regions, and what happens in the region we're living in is qualitatively duplicated in each of the other regions. A (more plausible) contrasting view is that there was at least some randomness in the initial conditions of the universe, such that different things can happen in different regions of the universe.[128]

Let's suppose that what the evidence suggests is right: the universe is in fact spatially infinite, and matter elsewhere in the universe is similar to matter here, and there was randomness in the initial conditions for different regions of the universe. (Below, when I talk of the universe being spatially infinite, I will be implicitly assuming that these other conditions hold as well.) What impact does the existence of an infinite number of planets have on arguments for God based on the origin of life?

Before answering that question directly, I will present another dart-throwing analogy. Alice is not very good at darts. Sure, Alice can hit the dartboard every time, but other than that Alice's aim isn't very impressive; only about 1 in 1000 throws of hers hit bull's-eye. But Alice likes to throw darts a lot. For example, the other day Alice threw a dart 10,000 times. How many bull's-eyes would you guess that Alice got? Well, if she gets bull's-eye on average of 1 in 1000 throws, and she throws 10,000 times, then you should guess that Alice got about 10 bull's-eyes. Similarly, if Alice throws 100,000 times, you should expect about 100 bull's-eyes, and so on.

What if Alice throws an infinite number of times? We should expect that she'll get infinitely many bull's-eyes. (If this isn't obvious, then tell me how many bull's-eyes you think Alice will get. I'll take that number, multiply by 1000, and tell you that that's about the number of throws it would take for Alice to probably get around the number of bull's-eyes you mentioned. But Alice is throwing more times than that; Alice is throwing infinitely many times.)

Moreover, note that we should expect Alice to get infinitely many bull's-eyes regardless of how unlikely it is for Alice to hit bull's-eye on any particular throw— as long as that probability is not zero. Even if Alice will only hit bull's-eye 1 in 1,000,000,000,000 times, we should still expect Alice to hit bull's-eye infinitely many times if she throws infinitely many times. (I use this "expect" terminology because it is still *possible* for Alice to never hit bull's-eye, even if she is throwing randomly an infinite number of times, just as it is possible to flip a fair coin over and over and keep getting heads, no matter how many times one flips.)

So what does this have to do with life in the universe? Well, let's go back to the question we considered above: how probable is it that life would spontaneously arise from non-life on a particular planet? As long as the probability is not zero, then if the universe is spatially infinite we should expect life to arise *somewhere* in the infinite universe, just as, if Alice throws an infinite number of times, we should expect her to hit a bull's-eye. In fact, we can draw a much stronger conclusion. We should expect life to arise at *an infinite number of places* in the universe—just as we should expect Alice, when she throws infinitely many times, to get infinitely many bull's-eyes.

My conclusion is that one shouldn't use the development of life from non-life to argue for the existence of a God-like designer—at least, one shouldn't do this if the universe is spatially infinite. As I mentioned above, my hypothesis that the universe is spatially infinite has built into it two further assumptions—that there are stars and planets throughout the universe, and that the initial conditions vary appropriately across different regions of the universe. It could be that the rest of the universe beyond what we can observe is barren of matter, and hence there are only a relatively small finite number of planets on which life could potentially arise. If this is the case, and the odds of life naturalistically developing on any particular planet really are 1 in $10^{100,000,000,000}$, it would be very unlikely for life to arise in the universe via naturalistic means, and hence the existence of life would provide some evidence for the existence of God. Moreover, it could be that there are stars and planets throughout the universe, but the initial conditions for all regions of the universe other than here are such that it is guaranteed that the planets can't support life—here again, the existence of life would provide some evidence for the existence of God. But assuming that the universe is spatially infinite and the two further assumptions hold, then the existence of life provides little to no evidence for the existence of God.

What the argument comes down to is a comparison of probabilities. Under the assumption that God exists, how likely do you think it would be that life would exist in the universe? Under the assumption that there is no God, how likely do you think it would be that life would exist in the universe? If the first number is higher, then the existence of life provides evidence for the existence of God. If the second number is higher, then the existence of life provides evidence against the existence of God. But if both numbers are about the same, then the design argument based on the origin of life doesn't do much to shift your probabilities regarding God either way.

My personal opinion is that, under the assumption that there's a God, it's quite likely that there would be life, while under the assumption that there's no God, it's pretty likely that there would be life, but not quite as likely as if there were a God. (I think there are more likely than not an infinite number of planets, but I'm nowhere close to certain about it.) So the argument for God based on the origin of life makes me think that it's a little more likely that God exists than I would think had I never heard the argument. The probability shift isn't significant enough though to stop me from being an atheist.[129]

There is an interesting side-note to make regarding my argument in this section. Antony Flew, an atheist for most of his life, recently (and famously) converted to theism. Flew discussed this conversion in a 2004 interview, saying:

I think that the most impressive arguments for God's existence are those that are supported by recent scientific discoveries…. I think the argument to Intelligent Design is enormously stronger than when I first met it.[130]

Elsewhere, Flew elaborates on this, citing the origin of life from non-life as an event that seemingly can't be accounted for via naturalistic means. He writes:

the evidential situation of natural (as opposed to revealed) theology has been transformed in the more than fifty years since Watson and Crick won the Nobel Prize for their discovery of the double helix structure of DNA. It has become inordinately difficult even to begin to think about constructing a naturalistic theory of the evolution of that first reproducing organism.[131]

He takes this problem of accounting for the existence of the first reproducing organism to provide evidence of the existence of God. He says that

one place where, until a satisfactory naturalistic explanation has been developed, there would appear to be room for an Argument to Design is at the first emergence of living from non-living matter.[132]

Now, if what I've been saying is right, then one *can* give a satisfactory naturalistic explanation of the first emergence of living from non-living matter. The specific biological details would need to be filled in, but such an event would be expected to occur, given the probabilistic resources one gets from a spatially infinite universe.

What About Evolution?

Most discussions of arguments for intelligent design focus on evolution-based arguments—proponents of intelligent design argue that there is biological evidence that complex life on Earth didn't come to exist simply as a result of the unguided process of natural selection. Intelligent design proponents like Michael Behe argue that, while it's reasonable to think that all life forms descended from a common ancestor, and while it's clear that natural selection does play a role in biological evolution, the Darwinian account of random mutation and natural selection is not sufficient to account for the complex life that actually exists.[133] Behe argues that some biological systems are irreducibly complex, in that they need all their parts in order to function at all, and such irreducibly complex systems would be unlikely to arise via Darwinian means. Here is Behe's exact definition:

> By *irreducibly complex* I mean a single system composed of several well-matched, interacting parts that contribute to the basic function, wherein the removal of any one of the parts causes the system to effectively cease functioning.[134]

Behe holds that the existence of irreducibly complex biological systems provides evidence for a designer.

As I've mentioned before, I find Behe's irreducible complexity argument weaker than the other intelligent design arguments I've considered. I've come to this judgment for a combination of two main reasons.

The first reason is that biologists have given promising accounts for how the systems Behe labels as irreducibly complex could plausibly have arisen via standard biological means.[135] To present these accounts requires a sophisticated and not easily summarizable discussion of the details of the biological systems in question, a discussion that I don't want to get into here. Since much of the debate over intelligent design has focused on Behe's irreducible complexity argument, the interested reader can follow this discussion by turning to the standard literature.[136]

The second reason is that, even in the absence of specific naturalistic accounts of how the seemingly irreducibly complex biological systems evolved, if the universe is spatially infinite we would expect such systems to arise naturalistically. My argument here is analogous to my argument above regarding the origin of life in an infinite universe—though, as we'll see, there are some interesting twists. Because this appeal to a spatially infinite universe has not been widely discussed in the context of the debate over irreducible complexity, I will elaborate on it in the next subsection.

IRREDUCIBLE COMPLEXITY IN AN INFINITE UNIVERSE

Critics sometimes portray Behe as arguing that it's *impossible* for irreducibly complex systems to arise via naturalistic evolutionary means. For example, Ken Miller writes:

> [Behe] observes, quite correctly, that science has not explained the evolution of the bacterial flagellum, but then he goes one step further. No such explanation is even *possible*, according to Behe. Why? Because the flagellum has a characteristic that Behe calls "irreducible complexity."[137]

But when Miller says that no such explanation is possible according to Behe, Miller is mischaracterizing Behe's view. Behe does not claim that it is *impossible* for there to be a naturalistic evolutionary explanation of the evolution of an irreducibly complex system. What Behe claims is that such an explanation is *unlikely*. Behe recognizes that an irreducibly complex system could arise via evolutionary means. Specifically,

Behe recognizes that it could arise via an indirect scenario, where (for example) the individual parts first came into existence via evolutionary means because they each performed some other useful function, and then they got co-opted to use in the irreducibly complex system. Here is what Behe says about this possibility:

> As the number of required parts increases, the difficulty of gradually putting the system together skyrockets, and the likelihood of indirect scenarios plummets. Darwin looks more and more forlorn.[138]

Thus, Behe's argument is probabilistic—it is highly improbable for an irreducibly complex system to arise via evolutionary means, so we should infer that irreducibly complex systems were likely designed.

What I want to point out now is that, if the universe is spatially infinite, we have the resources to reject Behe's design inference. The argument is a simple one: even though it is highly unlikely for irreducibly complex systems to arise on any particular planet, given an infinite number of planets, and sufficient variability in the initial conditions across the different planets, we should expect irreducibly complex biological systems to arise somewhere. In fact, we should expect them to arise in an infinite number of places.

In Behe's 1996 book *Darwin's Black Box*, where he originally gives the irreducible complexity argument, he does not discuss the possibility that the universe is spatially infinite. But in his 2007 book *The Edge of Evolution*, he takes up a related issue. Specifically, what he discusses is the possibility that there are many universes. Consideration of this possibility leads to the argument that there's no need to postulate a designer because, under the assumption that there is no designer, we would expect that most universes wouldn't have irreducibly complex biological systems, but given enough universes we would expect that some would. Thus, the fact that we find irreducibly complex biological systems existing in this universe does not provide evidence for a designer.

Unsurprisingly, Behe takes issue with this argument. The objections Behe gives to this argument prima facie carry over to my argument based on the spatially infinite universe, and so it's worth discussing Behe's objections. Before doing so, though, I want to point out that Behe seems unaware of my argument based on a single spatially infinite universe. He writes:

> Notice that the multiverse scenario doesn't rescue Darwinism. Random mutation in a single universe would still be terribly unlikely as a cause for life.[139]

It's true that, on a particular planet, it would be very unlikely for random mutation to lead to the development of life. But in a single spatially infinite universe, it would be incredibly likely for there to be some planets where random mutation did act as a cause for life. Thus, Behe is wrong to say that random mutation in a single universe would be terribly unlikely. While his claim would be true for some universes, it's false for a universe that's spatially infinite.

I'll now discuss the four objections Behe gives to the multiverse reply to his irreducible complexity argument. In doing so, I'll consider how these objections could be applied to my argument that appeals to a spatially infinite universe as a way of blocking the inference from the existence of irreducibly complex biological systems to the existence of a designer.

The first objection is that the multiverse scenario is "speculative."[140] While this is true, I want to point out that the hypothesis that the universe is spatially infinite is far less speculative—it's supported by standard scientific evidence, such as the WMAP observations.

The second objection is that "some multiverse models themselves require much fine-tuning to make sure that, if real, they would generate universes with the right possibilities."[141] This is true, and thus I don't think an appeal to those sorts of multiverse models is successful as a reply to the fine-tuning argument. It's worth pointing out that the hypothesis that the universe is spatially infinite also is not successful as a reply to the fine-tuning argument, since there would have needed to be fine-tuning to get a life-permitting spatially infinite universe in the first place. That's why the line of reasoning I'm endorsing here is not intended as a reply to the fine-tuning argument.

Behe's third objection is as follows. On the assumption that there are many universes where the properties of each universe are randomly established,

> we should very likely live in a bare-bones world, with little or nothing in life beyond what's absolutely required to produce intelligent observers.... Yet it certainly seems that life in our world is quite lush and contains much more than what's absolutely needed for intelligence. Just as one familiar example from this book, the bacterial flagellum seems to have little to do with human intelligence, but is tremendously unlikely. If I am correct that it isn't required to produce intelligent observers, the only one in a very large number of universes that had intelligent observers should be expected to also have bacteria with flagella.[142]

Behe is assuming that, out of the panoply of universes in the random multiverse scenario, there are more bare-bones universes with intelligent life than lush universes with intelligent life (where "bare-bones" and "lush" refer to the quantity of life in existence that's not causally related to the production of intelligent life). Let's not take issue with that, but instead let's consider an analogue of this argument in the spatially infinite universe case. As I'll now show, this analogous argument provides evidence *against* a designer.

On the assumption that life in the universe arose randomly, one would expect a bare-bones universe, with most of the universe barrenly devoid of life. On the assumption that life in the universe arose as a result of a designer, one would expect a lush, non-barren universe. In fact though, the universe, as far as we can tell, is mostly a barren place. We don't find life abundant throughout the universe; so far we've only found life here. Thus, the observed distribution of life in the universe provides evidence against a designer.

Behe clearly wouldn't be happy with this line of reasoning; in reply he might give a pro-designer argument that appeals to the type of life we have here. As Behe points out in the above quotation, we have bacterial flagella, and yet bacterial flagella aren't needed for intelligent life. Behe takes this as evidence for a designer; he would presumably say (in the context of the spatially infinite universe hypothesis) that, under the assumption that there's no designer, it would be much more likely for there to be intelligent life on a bare-bones planet than on a planet with lush life.

In contrast, I believe that the existence of bacterial flagella that have nothing to do with intelligent life provides evidence *against* a designer. Random undesigned evolutionary pathways would be expected to lead to all sorts of life, including life that was not especially intelligent. But I would expect a designer not to desire the existence of bacterial flagella. Thus, given that there are bacterial flagella, that provides evidence against there being a designer. (I recognize that this argument is speculative, because it depends on the intentions of the hypothesized designer. But it shares this speculative feature with all the design arguments of which I'm aware.)

Another reply to Behe's objection is that unlikely events would be expected to happen on any planet during the long evolutionary process that led to intelligent life. It is plausible to hold that the vast majority of planets with intelligent life wouldn't have bacterial flagella, but they would have other types of life with unlikely features. What Behe would have to argue is that our planet has a much greater number of unlikely types of life than one would expect for a planet where intelligent life evolves via unguided evolution, or Behe would have to argue that our planet has forms of life that are much more unlikely than one would expect for a planet where intelligent life evolves via unguided evolution. But he has not given such an argument.

Here is the fourth and final objection from Behe. Behe argues that, if there are an infinite number of universes, there are an infinite number of "freak observers," where matter spontaneously arranges itself so as to form a conscious brain for some interval of time. This would be very unlikely to happen in any particular finite region of spacetime, but

> In an infinite multiverse, probabilities don't matter. Any event that isn't strictly impossible will occur an infinite number of times.[143]

If you are one of the infinite number of freak observers, then you would have no reason to trust your senses. Behe argues that this is problematic:

> Infinite multiverse scenarios are no different from brain-in-a-vat scenarios. If they were true, you would have no reason to trust your reasoning. So anyone who wants to do any kind of productive thinking must summarily reject the infinite multiverse scenario for intelligent life and assume that what we sense generally reflects the reality we know exists.[144]

I have two replies to Behe's reasoning here. First, even if you thought that you might be a brain in a vat, or a freak observer, you could still do some productive reasoning. For example, you could make judgments about how things appeared to you, you could evaluate your phenomenal experience for signs that you are a brain in a vat or a freak observer, and you could engage in a priori reasoning.

Second, contrary to Behe's claim that "probabilities don't matter," one is able to make reasoned probabilistic judgments in a spatially infinite universe or an infinite multiverse. Even if events occur an infinite number of times, we can still make probabilistic judgments about them, or judgments that are functionally equivalent to probabilistic judgments. For example, imagine a spatially infinite universe divided up into an infinite number of equally big cube-sized regions, and suppose that in each region there are many regular observers and one freak observer. If I was to learn that I were a part of this universe, I would assume that I was probably a regular observer, since in each of the equal cube-sized regions there are more regular observers than freak observers.

Now, it is true that one could divide this universe up into gerrymandered regions where each region contained one regular observer and many freak observers. But this gerrymandering wouldn't respect the spatial metric of the universe, and (in the absence of any motivation to the contrary) it makes sense to use the spatial metric to make probabilistic judgments in the infinite space.[145]

I conclude that Behe's four objections to the multiverse/infinite universe reply to his irreducible complexity argument aren't successful. Thus, if the universe is spatially infinite, that fact can be used to block design inferences based on the existence of irreducibly complex biological systems.

THEISTIC EVOLUTIONIST CRITIQUES OF EVOLUTION-BASED INTELLIGENT DESIGN

As an atheist, I expect there to be a naturalistic explanation for how complex biological systems came to exist. But if I were to become a theist, I would think it prima facie plausible that God played some sort of role in evolutionary processes, and other things being equal I would expect us to be able to find evidence of that role upon investigation. Thus, I wouldn't be inclined to be a theistic evolutionist—

that is, I wouldn't be inclined to both believe in God and believe in the standard naturalistic biological account of evolution.

Interestingly, some of the strongest criticisms of intelligent design have come from theistic evolutionists. It would be fascinating to delve into the different theological views that theistic evolutionists and intelligent design proponents have, and to explore the relationship between these theological views and the approaches toward science that these people take. I haven't seen a good discussion of this, but alas I'm not going to provide such a discussion here—that could easily be a book-length project in itself. Instead, I'm just going to explore a few lines of critique of evolution-based intelligent design arguments given by two prominent theistic evolutionists, Ken Miller and Denis Alexander.

Ken Miller

I'll start with Ken Miller's 2008 book *Only A Theory: Evolution and the Battle for America's Soul*. In addition to giving straightforward biology-based criticisms of Behe's irreducible complexity argument (the "Evolution" part), Miller also has a more fundamental critique of intelligent design (the "Battle for America's Soul" part).

Miller makes the claim that the intelligent design movement doesn't just want to "win the battle against Darwin"; the intelligent design movement wants to "win the greater war against science itself."[146] This claim that the intelligent design movement is anti-science is quite a strong claim. The way intelligent design proponents typically portray their activity is that they are looking for scientific evidence for the existence of a designer. This may be confused science, but it's not anti-science. Moreover, some intelligent design proponents, like Behe, are tenured professors in science departments at legitimate academic institutions, who publish standard scientific articles in standard scientific journals. It would greatly surprise me if these people were anti-science. Perhaps *some* intelligent design proponents do argue in a way that is anti-science, but those aren't the most intellectually respectable proponents of intelligent design; those aren't the proponents of intelligent design who should be taken seriously.

Miller makes this strong claim that intelligent design is trying to win a war against science, but unfortunately he provides minimal evidence for this claim. In fact, as far as I can tell, the only prima facie plausible textual evidence he cites is a single passage by William Dembski:

> The implications of intelligent design are radical in the true sense of this much overused word. The question posed by intelligent design is not how we should do science and theology in light of the triumph of Enlightenment rationalism and scientific naturalism. The question is rather how we should do science and theology in light of the impending collapse of Enlightenment rationalism

and scientific naturalism. These ideologies are on the way out ... because they are bankrupt.[147]

Miller says that "There can be no mistaking the target in Dembski's crosshairs,"[148] but in fact I maintain that this passage by Dembski is ambiguous. There is a way of reading it such that it is anti-science, and a way of reading it such that it is not.

On the anti-science way of reading the passage, one would hold that science is a key part of Enlightenment rationalism, and that naturalism is a key part of science, and since intelligent design is opposed to Enlightenment rationalism and scientific naturalism, intelligent design is opposed to science.

On the pro-science way of reading the passage, one would hold that *naturalism* is a key part of Enlightenment rationalism, and that there is a view of science which takes the assumption of naturalism to be part of the methodology of science. One would hold that intelligent design is opposed to the naturalism in Enlightenment rationalism, and the naturalistic view of science, but one would not hold that intelligent design is opposed to science itself.

It is pretty clear to me, judging from everything I've read by Dembski, that he intends the latter, pro-science, reading. I couldn't fully defend this by giving an example or two; the only way to really defend this claim is to read a lot of Dembski's work, and (in my opinion, at least) it becomes clear that Dembski is pro-science; he's just not pro-naturalism, and hence he's not pro-naturalism-as-a-scientific-methodology.[149] But as a partial defense, I'll give a couple of examples. First, Dembski calls intelligent design "a scientific research program,"[150] but someone who was really anti-science wouldn't brand a doctrine he endorses that way. Second, Dembski states that "intelligent design is perfectly compatible with common descent";[151] this certainly makes him sound quite different than, for example, an anti-science young earth creationist.

Now, Miller thinks that naturalism is an essential part of science. He holds that if one drops the constraint of methodological naturalism, then science will stop, because one can simply appeal to God as an explanation of any scientific phenomenon. Miller writes:

> A theistic science ... will no longer be the science we have known. It will cease to explore, because it already knows the answers.[152]

But as I've explained in Chapter 2, that is a bad line of reasoning. The reason it's a bad line of reasoning is that, while theistic scientists could choose to stop investigating the world, and be satisfied with the answer "God did it," they need not. What theistic scientists can do is investigate questions like: "What structure did God choose to give the world?" If they try to answer this question, it follows that they won't be satisfied with the answer "God did it"; they'll want to investigate what exactly God did. Moreover, theistic scientists, like everyone else, can continue to ask the question "Is there a naturalistic explanation of this phenomenon?," even if the theistic scientists think that the right explanation is supernatural. As long as theistic scientists are willing to investigate those questions, then science can go on in pretty much the standard way; allowing supernatural hypotheses won't fundamentally change science. Miller is wrong to say that a theistic science would cease to explore, and thus, Miller's claim that intelligent design is anti-science doesn't hold up.

There's one final issue I want to take up regarding Miller. Miller is right that intelligent design proponents have a somewhat different conception of how science would go than atheists and theistic evolutionists. Intelligent design proponents think that God (or some sort of designer) plays an identifiable role in evolutionary processes, while atheists and theistic evolutionists wouldn't endorse this. Here's what Miller has to say about this:

> [Intelligent design would] reduce science to just another relativistic discipline.
> It would tell us that thinking the right spiritual thoughts is essential to the
> scientific process, and that there are no absolutes in nature.[153]

I mostly agree with the "right spiritual thoughts part," but I disagree with the "relativistic/no absolutes" part.

Initially it sounds bad to my atheist ears to hear that thinking the right spiritual thoughts is essential to the scientific process. But if science is ultimately a quest for truths about the world, and there is a God who sometimes intervenes in the world, then to have a completely accurate scientific account of the world, that account would have to include the fact that God sometimes intervenes in the world. If science tells us that God doesn't intervene, but God does, then science is getting some things wrong. Science would be based on the wrong spiritual thoughts, and as a result the scientific theories developed wouldn't be as good as they could be. One could still potentially do a lot of good science, even without including the God hypothesis, so in that sense I wouldn't say that having the right spiritual thoughts is *essential* to the scientific process. But some spiritual thoughts certainly would be relevant.

What about Miller's claim that intelligent design is a relativistic discipline that tells us that there are no absolutes in nature? That claim is, as far as I can tell, completely unfounded. Behind the hypothesis that thinking the right spiritual thoughts is essential to the process of science is the assumption that one set of spiritual thoughts is right, and all the competing sets are wrong. That is the opposite of relativism.

Denis Alexander

Denis Alexander is a biologist at Cambridge University, and is the editor of the journal *Science & Christian Belief.* Like Miller, he's a theistic evolutionist who is opposed to intelligent design. In his 2008 book *Creation or Evolution: Do We Have to Choose?,* in addition to giving the standard biological objections to evolution-based intelligent design arguments, he has another intriguing line of argument. Alexander criticizes intelligent design proponents for giving a "God-of-the-gaps" argument—an argument where one points to a gap in our scientific understanding of the world and claims that that gap provides evidence for the existence of God. I'll take issue with his claim that that's what intelligent design proponents are doing, but I'll also argue that, even if that's what they are doing, God-of-the-gaps arguments aren't as bad as people generally think.

Before taking up the God-of-the-gaps discussion directly, I'll start with a related claim by Alexander, that intelligent design arguments are instances of the fallacious "argument from ignorance" form. Alexander writes:

> The ID proponents are saying that because we don't know exactly how a complex entity evolved, therefore it didn't evolve, therefore it was 'designed.' But that is a non sequitur.[154]

I agree with Alexander that, if that's the argument form that intelligent design proponents are using, then intelligent design proponents are following a flawed argument form. Just because we don't know exactly how, for example, the first dinosaur evolved, it doesn't follow that the first dinosaur was designed. However, I disagree with Alexander's claim that the flawed argument form he identifies is an argument form that sophisticated intelligent design proponents are using. When Behe appeals to irreducibly complex biological systems, he is not simply saying that we don't know how such systems evolved. He's giving a positive argument that it's unlikely for such systems to evolve without the intervention of a designer. There are lots of biological systems for which it's the case that we don't know exactly how they evolved, but Behe's argument doesn't utilize all of those. Instead, Behe picks out certain biological systems that ostensibly have the special property of being irreducibly complex.

Now, I'll turn to Alexander's accusation that intelligent design proponents are giving a "God-of-the-gaps" argument. Such arguments are generally maligned, because it's generally believed that such arguments will have the gaps filled in by further scientific investigation. (More specifically, it's generally believed that the gaps will be filled in naturalistically, without appeal to a supernatural designer.) Alexander writes:

The history of science is full of examples where people thought they had encountered a completely insoluble mystery, or thought that science could not advance any further, only for that mystery to be resolved....[155]

Alexander then concludes that the God-of-the-gaps argument that Behe is giving will similarly have the gaps filled in by future naturalistic scientific investigation. But there are three problems with using this line of thought as a criticism of intelligent design.

First, despite how it's typically portrayed in the anti-intelligent design literature, I maintain that Behe's irreducible complexity argument is not a God-of-the-gaps argument at all. Behe is not saying that we don't know (or can't know) how irreducibly complex systems like the bacterial flagellum could plausibly arise naturalistically. Instead, Behe is giving positive reasons that the sequence of events that would have to happen for irreducibly complex systems like the bacterial flagellum to arise via an undesigned process is an improbable sequence, and hence the design hypothesis should be taken seriously.

To see my point, an analogy is perhaps helpful. Consider a standard coin, such as an American penny. It's generally assumed that the probability of getting heads if this coin is flipped is one-half, but in fact the probability is somewhat different— there seems to be more raised weight on the heads side than the tails side, and thus the coin probably isn't perfectly evenly weighted, and thus it's probably somewhat more likely to land on one side than the other. Now, imagine that a penny is flipped 100 times, and each time the penny lands heads. We don't know exactly what the probability is of this happening by chance, but we think the probability is low, and this leads us to take seriously alternative hypotheses, such as that the person doing the flipping is doing a magic trick, and hence the sequence of heads occurred by design. It would be unreasonable for someone to come along and say: "you might think that getting that sequence of heads by chance is improbable, but you shouldn't take the design hypothesis seriously; there's just a gap in our understanding, and that gap will surely be filled in by future scientific investigation." The reason this is unreasonable is that our judgment of the low probability of getting the sequence of heads by chance isn't a judgment based on a lack of understanding; it's an informed judgment. Behe would (I think) say the same thing about his irreducible complexity argument—he holds that he has good reason to think that it's improbable for irreducibly complex systems to arise via an undesigned process; the judgment isn't just based on our lack of understanding.

Here's the second problem with Alexander's move of maligning the intelligent design arguments by calling them God-of-the-gaps arguments. Just because gaps in the past were filled in with further naturalistic scientific investigation, it doesn't follow that every gap in the future will be similarly filled in. Alexander's argument to the contrary is a relatively weak inductive argument. To see this, consider an analogous argument. If one looks at the history of science, one sees that all scientific theories before the ones that we currently favor have been shown to be false. Does it follow that the scientific theories we currently favor will be shown to be false too? While some philosophers have endorsed this argument (called "the pessimistic induction argument"), most think that the argument is not that strong. The reason the argument is not that strong is that we could well have good reason to think that our currently favored theories are true, reasons that didn't exist for the past false theories. Just as that's a reasonable response to give to the pessimistic induction argument, so Behe could have the resources to give an analogous reasonable response to Alexander. Behe could say that he has good reason to think that the gaps he highlights won't be filled in naturalistically, reasons that didn't exist for past failed God-of-the-gaps arguments.

Here's the third and final problem with Alexander's critique of intelligent design arguments by way of critiquing God-of-the-gaps arguments. Alexander says that the history of science is full of examples where there was a seemingly insoluble gap in our understanding, but where that gap was filled in naturalistically by further scientific investigation. While this is true, what Alexander doesn't point out is that it's also the case that the history of science is full of seemingly insoluble gaps in our understanding that have never been filled in naturalistically. For example, we don't know what the nature of consciousness is, or how conscious mental activity arises out of physical brain activity. We don't know why the universe exists—we don't know why there is something rather than nothing. We don't know why the universe has three spatial dimensions and one time dimension. We don't know what the nature of mass is. We don't know what the universe is made of (most of it seems to be "dark matter," but we don't know what dark matter is). We don't have a single fundamental theory of physics (the two theories we do have, general relativity and quantum theory, are incompatible). The list could go on, but I've said enough to make my point. One can't just say: all gaps in the past have been naturalistically filled in, so future gaps will be naturalistically filled in as well, because in fact there are some persistent gaps that have never been naturalistically filled in. Thus, it's reasonable to be cautious in assuming that any new gap we discover will be naturalistically filled in as well.

BEYOND EVOLUTION-BASED ARGUMENTS

As I've explained, I find evolution-based intelligent design arguments less strong than the other intelligent design arguments I've considered. My view is seemingly not shared by the majority of intelligent design proponents, who generally put their focus on evolution-based arguments. I'm not sure why they do this. Perhaps they just happen to think that evolution-based arguments are the strongest arguments for a designer. Or perhaps they are especially concerned to show that we humans are not the product of an unguided process.

But if the goal is just to show that we are not the product of an unguided process, finding *any* sort of evidence for a designer can help to show that. That is, even if the successful argument for a designer is non-evolution-based, finding evidence for a designer can have consequences for our understanding of evolution. For example, if we decide that the fine-tuning argument is successful, then we would conclude that a designer exists, and that the designer wants the universe to have life. Given that such a designer exists, it's perfectly reasonable to think that the designer would have ideas about what sort of life the designer wants to exist, and would ensure that the universe proceeds in such a way that that sort of life comes to exist.

It's important to note that the designer could do this even in a situation where, from a biological perspective, it looks like life evolves via random mutation and natural selection. It could turn out that, while the mutations appear random, the designer is actually involved in ensuring that the mutations occur exactly when and where they do. For example, we know that some mutations are caused by cosmic rays from space; it could turn out that those cosmic rays are being produced by the designer. Or, it could turn out that the designer set up the initial conditions of the universe in such a way that there would be cosmic rays that would produce exactly the mutations that the designer wanted to be produced.[156]

These considerations show that, if one is looking for scientific evidence for a designer, it's important to not just focus on evolution-based investigations. It may be that, when we look at biological processes, we find no strong evidence for the existence of a designer, but when we look at, for example, cosmic ray production, we do see clear evidence for the involvement of an intelligent cause.[157]

The Simulation Argument

So far, the intelligent design arguments we've been considering in this chapter are theistically oriented, in that the arguments are generally given by theists to provide evidence for the existence of God. In this section I'm going to consider a non-theistic intelligent design argument, called *the simulation argument*. The conclusion of the argument is that there's a highly intelligent being (or beings) running a computer simulation of our universe, and we're just a part of that computer simulation. I consider the simulation argument to be a type of intelligent design argument, because it's arguing that the universe we're living in has been designed by an intelligent being, and because we can in principle get scientific evidence for this claim.

The original version of the simulation argument is due to the philosopher Nick Bostrom.[158] (The argument I'm going to be presenting is somewhat different, but it will be evident that I got inspiration from Bostrom's argument.) Now, Bostrom doesn't actually fully believe that we are living in a computer simulation—he thinks there's about a 20 per cent chance that's the case. In fact, I don't know of anyone who believes that we're living in a computer simulation, and I wouldn't expect you to believe it either. The hard part though is to say where the argument goes wrong.

So, without further ado, here is (my version of) the simulation argument. Let's start by supposing that (as discussed in the previous section) the universe really is spatially infinite, with an infinite number of planets. This would mean that there are an infinite number of intelligent civilizations in existence, and some of them are going to be a lot more technologically advanced than our civilization. We would expect some of these technologically advanced civilizations to run computer simulations of civilizations—perhaps for research, perhaps for fun. Now, there are different ways these civilizations could run simulations. They could just specify what each person in the civilization does—that would be a behaviorist simulation, where just the behavior of the people would be modeled. They could, however, run a more detailed simulation, where instead of just simulating the behavior of the person, they simulated the actual *brain state* of the person. The physical processes that go on in a person's brain would be replicated in fine-grained detail by the computer. Given a commonly accepted assumption that cognitive scientists and philosophers of mind make, the assumption of *substrate independence*, if a computer simulates a brain state in an appropriate way, there will be *conscious experiences* associated with that simulation. In other words, by simulating a brain, the computer will have produced an actual mind.

I'll say more about substrate independence below, but first let me finish the argument. Suppose that substrate independence is right, and that computers can make minds. Now, think back to this civilization running computer simulations of people. Since the civilization is so advanced, they could run lots and lots of computer simulations of people. Bostrom actually does some back-of-the-envelope calculations to show that advanced civilizations would in principle have the computational power to easily run lots of simulations of civilizations. (He estimates that to simulate the whole history of our civilization, it would take about 10^{35} computer operations, whereas an advanced computer could easily do 10^{42} operations per second. Obviously the numerical details don't matter, as long as the general argument is right that it wouldn't take much computing power to run a simulation.)

So, take some very large region of the universe, where there are lots of regular civilizations (living on a single planet, not very technologically advanced) and comparably fewer highly advanced civilizations. All these highly advanced civilizations would have the computational power to easily run simulations, but let's suppose that not many actually do. Still, we can expect that some of them would. Since it wouldn't take much computational power for such an advanced civilization to simulate a civilization on a computer, they could run vast numbers of civilization simulations. (The image that pops into my head is that of an advanced civilization where the desktop computers are so powerful that there are civilization-simulation screensavers—when the screensaver comes on, civilization-simulations start. The picture is surely anachronistic, but it gets the idea across that they have so much computational power that running vast numbers of civilization-simulations is easy.)

Now, think about all the minds that exist in this very large region of the universe. According to the simulation argument, there are so many minds that are associated with the computer simulations being run by the few highly advanced civilizations, that *the vast majority* of the minds in this region of the universe would be minds produced as a result of the simulations. Now, think about yourself. Would you expect your mind to be one of the few minds that exists in a real civilization, or would you expect your mind to be one of the many minds that exists in a simulated civilization? Well, if you discovered that *every* mind in the universe were a result of a computer simulation, then surely you would believe that your mind is a result of a computer simulation. Here though, you're discovering something slightly weaker—you're discovering that *almost every* mind is a result of a computer simulation. In that situation, absent further evidence, you should conclude that your mind is *almost certainly* part of a computer simulation.[159]

So, that's the simulation argument. If your attitude is incredulousness, I'm on your side. But expressing incredulousness doesn't show that the argument is wrong. After reflection, my opinion is that the argument is somewhat plausible. I'll start by defending the argument against some criticisms that I think are unfair, and then I'll tell you why I don't fully endorse the argument.

IS THIS SKEPTICISM?

Suppose for the moment that the simulation argument is right, and that you are living in a computer simulation. What this means is that the vast majority of your beliefs about the world are false. For example, you think that there's a book in front of you, but in fact there's not; in fact your visual experience of a book being in front of you is being produced by a computer. You think that you have a hand, but in fact you don't; in fact your sensory experiences of having a hand are being produced by a computer. Philosophers would call the hypothesis that you are living in a computer simulation a *skeptical hypothesis*, since it entails the falsity of so much that we believe about the world.

The traditional skeptical hypothesis is due to Descartes, writing in the 1600s. Descartes considered the possibility of an evil demon who deceived you into believing what we believe about the world (that there are books, that you have a hand, and so on) even though those beliefs are actually false. (Descartes didn't actually believe this hypothesis though; he argued that God existed, and God wouldn't deceive us.)

The more contemporary, flashier version of the skeptical hypothesis is that you are a brain in a vat—there are lots of electrodes hooked up to your brain, stimulating the appropriate nerves so that you have the sensory experiences you do, even though there's nothing in reality that corresponds to these sensory experiences.

Some philosophers use skeptical hypotheses to argue that we don't know much of anything about the world. For example, you *think* that you have a hand, but all your experience is compatible with your being a brain in a vat, so you don't *know* that you have a hand; for all you know you're really a brain in a vat. I don't want to go into the details of whether or not these arguments are good—there are enough philosophy books out there that do that sort of thing. What I want to point out is one important way that these skeptical arguments are different than the simulation argument. The skeptical arguments don't actually give you a positive reason to think that you're a brain in a vat; they just argue that your being a brain in a vat is compatible with your experience. The simulation argument, on the other hand, is much stronger than these skeptical arguments. The simulation argument gives you a positive reason to think that you're living in a computer simulation—most minds are part of computer simulations, so it's probably the case that your mind is as well.

CAN A COMPUTER MAKE A MIND?

Let's go back to the assumption of substrate independence I talked about above. This assumption has the consequence that if a computer simulates a brain state in an appropriate way, there will be *conscious experiences* associated with that simulation. But the assumption is more general than just that. What the assumption holds is that it doesn't take the particular physical stuff a brain is made of in order to produce a mind. As long as one has the right sorts of physical processes going on, it doesn't matter what is instantiating those processes; a mind will be associated with those processes.

This is a purposefully vague account, in large part because we don't know the details of what it actually takes to produce a mind. But even though we don't know the details, there are strong arguments that something like substrate independence must be right. I'll give one of the arguments here.

First, imagine the brain of some person—let's call that person "Bababooey." Bababooey currently has conscious experiences associated with his brain activity. The brain activity consists of interactions of neurons, where each neuron is capable of producing electrical impulses or releasing chemicals that affect other neurons. Now, imagine we take one of Bababooey's neurons, and replace it with an artificial neuron. The artificial neuron isn't made of the same stuff that a real neuron is made of, but it does the same thing—it reacts to chemical and electrical inputs the same way that the real neuron it replaced would, and it produces the same chemical and electrical outputs that the real neuron it replaced would. Surely, Bababooey would still have the same sort of conscious experiences after we replaced the neuron. (Well, he would as long as we replaced the neuron in a sufficiently non-invasive fashion. So let's suppose that we have the ability to magically switch real neurons with artificial ones.)

Now, imagine that we keep replacing real neurons with artificial ones, one by one. Bababooey would continue to behave the same way, since it's part of the hypothesis that the artificial neurons do the same things that the real neurons do: just as the real neurons sometimes send signals to Bababooey's muscle fibers to move his arm, so the artificial neurons would. Just as the real neurons sometimes send signals to Bababooey's muscle fibers to move his mouth, so the artificial neurons would. And so on. If you were standing there watching Bababooey as his neurons were replaced, one by one, you wouldn't notice any changes—he would continue to gesture and talk and be just as animated as ever. So after all his neurons had been replaced, it just wouldn't be plausible to say that he lacks conscious experiences—he's behaving just the same way he did before; it just wouldn't be plausible to say that he's doing all that without being conscious. So this is an argument for substrate independence—Bababooey right now is a conscious being, and if we replaced all his neurons with artificial neurons he would continue to be conscious. Thus, it doesn't take the particular physical stuff that makes up real neurons to produce a mind. In other words, substrate independence holds.

We can push this thought experiment further. In the story I told above, it's natural to think of the artificial neurons being of the same size as the real neurons. But notice that there's nothing essential to my story that requires that. So we can imagine replacing the full-size artificial neurons with smaller artificial neurons that do the same thing. (Perhaps we'll have to replace other parts of the brain too with small artificial parts, so it all fits together appropriately.) We're all familiar with this idea of making processors smaller; computers used to be room-sized but now they're laptop-sized, and they keep getting smaller.

So the picture here is that there's a tiny brain sitting inside Bababooey's skull, but still with all the appropriate connections between the brain and other parts of the body (like the muscle fibers). With his miniaturized artificial brain inside his skull, Bababooey would still behave the same sort of way, and so it would be completely reasonable to attribute to him the same sort of conscious experiences. So this is a slight extension of the substrate independence idea—just as the particular stuff making up a brain doesn't matter for conscious experience being produced, so the size of the stuff doesn't matter either.

Let's push the thought experiment even further. As long as the brain is receiving the appropriate inputs and producing the appropriate outputs, it doesn't matter whether the brain is hooked up to a body or to a computer. If the computer is sufficiently powerful, it could simulate all the inputs that the brain would experience as a result of its senses, and the computer could modify the inputs in an appropriate way based on the outputs coming from the brain. So if we did this to Bababooey's miniaturized artificial brain, he would still think that he's living a normal life, interacting with things like chairs and microphones, even though all the conscious experiences he has would actually be associated with a miniaturized artificial brain inside a computer.

From here it's not hard to imagine that it's not just Bababooey who's existing in this way, but that we all are. In sum, it's *possible* that we're all living in a computer simulation. The point of the simulation argument is to argue that we actually probably *are*.

DR. EVIL

I want to turn to an objection to the simulation argument which takes issue with the way the argument gets from the claim that most observers are living in a computer simulation to the claim that we are probably living in a computer simulation. To better evaluate this step in the argument, let's consider a thought experiment first described by Adam Elga, the Dr. Evil thought experiment.[160]

In this thought experiment (at least, in the version of the thought experiment I'm interested in), Dr. Evil is told by a group of philosophers that, at midnight tonight, a duplicate of him will be created. This duplicate will have all the same memories, beliefs, personality traits, and so on of Dr. Evil. Moreover, the duplicate will be created on a duplicate Earth, that looks just like the actual Earth. Dr. Evil, being a credulous sort, fully believes what the philosophers tell him—and indeed, what they tell him is true. When Dr. Evil wakes up the next morning, what probability should he assign to the hypothesis that he is the duplicate?

I maintain that the answer is 1/2. Since there are two beings out there, with exactly the same conscious experiences, Dr. Evil doesn't know which of the two beings he is, and has no reason to favor one over the other. Thus, what he ought to do is hold that there's a 50/50 chance that he's the duplicate.

Before considering objections to this, let me consider a variant on this thought experiment, so you can see how this relates to the simulation argument. Consider the thought experiment where, instead of one duplicate being created at midnight, 999 duplicates are created. Now, when Dr. Evil wakes up the next morning, what probability should he assign to the hypothesis that he is a duplicate?

I maintain that the answer is 999/1000—he should feel pretty certain that he's a duplicate. The reasoning is of the same sort I gave above: there are 1000 beings out there with exactly the same conscious experiences, and Dr. Evil doesn't know which of the 1000 he is, and he has no reason to favor any one over the other. Thus, what we ought to do is hold for each of the 1000 beings that there's a 1 in 1000 chance that he's that being.

This is an interesting result. What this shows is that one can go from feeling certain that one is the original to feeling almost certain that one is a duplicate, without having any new experiences that directly show that one is a duplicate. (Dr. Evil's only relevant experience is that of the conversation he had with the philosophers, when they tell Dr. Evil what they're going to do.) Further, note that the time at which the philosophers tell Dr. Evil about their duplication activities doesn't really matter. Suppose that the philosophers secretly create the 999 duplicates of Dr. Evil, and only later tell Dr. Evil what's happened. (Duplicate philosophers on duplicate Earths will tell the duplicate Dr. Evils what's happened as well.) Once Dr. Evil is told about this, he should think it's pretty certain that he's a duplicate. Thus, whether the duplication happens before or after Dr. Evil is told about the duplication doesn't matter.

Now one can see the similarities between the Dr. Evil thought experiment and the simulation argument. In both, there are some minds associated with one type, and comparatively more associated with the other type. In both, you start out thinking that you are of a particular type, but then you find out that there are more minds associated with a different type. This (arguably) leads you to shift your probabilities in favor of thinking that your mind is one of the more numerous type.

Of course, there are differences as well. The main difference is that, in the Dr. Evil thought experiment, it's guaranteed that the duplicates are exactly like the original. In the simulation argument, however, it's not specified that the simulated minds are exactly like non-simulated minds. So just because one endorses the answer I give in the Dr. Evil thought experiment, one need not give the same sort of answer in the simulation argument. Nevertheless, the Dr. Evil thought experiment is useful, because it isolates one part of the reasoning that goes into the simulation argument. As you might have guessed, people have objected to the answer I endorse in the Dr. Evil thought experiment, and presumably these people would object to the simulation argument in the same way. So it's worth looking at the objections people have given to the claim that Dr. Evil should think that there's a 50/50 chance he's the duplicate (in the case where one duplicate is created) and the claim that Dr. Evil should think he's most likely a duplicate (in the case where 999 duplicates are created).

There's a standard objection to this line of reasoning that I've heard from various people. The objection has never (as far as I know) been worked out in any detail, but it's worth discussing here, because I think it's an objection that many people inchoately have in mind if they balk at the reasoning I've defended. In informal surveys I've taken, about two-thirds of people are perfectly happy to say that there's a 50/50 chance that they're the duplicate (in the original Dr. Evil case described above), while about one-third of people are dissatisfied with that answer. The people who are dissatisfied tend to say that the probability is 1, or almost 1, that they are the original. Here's what I take to be the best defense of that answer:

Look, the morning after duplication, Dr. Evil has all sorts of memories about his past, memories that he'd have to reject if he thought there was a 50/50 chance he was the duplicate. For example, Dr. Evil believes that he had a croissant for breakfast a year ago, but he'd have to—somehow—get rid of that belief if he thought there was a 50/50 chance he was the duplicate. But that is really too much to ask; is anyone really capable of getting rid of all their beliefs about the past like that? And anyway, it's not like Dr. Evil has been given *positive evidence* that his beliefs about the past are false. It would be one thing if he was shown a videotape of him eating a bagel, not a croissant, for breakfast, with the time/date stamp on the video showing that this occurred a year ago. This is the sort of positive evidence that would lead him to drop his belief that he had a croissant for breakfast a year ago. In the Dr. Evil story, though, there's no such positive evidence.

No one has actually said exactly those words, but that's what I think people should say if they want to give this sort of objection. Or at least, that's the best I can come up with, because I find the objection pretty unconvincing.

First of all, just because we aren't capable of getting rid of our beliefs, it doesn't follow that there are never circumstances when we shouldn't try. Suppose Dr. Evil has trouble ridding himself of the belief that he had a croissant for breakfast a year ago. When he's asked about it, his initial inclination might be to say that he did have a croissant, but then he should remind himself that actually he doesn't know that, because for all he knows he's the duplicate who has a false memory of having a croissant. Whenever issues about the past come up, he should remind himself that, for all he knows, he's the duplicate. Whether he is actually capable of getting rid of his beliefs is a psychological issue, but when he's reasoning about the past in a considered fashion, he surely is capable of remembering what the philosophers told him, and hence he certainly is capable of reasoning in such a way that doesn't take for granted that he's the original.

There's a second reply I want to give to the people who say that Dr. Evil should hold that the probability is 1, or almost 1, that he's the original (even after duplication). I've presented these people as holding that Dr. Evil doesn't have positive evidence that he's the duplicate. But this notion of positive evidence is fishy. Why doesn't the discussion with the philosophers who generate duplicates count as positive evidence? Dr. Evil fully believes what the philosophers tell him, after all. I see how one *could* generate a distinction between (for example) the videotaped breakfast evidence and the philosophers' account of duplication, but I don't see how this distinction could be used in a principled way to establish whether or not one can ignore the evidence in question. Maybe the distinction could work that way, but I'd have to see the argument—I can't come up with a plausible-sounding argument on my own.

A PRAGMATICALLY SELF-DEFEATING ARGUMENT

There's something strange about the simulation argument, as I've presented it. The argument starts with the premise that we're living in a spatially infinite universe (where the main support for that premise is the empirical evidence like the WMAP observations I cited in the previous section). Then the argument concludes that we're probably living in a computer simulation. But if we're living in a computer simulation, then how can we know anything about the actual structure of the (real, physical) universe? Why should we think that the real, physical universe is spatially infinite? Sure, our simulated universe is spatially infinite, but that presumably doesn't tell us much about the real universe, the universe that the being running the computer simulation is living in.

So, a premise of the argument is that the real, physical universe is spatially infinite. Suppose we believe that premise, and we find the rest of the argument plausible, so we come to believe the conclusion. The problem is that, as a result of believing the conclusion, we don't have much reason anymore to believe the premise! And once we stop believing the premise, we will no longer believe the conclusion. But our belief in the conclusion was the only reason that led us to call into doubt the premise. So now that we no longer believe the conclusion, we can believe the premise again. But now we believe the premise, and we still find the rest of the simulation argument plausible, so....

You see where this is going. The argument is *pragmatically self-defeating*. (This is my terminology, because as far as I know philosophers haven't talked about this sort of argument before.) What I mean by the "self-defeating" part is that the conclusion of the argument leads one to call into question one of the premises of the argument. What I mean by the "pragmatic" qualifier is that it doesn't *follow* from the conclusion that the premise is false; it's just that, if one believes the conclusion, then one has no reason to believe the premise. It could be the case that we're living in a computer simulation and the universe is spatially infinite. It's just that, if we're living in a computer simulation, we don't have much reason to think that the real, physical universe is spatially infinite.[161]

This situation is somewhat similar to a paradox that's familiar to philosophers, *Moore's paradox*. Suppose my friend Katie says "It is raining and I believe that it is not raining." Katie is making two claims here: (1) it is raining, and (2) she believes that it is not raining. These claims aren't inconsistent; it could be true that it's raining, and it could be true that Katie has the false belief that it's not raining. But there's something weird about *Katie* asserting both those claims. Katie's statement is pragmatically inconsistent; she could have no reason to believe both claims.

Moore's paradox is about a single statement, whereas the pragmatically self-defeating nature of the simulation argument arises not as a result of any single statement in the argument, but as a result of the structure of the argument as a whole. So the paradox I'm pointing out in the simulation argument isn't the same as Moore's paradox. It is, I think, just as interesting as Moore's paradox—and given all the philosophical literature on Moore's paradox, that makes it quite interesting indeed.

So what should one do if faced with a pragmatically self-defeating argument? Let's be clear about the situation: one is faced with an argument where one fully believes that the conclusion follows from the premises, and one initially believes all of the premises. One comes to believe the conclusion, and then one realizes that, as a result of believing the conclusion, one no longer has much reason to believe in one of the premises. So, in this situation, what should one do?

I think this is a tricky situation, and I must admit that I don't really have a definite answer. But here are some considerations to keep in mind. The position where one strongly believes the controversial premise is an unstable one, since one will come to believe the conclusion, and that will call into question the reasons one had for believing that premise. But that doesn't merit believing that the premise is definitely false. So instead one should assign a probability to the premise that's neither close to 0 nor close to 1—a probability assignment like 1/2 would be good. Under the assumption that one fully believes the other premises in the argument, one then has to assign probability at least 1/2 to the conclusion, since the conclusion logically follows from the controversial premise in question—it would be impossible for the conclusion to be less probable than the controversial premise. The reason one might assign probability higher than 1/2 to the conclusion is that even if the controversial premise is false, it could be the case that the conclusion is true. But even though it would be reasonable for an agent to have other reasons to support the conclusion besides the argument I've given, the having of such reasons can lead to pragmatic self-defeat. If the probability assigned to the conclusion is greater than 1/2, this might lead one to assign a probability of less than 1/2 to the premise. A probability assignment of 1/2 to the premise and 1/2 to the conclusion doesn't lead to pragmatic self-defeat, but (as far as I can tell) any other probability assignment potentially does.[162]

HOW TO OBJECT TO THE SIMULATION ARGUMENT

I want to start this section by explaining how the version of the simulation argument I've presented differs from the original version presented by Bostrom. Here is Bostrom's version. Bostrom doesn't argue for the conclusion that we're probably living in a computer simulation; instead he argues that at least one of the following claims is true:

1. The fraction of all human-level civilizations that survive to reach a highly advanced technological stage is almost 0.

2. The fraction of all highly advanced civilizations that are interested in running computer simulations is almost 0.

3. The fraction of observers living in computer simulations is almost 1.

In my version of the simulation argument, the argument proceeded by claiming that (1) and (2) were both false. Bostrom would then conclude that (3) is true, since at least one of (1), (2), and (3) is true. From (3) Bostrom would conclude that we're probably living in a computer simulation.

In my version of the simulation argument, the argument for the falsity of (1) and (2) depended in part on the claim that the universe is spatially infinite. Interestingly, Bostrom doesn't explicitly endorse that claim in the context of giving the simulation argument (but he has endorsed that claim in other contexts). Perhaps Bostrom is aware of the pragmatically self-defeating problem that one runs into on that version of the argument. Nevertheless, Bostrom does seem to think that it's at least plausible that there are vastly many civilizations, some of which are running computer simulations, so to that extent he is utilizing the assumption that the universe is spatially infinite (or at least that the universe is very large).

Anyway, I think Bostrom is right to direct our focus to hypotheses (1) and (2). Even if the universe is spatially infinite, it could be the case that either (1) or (2) or both are true, and hence it could be the case that (3) is false. For example, (1) could be true, because it could be the case that almost every civilization manages to destroy itself before it reaches a highly advanced technological stage. Or, (1) could be true, because it could be the case that there are technological barriers we aren't aware of that prevent civilizations from reaching a highly advanced stage. Also, (2) could be true, because it could be the case that most all highly advanced civilizations find that they have better things to do with their computing power than to run civilization simulations. Or, (2) could be true, because it could be the case that most all highly advanced civilizations determine that it's unethical to run civilization simulations, and hence prevent the members of their civilization from doing so. It would naturally follow on any of these hypotheses that most observers are not living in computer simulations; hence it would follow that we are probably not living in a computer simulation.

I've just given examples of how one could have reason to endorse (1) or (2); the examples aren't meant to be exhaustive. But perhaps you find one of those reasons plausible, or perhaps you have a different reason to endorse (1) or (2). If so, you have an objection to the simulation argument. My personal opinion is that various reasons along these lines are somewhat plausible, and hence the probability I assign to both (1) and (2) is pretty high, which allows me to assign a pretty low probability to (3). But I don't have any knock-down reasons to think that (1) and (2) are true; we're at the level of hunches here.

Since we're at that level, here's one final worry of mine to report. I'm not completely convinced by the substrate independence argument, and if substrate independence is false then perhaps it is too difficult for even highly advanced civilizations to run consciousness-producing simulations. If that's the case, then (1), (2), and (3) could all be false—there could be lots of highly advanced civilizations all of which want to run simulations, but they aren't able to, and hence there are no conscious observers living in a simulation.

WHERE IS THE EVIDENCE FOR SIMULATION?

I consider the simulation argument to be a type of intelligent design argument, in part because it's arguing that the universe we're living in has been designed by an intelligent being (the being running the computer simulation). Moreover, the simulation argument, as I've presented it, appeals to scientific evidence—the evidence that the universe is spatially infinite—and argues on the basis of this evidence for a designer.

In this (final) section, I want to point out that one could in principle get more scientific evidence that we're living in a computer simulation, and I want to consider the consequences of this for our actual situation, where we don't have such evidence.

What sort of scientific evidence could one in principle get for the thesis that we're living in a computer simulation? Here is one example. In a computer (as we understand computers, at least), irrational numbers can't be fully accurately represented. (An irrational number is a number that can't be represented as a fraction; its decimal representation goes on infinitely.) Suppose it turns out that no fundamental physical constants are irrational—suppose it turns out instead that all the fundamental physical constants have decimal representations that go out to 16 digits, and then stop.[163] It's hard to see what physics-based reason there could be that the fundamental constants would be like this, but if we are living in a computer simulation it is easy to see why the fundamental constants would be like this—the computer running our civilization would have been programmed to only represent constants out to 16 digits.

So, that's an example of scientific evidence we could get for the simulation hypothesis. This leads to a further question: does the fact that we don't have such evidence provide support for the claim that we're *not* living in a simulation? To think about this question, it's helpful to have a more prosaic analogy. Suppose you think that an explosion might go off in the distance at 3 pm. You know that the explosion is too far away to see, but you think that perhaps you'll be able to hear the explosion if it happens; you're not sure. You wait until well after 3 pm, but you don't hear anything. Does this provide evidence that the explosion didn't happen?

The answer is that it does provide some evidence, but how much evidence it provides depends on how likely you thought it was that you would hear the explosion, given that it happened. For example, suppose you thought that there was a 99.9 per cent chance that you'd hear the explosion if it happened. The fact that you don't hear anything, then, provides pretty strong evidence that the explosion didn't happen. But now suppose you thought there was only a 10 per cent chance that you'd hear the explosion if it happened. In this case not hearing anything provides only a small amount of evidence that the explosion didn't happen. If one initially thought that the probability of an explosion was 20 per cent, then not hearing anything leads one to decrease one's probability for an explosion just a little bit, to about 18.4 per cent.[164]

This analogy carries over to the simulation case. Suppose that we initially thought that the probability that we're living in a computer simulation is 20 per cent. But now we take into account a new bit of evidence that we hadn't considered before, the evidence that in fact the fundamental constants have decimal representations longer than 16 digits. If we thought that there was a 10 per cent chance that, if we were living in a simulation, the decimal representations would only go out to 16 digits, then the evidence that in fact they are longer should lead us to decrease our probability for simulation to about 18.4 per cent.[165]

Of course, the hypothesis that the decimal representations of the fundamental constants would only go out to 16 digits is just one hypothesis for what evidence we could get that we're living in a simulation. The way to do the full calculation would be to think about all the evidence we could get that we're living in a simulation, and to think about how likely it would be that we would get that evidence if we actually were living in a simulation, and then to calculate how much the probability that we're living in a simulation goes down because we don't have any of that evidence. I won't try to do that calculation here.

Let's step back. My overall point of this section is that the simulation argument is a science-based argument for the existence of a (non-supernatural) designer. I don't find the argument that plausible, but I think it's worth taking seriously. Some people are quick to completely dismiss the argument because of the incredulousness of its conclusion, but I don't see how such dismissal is warranted. I've given ways to question the force of the argument, but by my lights, at least, the argument cannot be conclusively refuted. Thus, the simulation argument is another example of a somewhat plausible intelligent design argument.

CHAPTER 4

Should Intelligent Design Be Taught in School?

Three Worries

The topic of intelligent design sometimes engenders emotional responses, and nowhere does this happen more than with the issue of what should get taught in school. I find the arguments that intelligent design should not be taught to be uncompelling, and I can see benefits in its being taught. In saying this to fellow secularists, I have gotten some of those emotional responses. In this final chapter, I'm going to do my best to set aside the emotion and acrimony, take a step back, and think carefully about whether intelligent design should be taught in school. I will argue that there are some situations where it is appropriate and even helpful to do so—as long as it is taught in an intellectually responsible, non-proselytizing way.

Before making this argument, I want to register three worries I have about engaging in this project, and explain why I'm doing so in spite of these worries.

The first worry is that I'm not an expert on the topic of educational policy. As I said in the paper that I wrote in response to the Dover trial, the paper that was reproduced in Chapter 2: "I am trained as a philosopher; I have no special insight as to whether intelligent design should be taught in science class." Well, it's still the case that I am trained as a philosopher, but I've been thinking more about this issue of whether intelligent design should be taught in school, and I've decided that I do have something worthwhile to say on the topic. One of the factors that spurs me to do this is that I've read more of the literature on the issue of whether intelligent design should be taught in school, and I've seen a lot of problems with what has been said. Since I haven't seen my own viewpoint represented in the literature, I thought it would be worth putting on the table.

The second worry is that the issues I've talked about so far in this book, like whether intelligent design is science, and what the evidence for intelligent design is, should really be kept separate from the issue of whether intelligent design should be taught in school. The issues surrounding what should get taught in school depend so heavily on particular details of our society, in a way that the abstract philosophical issues I've been discussing don't. For example, we generally think that what is appropriate to teach in school depends in part on where the funding is coming from: doctrines about God can be taught in Catholic private school that can't be taught in religiously neutral public school. But these societal details aren't relevant to the philosophical issues associated with intelligent design. The answer to the question of whether intelligent design is true doesn't depend on what type of school one is in.

I agree that the issues should be kept separate, in the sense that the positions people take on the issues I've discussed in the previous chapters shouldn't stem from the positions people take regarding what should get taught in school. But it's permissible and even advisable for the dependence to go the other way. That is, it makes sense that the position one takes on what gets taught in school depends on whether one thinks intelligent design is inherently theistic, whether one thinks intelligent design is science, and whether one thinks there's any evidence for intelligent design. Now that I've given my opinions on those issues, it's only natural that I move on to evaluate what influence they have on the debate over whether intelligent design should be taught in school. I want to make clear, though, that the first three chapters are self-contained; if you're not interested in the issue of whether intelligent design should be taught in school you won't lose anything by stopping reading now. But since so many people are interested in that topic, and since I thought I had something insightful to say, I decided to weigh in.

The third and final worry I want to express before moving on is the worry that, by arguing that there are some situations where it's good for intelligent design to be taught in school, I'm playing into the hands of those critics who say that the goal of the intelligent design movement is to get religion into school. Recall the Barbara Forrest quotation I started this book with:

> In promoting "intelligent design theory"—a term that is essentially code for the religious belief in a supernatural creator—as a purported scientific alternative to evolutionary theory, the intelligent design movement continues the decades-long attempt by creationists either to minimize the teaching of evolution or to gain equal time for yet another form of creationism in American public schools.

And now, after discussing the philosophical issues surrounding intelligent design, here I am arguing that it should be taught in school. Am I just providing more evidence that getting creationism taught in school is really what intelligent design is about?

First of all, I want to make clear that I do not at all consider myself to be part of the intelligent design movement. I'm an atheist, so I don't have religious belief in a supernatural creator, but other than my atheism I consider myself to be a neutral objective observer of the intelligent design movement (to the extent that there is such a "movement"). I have been accused of being a closet creationist before, and I'm not sure how to respond to such charges, except to assert: no, I really am an atheist. Yes, I am on the editorial board of Oxford Studies in Philosophy of Religion; yes, I've been to multiple Society of Christian Philosophers conferences; yes, I participated in a debate in Fort Worth where I helped represent the "pro-ID" side, but I'm still a committed atheist. (I was invited to be on the editorial board I think in part because they were looking for intellectual diversity; I was invited to participate in the Christian Philosophers meetings because I was doing work they were interested in; and the position I took in the debate was a summary of the position you've seen me take so far in this book.)

Furthermore, I want to make clear that I am not writing this book with the goal of getting intelligent design taught in school. My main focus was really the first three chapters; this chapter is an extra free bonus. For better or for worse, the issue of what should get taught in school has been inextricably linked to all the other issues surrounding intelligent design—in part as a result of critiques like Forrest's, where people giving the philosophical and scientific arguments for intelligent design are accused of having the hidden nefarious goal of getting intelligent design into school. Since the issue of teaching intelligent design in school has become such a focus, and since lots of bad arguments are being given, I feel compelled to weigh in.

Where the Controversy Lies

People often frame the debate as being about the question of whether intelligent design should be "taught in school," and so far I've been following their lead. But now I want to clarify that the "taught in school" phrase is shorthand for something much more specific.

Consider first that the debate isn't about what should be taught in college. I take up intelligent design in some of my philosophy of science and philosophy of religion classes, but no one is complaining about that. One might think this is because people in college are adults (by United States legal standards, at least), and the opponents of teaching intelligent design are only concerned about what minors are being taught. But there are some minors in college; I haven't heard any suggestions that such minors should be prevented from taking college classes where intelligent design is taught.

Moreover, the debate isn't about what children should be taught. Parents are allowed to teach their children about intelligent design, and they're even allowed to teach their children that intelligent design is true. (At least, they're allowed to do this in the United States—I'll keep my focus on that country, since that's where the "intelligent design in school" controversy is most conspicuous nowadays.) I haven't heard any suggestions that parents shouldn't be allowed to teach their children about intelligent design.

Moreover, the debate isn't about whether intelligent design can be taught to children in school. Parents are allowed to send their children to private religious schools, and these private religious schools are allowed to have a religious component to their curriculum. Since (as far as I know) secularists aren't complaining that some children in private school have to learn the Catechisms of the Catholic Church, so they shouldn't complain that some children in private school have to learn the doctrines of intelligent design. (There would, I take it, be a controversy if these children had to learn the doctrines of intelligent design, and *not* the theory of Darwinian evolution. But as long as both are taught, I don't see the opponents of intelligent design raising objections.)

Moreover, the debate isn't about whether intelligent design can be taught to children in *public* school. There are world religion and comparative religion classes in some public schools. Since opponents of intelligent design brand intelligent design as inherently theistic, presumably they would think the proper place for intelligent design is in a comparative religion class.

The issue of comparative religion classes is worth elaborating on, because some people I talk with are surprised to hear that there are comparative religion classes in public school. To give a specific example, consider the following description of an elective course at Montgomery Blair High School, an award-winning public high school in Silver Spring, Maryland:

> *Comparative Religion* (10th/11th/12th grades; 1/2 credit)—This single semester course surveys the basic elements and historical developments of world religions. After establishing a common definition of the purpose of religion and ways to study religion, students study Buddhism, Taoism, Hinduism, Judaism, Christianity, and Islam. Speakers, student projects, and an emphasis on class discussion guide students to an understanding of the major religions of the world. Other religions are studied as time and interest permit. The course is structured in such a way that interested students of any level can be successful.[166]

I don't know whether intelligent design has been taught in such a class, but if all those different religious views are being taught, I don't see how it would be problematic for intelligent design to be taught as well. (I assume that opponents of intelligent design wouldn't object to comparative religion classes, because they give students a better understanding of a key aspect of society, without teaching students that the religious beliefs are true. In fact, by situating a student's own religious beliefs in the context of other religious traditions, such a class can very well lead a student to think more critically about the religious beliefs he or she was raised with. Some *proponents* of intelligent design might object to intelligent design being taught in a comparative religion class, since they hold that intelligent design isn't inherently theistic.)

What the debate over intelligent design in school is really about is whether intelligent design should be taught in public school science classes. Moreover, the debate isn't just about whether intelligent design should be presented as true; the debate is about whether intelligent design should be discussed at all in such classes. Proponents of intelligent design use the slogan "teach the controversy." They aren't promoting the idea that intelligent design should be taught as true, they are just promoting the idea that intelligent design should be presented as one of the options on the table (in the same way that the various competing religions are taught in a comparative religion class).

Well, I'm sure some proponents of intelligent design want it taught as true. But the Discovery Institute is at pains to argue that that's not what they're trying to achieve. Here is a selection from their "Frequently Asked Questions" page:

> *Should public schools require the teaching of intelligent design?*
> No. Instead of mandating intelligent design, Discovery Institute recommends that states and school districts focus on teaching students more about evolutionary theory, including telling them about some of the theory's problems that have been discussed in peer-reviewed science journals. In other words, evolution should be taught as a scientific theory that is open to critical scrutiny, not as a sacred dogma that can't be questioned. We believe this is a common-sense approach that will benefit students, teachers, and parents.

> *Is teaching about intelligent design unconstitutional?*
> Although Discovery Institute does not advocate requiring the teaching of intelligent design in public schools, it does believe there is nothing unconstitutional about discussing the scientific theory of design in the classroom. In addition, the Institute opposes efforts to persecute individual teachers who may wish to discuss the scientific debate over design in a pedagogically appropriate manner.[167]

Of course, the Discovery Institute may not be being forthright here—perhaps they secretly want intelligent design taught as true, and evolution not taught at all. (This is what many opponents of intelligent design would claim, at least.) If that's the Discovery Institute's real goal, then I'm opposed to it. But I'm not opposed to their stated goal. As I will argue below, I think it can be pedagogically useful to teach evolution as a theory that is open to critical scrutiny. (Moreover, I don't just think this about evolution; I think this way about teaching any scientific theory.)

So, the controversy is over whether intelligent design should be taught in public pre-college science classes. Moreover, the heart of the controversy isn't over whether intelligent design should be taught as true—even the Discovery Institute isn't publicly trying to get it taught as true. The controversy is over whether intelligent design should be discussed at all in public pre-college science classes. From now on, I'll continue to use the standard shorthand of referring to this controversy as the controversy of whether intelligent design should be taught in school.

It's worth noting that, historically, the creationist movement has called for "equal time" in science classes between evolution and creation. I am in no way advocating for equal time for intelligent design. My opinion is that intelligent design probably should be brought up in science classes, but not a lot of time should be spent on it. The Dover trial (discussed in Chapter 2) was about a 60-second mention of intelligent design ideas in class, and millions of dollars were spent adjudicating whether this 60 second mention was permissible. I see no problem with giving intelligent design ideas 60 seconds—or even longer—as long as intelligent design is discussed in an intellectually responsible, pedagogically useful, non-proselytizing way.

Evaluating the Question

So, the question is: "should intelligent design be taught in school?" It's worth thinking more about what work the "should" is doing in this context. We can separate out a number of questions. For example, is it pedagogically good for the children to be taught intelligent design? Will it further the cause of science if children are taught intelligent design? Is it good for society as a whole if intelligent design is taught in school? Is it legally permissible for intelligent design to be taught in school? Each of these questions leads to different criteria for evaluating the question of whether intelligent design should be taught in school.

Let's focus on the pedagogical and legal questions for the moment, and get clear on why they're different questions. It could be that it's a good idea for children to be taught intelligent design, in the sense that it would give them a better understanding of science and improve their critical thinking abilities, even though it is legally impermissible to teach it. (The law has gotten things wrong before—just think Dred Scott—so this possibility shouldn't be surprising.) Also, it could be that children would not benefit from learning intelligent design, even though it is legally permissible to teach it to them.

I am going to set aside the legal question as being too parochial. Laws (and constitutions) can be changed, so even if it is illegal now to teach intelligent design, it might not be illegal in the future. The important question is: is it beneficial, is it prudent, is it morally desirable to teach intelligent design in school?

It may be that there is no univocal answer to that question—in the sense that some students might benefit from having intelligent design be taught, while other students might not. Suppose that, for some students, learning about intelligent design gives them a better understanding of science. They see that there are controversies in science, and they start thinking more about evidence for and against theories, instead of just learning the content of the theories that are part of received science. Some of these students grow up to be scientists, and because of their early training in looking at arguments for and against received theories, and comparing those arguments with arguments for and against renegade competing theories, they end up being better scientists than they would have been had they not had such early training. In fact, they develop new theories that lead to all sorts of advancements that benefit society. For other students, however, learning about intelligent design just reinforces the religious beliefs they were raised with. This makes them more certain of the truth of their religious views, and as adults some of them enter politics and try to impose their religious views on society as a whole. (From my standpoint as an atheist, at least, this is not a desirable result; I don't want religion to have an influence on the way governments restrict my behavior.)

That's one story for how things could go, such that there's no univocal answer to the question of whether it's good to teach intelligent design in school. Here's one more story that doesn't provide a univocal answer. Suppose that, for some students, learning about intelligent design makes them think that appealing to God is a way to account for any unexplained phenomenon in the world. These students think that intelligent design allows them to explain anything in science with the claim "God did it." Some of these students would have grown up to be successful scientists, had they not learned about intelligent design, but because their inquisitiveness was stifled, they grow up to be minimally productive members of society. But also suppose that there are other students, raised in religiously strict households, where learning about intelligent design is an eye-opening experience for them. For the first time they see arguments both for and against some of the religious views they've been taught. They find the arguments against intelligent design to be stronger, and hence rebel against their religious upbringing. They grow up to champion secular society and fight the pernicious forces of theocracy in the world.

If one of these scenarios were true, I'd be hard-pressed to say whether intelligent design should be taught in school.[168] The fact that such scenarios are prima facie plausible shows that the question of whether it's a good idea to teach intelligent design in school may not have an easy answer. Ultimately, the issue of what's best for the students is an empirical question, even though it would be hard to get the empirical data that would definitively answer that question. Here is one proposal for how one could potentially test whether teaching intelligent design is pedagogically useful. We could take a school and randomly divide the students into two groups, and one group could be taught science the standard way, while the other group could be taught both the standard theories and their competitors, with arguments for and against the theories and the competitors would be evaluated. (The competing theories would include intelligent-design-based theories.) We could then evaluate the students in the two groups, and see which group fares better.

This leads to a key question though: what criteria would we use to decide which group fares better? We could give them exams at the end of the course that test the students on their knowledge of received scientific theories. Here we might expect the control group, the group that is taught science in the standard way, to do better. We could give them exams at the end of the course that test the students on their knowledge of how scientists give arguments for and against theories. Here we might expect the group that studied standard theories and their competitors to do better. Or we could wait and give them exams a couple of years after the course was run. Here it's not as obvious to me that the results would be the same—there are well-known results from the study of education that, if one learns a theory as an unrelated compendium of ideas, one easily forgets those ideas, whereas if one learns the reasoning behind a theory, one retains a better long-term grasp of a theory.[169] Perhaps the students who learned the arguments for and against standard theories would retain a better long-term grasp of the standard theories, because they would see more of the reasoning behind the standard theories.

But even those exams seem to be missing something important about the potential good and bad effects of teaching intelligent design. The issue isn't just what the students know right after the class, or even two years later, but how it affects their education and lives long-term (if it has any effect at all). Here's why it's the long-term effects that matter. Suppose that the students in the two groups performed differently on the exams given right after the classes were over, but performed the same on the exams given two years after the classes were over, and performed the same on every other metric given from then on. I would conclude that it doesn't really matter which type of science course the students take, since the course has no long-term effect.

But perhaps the two courses do have different long-term effects; if that were the case, it would be interesting and important to know what the long-term effects were. Unfortunately, this is difficult to study. We'd have to chart the progress of these students over the long run, and we'd have to determine which metrics were the appropriate metrics to use to judge the lives of these students. How many become scientists? How many become bad scientists? How many become top scientists? How many go on to promote theocracy? This is just the start of the list of questions I'd want asked. And to get statistically significant results, we'd need quite a large sample. As far as I know, no research like this has been done—or is even in the process of being done—on the effects of teaching intelligent design. In the absence of such research, it seems to me that anyone who expresses an opinion on the topic is just engaging in speculation.

How Not to Teach Intelligent Design

With that said, let the speculation begin. Actually, I'm going to start with a point that I'm pretty sure of—the way the Dover school board mandated that intelligent design be taught is *not* the right way to teach intelligent design. My main problem with what the school board did isn't that they tried to get intelligent design in school; my main problem is that their method for doing so was remarkably bad from a pedagogical standpoint.

Recall from Chapter 2 that the Dover school board wanted the following disclaimer to be read to ninth-grade biology students before they learned about evolution:

> The Pennsylvania Academic Standards require students to learn about Darwin's Theory of Evolution and eventually to take a standardized test of which evolution is a part.
>
> Because Darwin's Theory is a theory, it continues to be tested as new evidence is discovered. The Theory is not a fact. Gaps in the Theory exist for which there is no evidence. A theory is defined as a well-tested explanation that unifies a broad range of observations.
>
> Intelligent Design is an explanation of the origin of life that differs from Darwin's view. The reference book, Of Pandas and People, is available for students who might be interested in gaining an understanding of what Intelligent Design actually involves.
>
> With respect to any theory, students are encouraged to keep an open mind. The school leaves the discussion of the Origins of Life to individual students and their families. As a Standards-driven district, class instruction focuses upon preparing students to achieve proficiency on Standards-based assessments.

Because some teachers didn't want to read the disclaimer, an administrator would come in to the classroom and read it to the students. After the disclaimer was read, students were told that there would be no discussion of it in class.

So what's wrong with this? Well, to start, the disclaimer was only read to the students, but some people learn better visually than auditorily. I'm one of those people: if I were to hear that disclaimer just once, I would be confused about what exactly was being said, whereas if I could read it I would have a much better understanding of what was being communicated.

Another thing that's wrong with this is that the students are being taught bad ideas. Even though I'm a philosopher of science, and I've read lots of literature on what a scientific theory is, I've never heard of a theory being defined as "a well-tested explanation that unifies a broad range of observations." The definition is problematic. Normally we think of a scientist being able to come up with a theory, and then going on to do experiments to test whether the theory fits the experimental evidence. But by the definition of the Dover school board, that scientist has not come up with a theory, because she has not yet run the experiments to test it—the explanation she's come up with is not "well-tested." Einstein's theory of general relativity is a classic example of a theory that didn't have a lot of experimental support when it was first proposed. By the lights of the Dover school board, at the time that Einstein proposed general relativity, everyone was wrong to call it a "theory," because it hadn't been well-tested. I would love to hear what the rationale is for the definition of a theory as given in the disclaimer—but the students aren't given the rationale, they're just told the definition as if it's definitively true.

Now, one could teach this proposal about what a theory is in a way that doesn't treat the proposal as if it's true. The teacher could tell the students that some people endorse this proposal, and the students could consider what arguments one might give for or against the proposal. Moreover, one can do this without having the students or the teacher actually say whether or not they endorse the proposal.

For example, I've taught philosophy of religion before, where at the end of my teaching students come up to me wondering what I actually believe about God. We've spent hours talking about the existence of God, and yet the students still don't know what I think, because I'm not telling them what I think is true; I'm just presenting arguments for and against various views. This skill of not letting on what one actually thinks isn't that difficult; I have a number of students in such classes who do it too. I've had students who were very talkative, and would express opinions on the relative merits of particular arguments, but the topic of whether they were theists or atheists would never come up.

This leads to one more thing that's wrong with the Dover school board's approach. (There's lots more that could be said, but I'll stop after this.) By not allowing discussion, the Dover school board is denying the students the best opportunity to learn. You can't just tell students that "Gaps in the Theory exist for which there is no evidence." Inquisitive students would wonder what that actually means, and would wonder what the gaps are. (Students who are on their way to becoming philosophers would ponder how there can be evidence for a gap, and would wonder whether a category mistake is being made.) Without giving the students the evidence to support the claim that there are gaps, the students are being asked to believe the claim solely on the authority of the teacher (or administrator). This is the worst form of proselytizing teaching, an argument from authority. The students in Dover deserve better.

Six Thoughts on Teaching Intelligent Design

So how should intelligent design be taught? Well, I'm not going to start formulating teachers' lesson plans here. But I am of the opinion it could be taught in a manner that furthers the intellectual development of the students. What follows are six lines of thought to support that opinion.

A NEW MODEL FOR SCIENCE EDUCATION

There is a push in science education nowadays away from fact-based education and toward inquiry-based education. The underlying ideas behind these approaches are that in fact-based science education, one learns the content of particular scientific theories, whereas in inquiry-based education, one learns how scientists think. Carl Weiman is a Nobel-prize-winning physicist and a part-time colleague of mine at University of Colorado, and he is one of the people spearheading the inquiry-based science education movement. He points out that there is research that has been done on how science students best learn:

> The results of this research, and the dramatically improved gains in learning and interest achieved in associated teaching experiments, show that there are tremendous opportunities to improve university science education. Realizing these opportunities, however, will require a different pedagogical approach, one that treats science education as a science, with rigorous standards for teaching effectiveness. It also requires abandoning the longstanding and widespread assumption that understanding science means simply learning a requisite body of facts and problem-solving recipes, and that mastery of those facts is the sole qualification needed to be a science teacher. Science education research clearly shows that a true understanding of science, as demonstrated by how it is practiced, is not merely about learning information. Rather, it is about developing a way of thinking about a discipline that reflects a particular perception of how "knowledge" is established, its extent and limitations, how it describes nature, and how it can be usefully applied in a variety of contexts. Developing such a way of thinking is a profoundly different experience from learning a set of facts, and requires very different teaching skills.[170]

Here we see Weiman championing the idea that learning science isn't fundamentally about learning facts, but it's about learning how scientists think; that's what leads to a better understanding of science.

I am not saying that Weiman would endorse the teaching of intelligent design in school. What I am saying is that the model of inquiry-based science education can be used as a first step in an argument in favor of teaching intelligent design in school. One way to see how scientists think would be to see the arguments they use for Darwinian evolution, and one way to see what arguments scientists give for Darwinian evolution would be to consider the reasons they have for rejecting competing theories. Intelligent-design-based biology arguments, like Michael Behe's irreducible complexity argument, could provide an appropriate foil. There are many biologists who give arguments against Behe's irreducible complexity argument; it could be helpful for students to see what arguments they give, so that students get a better understanding of how scientists present evidence against a particular view.

THEY'RE GOING TO HEAR ABOUT IT ANYWAY

I'm arguing that a reason for students to take up the intelligent design controversy is so that they can get a better understanding of how science reasoning happens. One could object to this by saying that there's no special reason for them to take up the intelligent design controversy, as opposed to some other controversy. For example, they could take up the historical controversy of whether Mars has canals, or the current controversy over the nature of dark matter. This way, students can see how scientists reason, without having to wade into the controversies associated with teaching intelligent design.

Well, I would be happy with the students learning about the Martian canal controversy and the dark matter controversy too. I agree that from the standpoint of seeing how scientific reasoning happens, there's no need to take up intelligent design. But here is another reason to take up intelligent design, a reason that doesn't hold as strongly for the Martian canal and dark matter controversies. The reason is that enough students are going to hear about the intelligent design controversy anyway, regardless of whether it gets taught in school. And given that they're going to hear about it anyway, it seems best to have it discussed in an intellectually sophisticated way in the classroom. (Arguments for sex education in school have a similar rationale.)

But how will students hear about the intelligent design controversy? There are a variety of ways. Intelligent design proponents have done a good job of getting intelligent design into mainstream public discourse. Cases like the Dover trial have received national publicity, so any student who follows the news could very well hear about the next iteration of that legal battle. Students who grow up in religious households could hear about it from their parents, students who go to church could hear about it from their pastor, students who grow up in religiously oriented communities could hear about it from their friends and neighbors. Only about one-quarter of American adults believe in the standard unguided Darwinian account of evolution, so most students who talk about the issue with their parents will hear an account that's not the standard account of biologists.[171] All it takes is a single student to ask a question in class, and at that point all the students in class will have heard about it. It's up to the teacher to decide how to handle such questions, but I would be in favor of dealing with such a question by having an intellectual discussion about the issues, not telling the students that that issue can't be talked about in school. (Of course, for some students, hearing that intelligent design can't be talked about in school will motivate them to do research on their own. If enough students are like that, then perhaps those who want more students to hear about intelligent design should encourage schools to treat it as a forbidden topic, to pique students' interest.)

While I think it can be a good idea to teach intelligent design in school, there are lots of good ideas for what should be taught in school and, given time limitations, tradeoffs need to be made. I personally am in favor of leaving a lot of these decisions up the individual teacher. (For example, if one of the students' parents is studying dark matter, and none of the students seems to care about intelligent design, I'd be all for having the students study the dark matter controversy instead.) But if I were the teacher, I would take up intelligent design, because I would figure that the students are eventually going to hear about it anyway, and I'd like them to hear about it in an intellectually well-informed climate.

This leads to one point I'd like to make regarding legal matters. The Dover case was a highly non-ideal test case for whether intelligent design is legally allowed to be taught in school, because the disclaimer was mandatory, the disclaimer was poorly thought out, and it was clear that the school board had religious reasons for wanting the disclaimer to be read. I would love to see a test case that stemmed from an individual teacher choosing to take up the issue of intelligent design in an intellectually informed, non-proselytizing way.

Perhaps there will be one in Louisiana, as a result of the Science Education Act, which passed the legislature and was signed into law in June 2008. This act says:

> The State Board of Elementary and Secondary Education, upon request of a city, parish, or other local public school board, shall allow and assist teachers, principals, and other school administrators to create and foster an environment within public elementary and secondary schools that promotes critical thinking skills, logical analysis, and open and objective discussion of scientific theories being studied including, but not limited to, evolution, the origins of life, global warming, and human cloning.[172]

As you can see, this act allows for intelligent design to be taught in school, as part of the open discussion that could take place regarding evolution and the origins of life. Depending on what the school administrators say, this teaching need not be mandatory; it could be up to the individual teacher to decide whether to take up the topic of intelligent design.

NON-PROSELYTIZING TEACHING

It is clear that the concern many people have about intelligent design being taught in school is that it will (implicitly or explicitly) be taught in a proselytizing way. And even if it is not taught in a proselytizing way, people are concerned that it will be taught as a well-respected competitor to standard scientific theories, and as a result students will get a confused idea about what the vast majority of scientists actually think about intelligent design.

Well, if students come away with such a confused idea, that would be the fault of the teacher. When I suggest that I want intelligent design to be taught, I am not suggesting that I want it to be taught *badly*. I am suggesting that I want it taught well, where the views of mainstream scientists are made clear, and the arguments on both sides are discussed. (If nothing else, I think this would be a lot more interesting to the students than the way science is standardly taught—controversies are invariably more interesting to study than basic facts. But just to make it clear, it's my opinion that a good science education requires the study of both.)

There is a problem with science education in general in this country; often students are taught in such a way that they don't get a good understanding of what the vast majority of scientists actually think. For example, when I learned physics in high school and early college, I was taught Newtonian physics and classical electromagnetism as if they were true theories; it was only later that I learned that they made false predictions, and had been supplanted by quantum mechanics and general relativity. From talking with other people who learned physics via the American educational system, I see my experience was completely normal. So physics has been taught badly in our educational system, but this doesn't mean that physics shouldn't be taught; it just means that the teaching of physics needs to be improved. The same holds for the teaching of intelligent design—the fact that it may be taught badly doesn't entail we should stop teaching it; it just means that the teaching of intelligent design needs to be improved.

One of the key criteria for how intelligent design should be effectively taught is that it should be taught in a non-proselytizing way. I recognize a concern that many intelligent design opponents have—they worry that if intelligent design is allowed into science classes, then the teacher will teach it in a proselytizing way, even if the teacher is not supposed to. This is a concern I have too, but the same concern holds even if teachers aren't supposed to talk about intelligent design at all.

If a teacher is going to violate the rules, then having a rule that intelligent design can't be talked about at all isn't going to stop the teacher from doing so.[173] Perhaps teachers could benefit from rigorous training on how to teach intelligent design in a non-proselytizing way—just as they could benefit from rigorous training in other aspects of science education.

In fact, evidence suggests that intelligent design is being taught, despite rules against it. According to the results of a scientific survey published in May 2008, about 12 per cent of public high school biology teachers in the United States teach creationism or intelligent design as valid science.[174] It's worth noting, though, that, according to the same survey, a slightly higher percentage of the teachers teach creationism or intelligent design, but do *not* teach that it provides a "valid, scientific alternative to Darwinian explanations for the origin of species." It appears that a slight majority of the 25 per cent of public high school biology teachers who teach creationism or intelligent design are teaching it in a non-proselytizing way.

So far I've been talking about "non-proselytizing teaching" as if it's clear what I'm talking about. But it's not clear how exactly one could achieve completely non-proselytizing teaching— even if that's a good goal to have. To see this, let's set aside intelligent design for a moment, and consider some other scenarios. Suppose that a history teacher is teaching students about World War II, and suppose that one student denies that the Holocaust happened. How should the teacher handle this? If the teacher tells the student that he's wrong, and penalizes him for denying the Holocaust on his history exam, the student's parents could get upset—perhaps they too are Holocaust deniers. If the teacher instead decides to use the students' objection as a learning opportunity, this could upset other parents—they could argue that the teacher is wasting students' time giving credence to a theory that doesn't deserve it. The teacher could just state a disclaimer at the beginning of class of the form "I'm just teaching you what mainstream history says; it's up to you to decide what to believe" but this could leave the students wondering what the evidence is for the mainstream view of history, and what the mysterious alternative views are that they aren't being presented with.

Similar issues can come up in almost any context. Suppose a physics teacher asks the students to write up the results of an experiment they have just performed. A student could object to this project by claiming that the world was created one second ago, and everyone in class was created with the false memory of having done the experiment. The teacher can't prove to the student that the world wasn't created one second ago—all the evidence we have right now is compatible with that hypothesis. So how should the teacher handle this? Should the teacher act as if the student definitely has false beliefs? Should the teacher take this as an opportunity to teach about epistemological skepticism? Should the teacher just say "for the purposes of this class, let's pretend that the world wasn't created one second ago"? Or should the teacher do something else?

I don't think there are obvious answers to these questions. As a teacher myself, there are often times where I would acknowledge what the student has said but then shut down discussion, because I didn't want to be derailed from the main topic at hand. There are situations where it would be appropriate to do that if intelligent design issues were raised as well; perhaps the teacher is trying to talk about a different issue on that particular day, and doesn't want to get sidetracked. But there are other situations where talking about intelligent design might be appropriate in class—just as there are situations where talking about Holocaust deniers or newly-created-world believers might be appropriate. Whether the teacher ends up being viewed as proselytizing for the mainstream view will depend in part on what situation the teacher happens to be in at the time that the dissenting view gets raised.

Of course, proselytizing for the mainstream view (or at least, the scientifically mainstream view) is not the sort of proselytizing that the intelligent design opponents are concerned about. What they are concerned about is a teacher proselytizing for the non-mainstream view of intelligent design. In principle I am opposed to this sort of proselytizing too, but I want to point out that there are contexts where it might look like that's what a teacher who's teaching effectively is doing. Let's start with a non-intelligent design example. Suppose that a teacher is teaching epistemology, and she's trying to get the students to think about what evidence the students have that they have bodies. To do this, she could spend the whole class arguing that the students are actually brains in vats, hooked up to computers that are feeding the brains the non-veridical sensation of having bodies. Confused students could walk away from class thinking that that's actually what the teacher thinks, and that she was proselytizing. More savvy students would recognize that the teacher was just pushing them to think more clearly about what evidence they have for their belief that they have bodies.

The same sort of scenario could happen in an intelligent design context. After presenting the standard Darwinian theory of evolution, for example, the teacher could present the intelligent design view, and could give arguments for intelligent design in an attempt to get the students to think more clearly about what the evidence is that they have for the Darwinian view. Superficially, the teacher might look like she's promulgating intelligent design, but in fact she's just trying to get the students to think.

That said, the teacher would have to be careful. In a class where some students actually believed that they were brains in vats, the epistemology teacher might not want to take the approach I described—and the same holds for the biology teacher in a class where some students believe the intelligent design theory. In sum, it's easy to say that teachers shouldn't proselytize, but translating that goal into a prescription for what exactly teachers should and shouldn't do is tricky, because so much depends upon context.

TEACHING PHILOSOPHY OF SCIENCE

Some opponents of intelligent design act as if the philosophical issues associated with intelligent design are settled, and we can use those results to reach negative conclusions about intelligent design. We saw this back in Chapter 2, for example: Pennock acted as if it's settled that intelligent design is not science, whereas I pointed out that there's actually a controversy in the philosophy of science community on this issue.

This leads to another potential learning opportunity for students. Why not have students study the philosophical issues associated with intelligent design, such as the debate about whether intelligent design is science? Granted, this isn't the sort of issue that is standardly taken up in a science class, but this is the sort of issue that our educational establishment thinks is worth teaching—philosophy of science classes are standardly offered in college, and whether intelligent design is science is a topic that's standardly taken up (judging from anthologies, and from conversations with fellow philosophy of science professors).

In suggesting that the students could study the philosophical issues associated with intelligent design, I don't mean to suggest that these are the only philosophical issues they should study—I envision science courses having a philosophy of science component, where one potential sort of topic that could be taken up during that component are issues associated with intelligent design. (Ultimately, I'd want the details left up to the individual teacher; as a philosopher of science I'd be willing to provide sample lesson plans to give them options.) Philosophers of science have all sorts of interesting debates about big picture issues regarding how science works, and about whether we should believe what scientific theories tell us about the world. They also have interesting debates about somewhat narrower issues, like what role causation plays in science, and whether scientific research should be driven by demands for explanation. I regularly (and successfully) teach these topics to first-year college students; I am confident that, with suitable adjustments, I could teach these topics to high school students, and I could teach teachers how to do so as well.

My science education was disappointing: a particular group of scientific theories was taught as true, with little insight into how and why those theories were developed, almost no discussion of current scientific controversies, and minimal education on how scientists actually reason through these controversies. (And from what I gather, my experience with science education wasn't anomalous.) What I'd like to see is a move away from that stagnant model of science education, and a move toward a model where students get a more accurate picture of how science works—and also see that there is no fully-agreed-upon picture; there are lots of controversies. Theories would be set in historical context, open lines of research would be highlighted, and competing ideas regarding the nature of the scientific enterprise would be discussed. It would be reasonable for intelligent design to come up as a component in this sort of dynamic model of science education.

INTELLIGENT DESIGN ARGUMENTS ARE INTERESTING

It is probably clear by now that, even though I'm an atheist, I find intelligent design arguments interesting, important, and worth discussing. The fine-tuning argument, the cosmological argument, arguments about the origin of life and the infinite universe, and the simulation argument all fall into this category. Why not have these topics taught in school? What would be wrong with students reading something like Chapter 3 of this book, and discussing the issues? If the topics of Chapter 3 were taken up in science class, I could see this bolstering students' interest in science, because the topics are so much more interesting than what standardly gets taught.

Some would object that kids need to learn the basics first, and only then can they take up the topics that I discussed in Chapter 3. I would disagree with this, but to adequately address this objection, we'd have to get into the details of how science is taught. I'll offer one example to show where I'm coming from. When I took biology in high school, I recall spending at least a week learning the names for the various parts of a fish (dorsal fin, ventral fin, and so on), and then having a big quiz on it to make sure we learned all the names. I don't recall ever talking about competing theories regarding the origin of life from non-life. Looking back on it, I would have much preferred never learning the names of the various parts of the fish, and instead learning about competing theories regarding the origin of life. It's not clear to me that the names of parts of a fish are more basic than theories regarding the origin of life, or that one has to learn the parts of the fish before talking about the origin of life. Moreover, perhaps learning about the origin of life controversy would make more students want to study more biology, where they could eventually learn the names of the parts of a fish.

DISCUSSING WHAT SHOULD BE TAUGHT

I would love to run a high school class where I taught the students about intelligent design, and the controversy over whether it should be taught in school, and then I had the students debate whether other students at their educational level should be taught intelligent design. In my interactions with high school students, I get the sense that a fair number of them are sophisticated enough to understand these issues, and to have well-thought-out ideas on topics like this. If students are treated like intellectual peers, many will rise to the challenge. This will improve their intellectual abilities much more than just rote learning of the content of some particular scientific theory.

In general, I worry that those who don't want intelligent design taught in school are sometimes motivated by the thought that students are empty vessels, and that we want to be careful to only fill them with the right ideas. My idea—building off the new model for science education I talked about at the beginning of this section—is that students are budding critical reasoners, and we as a society want to do our best to improve their reasoning abilities. I don't see anything wrong with presenting them with the issues that we as a society debate now. The issues they'd be especially interested in are the issues involving them, such as the issue of whether intelligent design should be taught in school.

Objections

I'll now take up some of the arguments of those who claim that we as a society should not allow the teaching of intelligent design in school.

WE'D BE TEACHING RELIGION

One popular objection to teaching intelligent design in school is to hold that it's inappropriate to teach religiously-based ideas in school, and that intelligent design is religiously based. For example, consider this resolution, passed in May 2008 by the United Methodist Church:

> WHEREAS, the United Methodist Church has for many years supported the separation of church and State,
>
> THEREFORE BE IT RESOLVED that the General Conference of the United Methodist Church go on record as opposing the introduction of any faith-based theories such as Creationism or Intelligent Design into the science curriculum of our public schools.[175]

From what I've said so far in this book, you can probably see how I'm going to respond. First, I would highlight the arguments from Chapter 1 that intelligent design isn't fundamentally religious. For example, one could talk in science class about the idea of directed panspermia regarding the origin of life (that Earth was seeded by intelligent aliens), and this doesn't involve any religious beliefs. Second, I would point out that intelligent design arguments aren't faith-based—there is reasoning behind the arguments, as I've discussed in Chapter 3, and the reasoning is somewhat plausible.

How would the United Methodists reply to my response to their resolution? Well, they do give an official rationale for their resolution, which reads in full as follows:

> Creationism and Intelligent Design are appropriate topics in public education classes such as comparative religion, literature, or philosophy since scientific method incorporates critical thinking processes. All truth is God's truth. The promotion of religion or any particular religion in the public schools is contrary to the First Amendment.

I must admit that I don't completely understand this rationale. If the scientific method (assuming there is such a thing) incorporates critical thinking processes, then presumably we would want critical thinking taught in science classes. I would think that contrasting intelligent design with mainstream scientific views, and looking at the arguments for both sides, would help students' critical thinking abilities. The United Methodists' rationale allows for intelligent design to be taught in philosophy class, and if that happens then presumably scientific ideas would come up. (For example, the philosophy class could take up Michael Behe's irreducible complexity argument against Darwinian evolution—this would require some fairly sophisticated discussion of biology.) It's not clear to me, on the basis of what's said in this rationale, why it's appropriate to discuss the irreducible complexity argument in philosophy class, but not in science class—especially given that "scientific method incorporates critical thinking processes" (whatever exactly that means).

Note, by the way, that not everyone approves of intelligent design being taught in philosophy class in public school. Eugenie Scott approvingly cites a lawsuit that resulted from a 2006 attempt by the school district in Lebec, California to teach a "philosophy of intelligent design" class.[176] The case was settled, and the school district promised not to teach the subject in the future.

WE'D BE MISREPRESENTING THE CONTENT OF SCIENCE

Another popular objection to the idea that intelligent design should be taught in school is to hold that teaching intelligent design would make intelligent design ideas look like legitimate scientific ideas, whereas in fact they're not. For example, consider the following excerpt from the statement put out by the Australian Academy of Science and other leading Australian science organizations:

> Intelligent design … is not science. We therefore urge all Australian governments and educators not to permit the teaching or promulgation of ID as science. To do so would make a mockery of Australian science teaching and throw open the door of science classes to similarly unscientific world views—be

they astrology, spoon-bending, flat-earth cosmology or alien abductions—and crowd out the teaching of real science.[177]

I have two lines of response here.

First, it's not clear that intelligent design ideas aren't legitimate scientific ideas. Francis Crick took seriously the directed panspermia idea, and even wrote a book about it.[178] Michael Behe is a legitimate biochemistry professor at Lehigh University, and he endorses the pro-intelligent-design irreducible complexity argument. The fine-tuning argument is given credence by various physicists, even if they don't ultimately endorse the argument. So there are some legitimate scientists who take intelligent design ideas seriously.

One could respond to that by saying that intelligent design ideas aren't part of the *mainstream* content of science. This leads to my second response—if teachers are to discuss intelligent design ideas, they should make clear the status the ideas hold within the scientific community. I wouldn't want intelligent design taught at all if the teacher was going to pretend that it is widely scientifically respected, or if the teacher was going to give it equal time with mainstream scientific theories like Darwinian evolution. But remember, the Dover trial was about a 60-second mention of intelligent design ideas in class. I see no problem with giving intelligent design ideas 60 seconds—or even longer, as long as the ideas are brought up in a way that makes clear the worthiness the ideas are judged to have in the scientific community, and as long as arguments for and against the ideas are presented in such a way as to foster the intellectual development of the students.

The same reasoning could hold for taking up the other unscientific worldviews that the Australian scientists mentioned in their statement. For example, it would be a good exercise for the students to consider the evidence for and against astrology, as long as the teacher led the discussion in an intellectually responsible way. Many students have the unreflective view that there's something to astrology; perhaps by carefully looking at the arguments for and against astrology, more students would recognize that they shouldn't believe in it. In rejecting astrology on the basis of the evidence, the students would be thinking like scientists—and that, in my opinion, is the real goal of science education.

WE'D BE IGNORING CONSENSUS

Another argument for why intelligent design shouldn't be taught in school holds that what gets taught in school is the consensus view that scientists hold, and intelligent design is not part of the consensus. As Eugenie Scott (head of the National Center for Science Education) writes:

What gets taught in the pre-college science class is the consensus of scientific opinion on an issue.[179]

The first point to make about this is that what Scott says is not true. Newtonian physics is standardly taught in pre-college science classes, but Newtonian physics is a false theory—it predicts that clocks in stronger gravitational fields run at the same rate as clocks in weaker gravitational fields, whereas in fact clocks in stronger gravitational fields run slower, as correctly predicted by general relativity. Thus, assuming that current teaching practice is the right way to teach, the Newtonian physics example shows that figuring out what to teach in school is more complicated than figuring out what the consensus view is.

But the key point to make about what Scott says is that (in my opinion, at least) we are doing students a disservice by just teaching them the consensus view. In doing so, we are treating science as a monolithic body of facts, whereas in fact there are controversies and open questions and nascent ideas in science. By taking up these sorts of developments in science, teachers would give their students a more interesting and accurate picture of how science functions.

It's worth noting that Scott's position on teaching consensus is more stringent than other critics of teaching intelligent design in school. For example, Andrew Petto and Laurie Godfrey write:

> Although the science education curriculum can be enriched by a discussion of scientific controversies …, the goal of most science education is to provide students with a solid understanding of the current consensus in various scientific disciplines, not to present various untested and speculative ideas….[180]

The claim that *most* science education should focus on teaching the consensus view is quite different than the claim that *all* science education should have that focus. Holding that most of the focus should be on the consensus view is compatible with some time spent on non-consensus views, such as intelligent design views. For example, we could have one week of a high-school student's time in science class spent on learning scientific controversies, while all the other weeks can be devoted to learning the consensus view. Within that one-week period, 10 minutes could be spent discussing arguments for and against intelligent design, in an intellectually responsible way. Scott would be opposed to this, but I think the students would be intellectually better off than if they spent *all* their time in science class learning the consensus view.

WE WOULDN'T BE TEACHING CRITICAL THINKING

One argument for teaching intelligent design is that it could be a component of teaching critical thinking. That is what some proponents of teaching intelligent design say, but critics argue that they are just paying lip service to the idea of critical thinking, and that really they don't want it taught. Consider for example this passage by intelligent design critic John Cole:

> anti-evolutionists do not support models of critical thinking.... In fact, many of them become very upset with efforts to teach critical thinking, on the grounds that it teaches general questioning of authority—first textbooks, next parents and teachers, and then the Bible.... The subtler approach [that anti-evolutionists] have advocated in Texas, Louisiana, and other states is a textbook warning that *evolution alone* requires critical assessment.[181]

My stance is that critical thinking should be taught, and if that makes the anti-evolutionists upset, so be it. I want intelligent design to be taught in a fair-minded way, and this will mean presenting the strongest arguments for *and against* intelligent design. If—as most atheists think—the arguments against intelligent design are stronger than the arguments for, then the students who think critically and objectively about the arguments will come out against intelligent design. So yes, this will make some religious parents upset—but it will also make some atheist parents upset, because they don't want intelligent design to come up at all.

But this is what's best for the students. I want all the students—especially the committed atheists and the committed theists—to feel challenged. By teaching critical thinking well, the students should be led to not only question authority, but also to question their own beliefs, and the reasoning processes that got them to their beliefs. This will make some religious parents upset, but I am not endorsing the teaching of intelligent design in school to coddle parents' religious views; I'm endorsing it because I think that would best further the intellectual development of the students. If a student brings up the topic of intelligent design, I don't want the student just told to "discuss the question further with his or her family and clergy" (as is the policy in California public schools).[182] I want the topic discussed in an intellectually sophisticated way that will further the academic development of the students.[183]

Because of this, I agree with biologist Michael Reiss when he describes his view on teaching students who disagree with the standard biological theories:

> My experience after having tried to teach biology for 20 years is if one simply gives the impression that such children are wrong, then they are not likely to learn much about the science.... I realised that simply banging on about

evolution and natural selection didn't lead some pupils to change their minds at all. Just because something lacks scientific support doesn't seem to me a sufficient reason to omit it from the science lesson.... There is much to be said for allowing students to raise any doubts they have—hardly a revolutionary idea in science teaching—and doing one's best to have a genuine discussion.[184]

Reiss was the director of education for the prestigious British national academy of science, the Royal Society, until he made those comments, but the resulting furor led to his resignation.

WE WOULDN'T BE TEACHING A REAL CONTROVERSY

Some hold that intelligent design shouldn't be taught in school, because it doesn't constitute a real controversy. Intelligent design critics Petto and Godfrey, in the context of discussing the Discovery Institute's position that it would be helpful for controversies about Darwinian evolution to be taught, write:

If "controversies" are to be taught, they should be real matters of contention within the disciplines they are said to represent. But there is no controversy in biology over the occurrence of evolution.... The only controversy is one imposed from outside the discipline: It is about *teaching* evolution in public schools. This controversy is not *scientific* but socio-culturo-political.[185]

But intelligent design proponents (or at least, sophisticated intelligent design proponents, of the sort that are affiliated with the Discovery Institute) aren't trying to argue that evolution doesn't occur. Michael Behe, for example, believes that evolution occurred, and even is willing to believe in common descent—the idea that all life forms evolved from a single source. But Behe sees evidence of outside intelligent intervention in the evolutionary process. There is clearly a controversy between Behe and other evolutionary biologists, and moreover (as one can see by reading Behe's 1996 book, *Darwin's Black Box*), the evidence Behe cites is scientific, not socio-culturo-political. In fact, nowhere in the book does Behe even take up the issue of whether and how evolution and intelligent design should be taught in public schools. It is surprising to me that Petto and Godfrey can claim in 2007 that the controversy that the Discovery Institute has with evolution is socio-culturo-political, given the obviously science-based arguments that Discovery Institute fellows like Behe have given. It's one thing to say that Behe is giving bad arguments, but it's another thing to say that Behe is actually only concerned with the teaching of evolution, and is only giving socio-culturo-political arguments; the latter claims are manifestly false.

WE'D BE ASKING TOO MUCH OF THE STUDENTS

Some intelligent design proponents want scientific controversies within evolution to be taught, even if arguments for intelligent design are not. Some intelligent design opponents object to this idea by suggesting that we'd be asking too much of the students; the students aren't intellectually sophisticated enough to understand such controversies. Here is how Petto and Godfrey put it:

> If the scientific research community has not yet decided which of these ideas are tenable, can K-12 students (or their teachers) resolve them in the curriculum? Do they have the knowledge and the intellectual sophistication to decipher the complexities of these models and their implications? What can the introduction of such untested ideas produce, other than deep confusion?[186]

It is clear from context that these questions are rhetorical.

I would reply that Petto and Godfrey are confused about the goal of introducing students to scientific controversies. The goal is *not* to get the students and teachers to resolve the controversies. The goal is to get the students to see that there *are* scientific controversies. Presumably the students could be led to see this without having to go into all the complexities of the competing models. The reason for introducing untested ideas to the students is to show the students that there are untested ideas in science. Students should know that science is not a monolithic body of facts; students should know that science is a dynamic enterprise, one where the scientists themselves are sometimes confused about the implications of the theories they have and the observations they make. Introducing the students to scientific controversies can give them a better understanding of how science actually happens.

WE'D BE ASKING TOO MUCH OF THE TEACHERS

Let's continue discussing this issue of the intelligent design proponents wanting scientific controversies within evolution to be taught, even if arguments for intelligent design are not. Another objection to this idea is to hold that it's asking too much of the teachers. As Petto and Godfrey put it, only "the exceptional high-school teacher" has training which has prepared him or her to teach students the scientific controversies over evolution. Petto and Godfrey write:

> It is not that these teachers are incapable of performing this task; it is more that they are well prepared to perform a *different* task—one that is already very challenging and powerful: to produce a developmentally appropriate curriculum that will provide students with a fundamental knowledge of core scientific

concepts and theories in order to help them understand and apply scientific concepts in the future. This pedagogical objective results in a "survey" course—one based on an overview of a discipline and its key concepts and facts.

They summarize this as follows: "the training of high-school science teachers focuses on the consensus view."[187]

Let me start with a minor point. Petto and Godfrey's focus on training is somewhat misplaced, because teachers can be good at doing things that they haven't been trained to do. Teachers can learn how to do things on their own—self-study as well as training can prepare teachers to teach new topics.

On to the major point. Just because teachers have been trained to teach a certain way, it doesn't follow that we should stick with that way of doing things. It could be that that way of doing things is pedagogically bad for the students—or at least, it could be that there are pedagogically better ways out there. The key claim that Petto and Godfrey make is that the current way of doing things is "powerful"—this suggests that they hold that teaching the consensus view is good for the students.

Petto and Godfrey do not give justification for their claim that the current way of doing things is "powerful"; someone like Carl Weiman might disagree. As discussed above, Weiman says that there are tremendous opportunities to improve science education, but doing so will require a different pedagogical approach. Petto and Godfrey sound like they are endorsing the status quo of how students are taught, but this seems misguided, given that there is room for improvement.[188]

Some Final Thoughts

Debates about whether intelligent design is true, and about whether intelligent design should be taught in school, often get acrimonious. Some people think that the acrimony—the involvement of emotive rhetoric—is how minds are changed and decisions won. I don't know whether that's true or not; that's a psychological question that would need to be addressed with empirical research. I do know that I don't much care whether I change minds or win decisions in the public forum. What I care about is getting at the truth. I wouldn't want to change minds with bad argumentation, and whether I give good arguments for the views I think are right is more important to me than whether, say, intelligent design gets proselytized about in school.

Now, if giving a partial defense of intelligent design would somehow cause our society to become an oppressive theocracy, I would be concerned, and might even be willing to sacrifice my quest for truth in favor of political expediency. But I really don't think that's going to happen, and absent such extreme possibilities, I'm going to pursue good arguments, without worrying about the cultural or political effects that they have.

One thing to keep in mind here is that the focus on changing minds and winning decisions tends to be a short-term focus, while philosophy arguments are (hopefully, at least) around for the long term. This may be hopelessly Pollyannaish of me, but I envision my writings being read many years from now, in a cultural climate without the sort of heated rhetoric that we have now, and I picture those readers saying: "yes, Monton had it right." Those people are my real audience, not the people who are just looking for the latest salvo to defend their side in an ostensible culture war.

NOTES

Preface

1. For those who aren't familiar with Mother Teresa's doubts, see David van Biema, "Mother Teresa's Crisis of Faith," *Time Magazine*, 23 August 2007, http://www.time.com/time/printout/0,8816,1655415,00. html, archived at http://www.webcitation.org/5bTRPTLwa.

Chapter One

2. Barbara Forrest, "Understanding the Intelligent Design Creationist Movement: Its True Nature and Goals," *A Position Paper for the Center for Inquiry* (2007), 1, http://www.centerforinquiry.net/uploads/attachments/intelligent-design.pdf, archived at http://www.webcitation.org/5bYGV2skQ.

3. Forrest, 1.

4. For a book-length presentation of the evidence, see Barbara Forrest and David Gross, *Creationism's Trojan Horse: The Wedge of Intelligent Design* (New York: Oxford University Press, 2004). A major piece of evidence that Forrest and Gross cite is the Wedge Document, an internal planning document of the Discovery Institute, the leading intelligent design think tank. Forrest and Gross make much of the fact that this document says, for example, that the Discovery Institute "seeks nothing less than the overthrow of materialism and its cultural legacies." However, the document also says (in the very first paragraph, no less):

> The proposition that human beings are created in the image of God is one of the bedrock principles on which Western civilization was built. Its influence can be detected in most, if not all, of the West's greatest achievements, including representative democracy, human rights, free enterprise, and progress in the arts and sciences.

If they are celebrating Western civilization, and pointing out that the achievements of Western civilization include representative democracy and human rights, it doesn't sound like the Discovery Institute is on the level of the Taliban.

This could obviously be debated further, but I'm not going to do that in this book. The Wedge Document is available at http://www.antievolution.org/features/wedge.html, archived at http://www.webcitation.org/5c6ls3kRE.

5. Discovery Institute Staff, "Discovery Institute's Science Education Policy" (2008), http://www.discovery.org/scripts/viewDB/index.php?command=view&id=3164&program=CSC%20-%20Science%20and%20Education%20Policy%20-%20School%20District%20Policy, archived at http://www.webcitation.org/5bYGjkwyo. Here and elsewhere, typos will be corrected without comment.

6. Discovery Institute Staff, "The 'Wedge Document': 'So What?'" (2003), 3, http://www.discovery.org/scripts/viewDB/filesDB-download.php?id=349, archived at http://www.webcitation.org/5c6m3ONsE.

7. Some readers have taken issue with my claim here, admitting that ideally one should just evaluate the arguments, but pointing out that in situations where one is not capable of evaluating the arguments, then looking at the sociological issues has some merit. These readers say, for example, that someone who beats his or her spouse would be more likely to give disingenuous arguments. I'm not convinced that that's the case, though; establishing that would require empirical research of the sort that as far as I know has not been done. But even if that were the case, we'd have to look at the moral standing of both intelligent design advocates and intelligent design opponents before making any sort of comparative judgment. Anyway, the people who have raised this objection to me agree that the ideal situation is just to evaluate the arguments, and that's what I'm going to be doing in the rest of this book.

8. Eugenie Scott, "Creation Science Lite: 'Intelligent Design' as the New Anti-Evolutionism" in *Scientists Confront Intelligent Design and Creationism*, ed. Andrew Petto and Laurie Godfrey (New York: W.W. Norton, 2007), 69.

9. Discovery Institute Center for Science and Culture, "Top Questions," http://www.discovery.org/csc/topQuestions.php, archived at http://www.webcitation.org/5bYHCDXYw. For the record, I am reading "an intelligent cause" as "at least one intelligent cause." As long as there are at least some features of the universe or of living things that are the product of a particular intelligent cause, that statement of intelligent design comes out true. It doesn't matter whether there are other features of the universe or of living things that are the product of a different intelligent cause.

10. It was surprising to me that some readers objected to this line of thought, saying that squirrels and bees (and dogs, which I talk about below) aren't intelligent. Well, compared to us they're not, but compared to rocks and oceans they are, and it's the latter comparison that I have in mind.

11. If you're not happy with the "beings who have been in existence forever" argument, a similar argument could be given based on beings who have popped into existence, via, for example, a highly improbable quantum or thermodynamic fluctuation. If it turns out that some beings with the same sorts of powers as we humans have popped into existence and caused certain minor features of the universe, I don't think we'd cite this fact as support for intelligent design.

12. For details see J. Richard Gott, *Time Travel in Einstein's Universe: The Physical Possibilities of Travel Through Time* (Boston: Houghton Mifflin, 2001), Chapter 4.

13. I recognize that this is an oversimplification, but the details don't matter for my purposes.

14. I am considering lots of far-fetched scenarios in this chapter. This is a standard practice of philosophers, but it's worth making clear why it's legitimate. I'm not saying that any of these far-fetched scenarios are at all likely to be true; I'm just saying that these far-fetched scenarios show that there's something conceptually wrong with the statements of intelligent design I'm evaluating. Intuitively, we wouldn't want the doctrine of intelligent design to come out true because one of these far-fetched scenarios came out true, and hence to correctly capture the idea behind intelligent design, we have to formulate the doctrine of intelligent design in such a way that it's not made true by the far-fetched scenarios.

15. B.H. Roberts, *History of the Church of Jesus Christ of Latter Day Saints* (Provo, UT: Brigham Young University Press, 1930), 6: 305–06.

16. And indeed, it's a significant improvement—it avoids all the problems I've pointed out for alternative potential versions of the statement of intelligent design.

17. I should note that I am not an expert in evolutionary theory; my science background is in physics, not biology.

18. Stephen Meyer, "Not by Chance: From Bacterial Propulsion Systems to Human DNA, Evidence of Intelligent Design is Everywhere," *National Post of Canada*, 1 December 2005, http://www.discovery.org/scripts/viewDB/index.php?command=view&id=3059, archived at http://www.webcitation.org/5bckLNZuk.

19. As quoted in Discovery Institute Staff, "The Theory of Intelligent Design: A Briefing Packet for Educators," (2007), http://www.discovery.org/scripts/viewDB/index.php?command=view&id=4299&program=CSC%20-%20Science%20and%20Education%20Policy%20-%20News%20and%20Articles, archived at http://www.webcitation.org/5bckYeUuE.

20. Logan Paul Gage, "Deconstructing Dawkins: Alister McGrath's Challenge of Famous Atheist is Bracing—But Does Not Go Far Enough," *Christianity Today* (November 2007), http://www.discovery.org/a/4450, archived at http://www.webcitation.org/5bcmCXCfs.

21. Matt Young and Taner Edis, *Why Intelligent Design Fails* (Piscataway, NJ: Rutgers University Press, 2006), 4–8.

22. Young and Edis, ix.

23. Young and Edis, 18.

24. William Dembski, *Intelligent Design: The Bridge Between Science & Theology* (Downers Grove, IL: InterVarsity Press, 1999), 14.

25. Logan Paul Gage, "Shedding the Galileo Complex" (2008), http://insidecatholic.com/Joomla/index.php?option=com_content&task=view&id=2240&Itemid=66&ed=1, archived at http://www.webcitation.org/5bd4AQtff. By the way, I've been accused of not knowing who the leading intelligent design proponents are, because I spend some time talking about Gage, and he is not a leading intelligent design proponent. In fact, I'm well aware that Gage is not a leading intelligent design proponent, but he's said some interesting things, and there's nothing wrong with me talking about them.

   In general, I have much more to say about intelligent design, including much more to say about each of the leading intelligent design proponents, than I say in this book. If I put it all in, the book would be a monstrosity, whereas I'm trying to produce a pithy read. If you're wondering what I have to say about some particular issue that I don't talk about in this book, try my web page or blog (accessible via bradleymonton.com).

26. In fact, elsewhere Gage drops the "robust" qualifier. For example, he writes: "To see why Darwinism and theism are incompatible…," in "Deconstructing Dawkins."

27. For those who aren't familiar with this "weak" terminology, by saying that a doctrine should be weak, I'm not saying that the arguments given for the doctrine should be weak; I'm saying the doctrine itself should be formulated in such a way that it's more likely to be true.

28. Meyer, "Not by Chance."

29. Forrest, 1.

30. Rael, *Intelligent Design: Message from the Designers* (Surbiton, UK: Nova Distribution, 2006).

31. Elliott Sober, "Intelligent Design Theory and the Supernatural: the 'God or Extra-terrestrials' Reply," *Faith and Philosophy* 24 (2007): 72–82.

32. Sober, 79.

33. Sober, 73–74.

34. For the record, I think that there are other assumptions Sober is making besides the four that he highlights, but I'll just focus my discussion on the four he highlights. (I think another assumption comes into play in the step between point 5 and point 8, for example.)

35. Michael Behe, *Darwin's Black Box: The Biochemical Challenge to Evolution* (New York: Free Press, 1996).

36. A category mistake is made when a property is ascribed to something that couldn't possibly have that property. For example, if someone says "Bradley Monton is true," they're making a category mistake. Bradley Monton himself can't be true, though the claims Bradley Monton makes can be.

37. Sober, 75.

38. After Sober gives his diagram dividing the human mind up into six parts, he writes: "This division not only characterizes human beings; I suggest that it also describes the minds of intelligent beings who design and produce irreducibly complex systems, whether they happen to be human beings or not. This is the justification for premise (4)" (p. 74).

39. See for example Paul Churchland, *A Neurocomputational Perspective: The Nature of Mind and the Structure of Science* (Cambridge, MA: MIT Press, 1992).

40. Sober, 75.

41. See for example the discussion of the cyclic model in Paul Steinhardt and Neil Turok, *Endless Universe: Beyond the Big Bang* (New York: Doubleday, 2007). See also "The Cyclic Model Simplified," http://www.physics.princeton.edu/~steinh/dm2004.pdf, archived at http://www.webcitation.org/5c2naW8EI.

42. For more words of caution regarding making inferences from current physics, see my manuscript "Prolegomena to Any Future Physics-Based Metaphysics," http://philsci-archive.pitt.edu/archive/00004094/.

43. For details see J. Richard Gott, *Time Travel in Einstein's Universe: The Physical Possibilities of Travel Through Time* (Boston: Houghton Mifflin, 2001), Chapter 3.

Chapter Two

44. The paper is posted at http://philsci-archive.pitt.edu/archive/00002583/. I've made some minor edits to ensure stylistic compatibility with the rest of the book.

    Here's a general point I'd like to make about this chapter. While the specific arguments I give are mostly original with me, the general idea that it's legitimate to consider supernatural hypotheses in science is not. For some nice arguments for the thesis that it is legitimate, see Del Ratzsch, *Nature, Design, and Science: The Status of Design in Natural Science* (Albany, NY: SUNY Press, 2001), Chapters 9 and 10.

45. Judge Jones's decision, p. 2, http://www.pamd.uscourts.gov/kitzmiller/04cv2688-111.pdf, archived at http://www.webcitation.org/5bZpAS8Xe.

46. A Google search will reveal the details. Some places where it has been (approvingly) cited in print are in David K. DeWolf, John G. West and Casey Luskin, "Intelligent Design will Survive Kitzmiller v. Dover," *University of Montana Law Review* 68 (2007): 32; Yonatan Fishman, "Can Science Test Supernatural World Views?" *Science & Education*, forthcoming (published online August 2007); and Sahotra Sarkar, "The Science Question in Intelligent Design," *Synthese*, forthcoming.

47. Discovery Institute Center for Science and Culture, "Top Questions," http://www.discovery.org/csc/topQuestions.php, archived at http://www.webcitation.org/5bYHCDXYw.

48. Along the lines of, for example, Bas van Fraassen, *The Scientific Image* (New York: Oxford University Press, 1980).

49. Larry Laudan, "The Demise of the Demarcation Problem," in *But is it Science?*, ed. Michael Ruse (Amherst, NY: Prometheus, 1983), 349.

50. Judge Jones's decision, 64.

51. This note wasn't in the online paper, but as David Boonin has pointed out to me, I should have said that there are *at least* two problems with this criterion. For example, some would argue that a claim cannot be refuted by the scientific community if the claim itself is not scientific. So, if the scientific community can address and rebut intelligent design, then it automatically follows that intelligent design is scientific.

52. For more on this point, see Branden Fitelson, "Some Remarks on the 'Intelligent Design' Controversy" (2006), http://fitelson.org/id.pdf, archived at http://www.webcitation.org/5bd82TRGF.

53. Michael Behe, *Darwin's Black Box: The Biochemical Challenge to Evolution* (New York: Free Press, 1996).

54. For more on this argument, see the discussion in Chapter 3.

55. See for example Lee Strobel, *The Case for a Creator* (Grand Rapids, MI: Zondervan, 2004), 37–42.

56. I am not the first to present this sort of scenario; for a related scenario, see William Dembski, "The Incompleteness of Scientific Naturalism," in *Darwinism: Science or Philosophy*, ed. Jon Buell and Virginia Hearn (Foundation for Thought and Ethics, 1992), available at http://www.leaderu.com/orgs/fte/darwinism/chapter7.html, archived at http://www.webcitation.org/5bd7xoMzG.

57. Robert Pennock, Expert Report, 11, https://www.msu.edu/~pennock5/research/papers/Pennock_DoverExptRpt.pdf, archived at http://www.webcitation.org/5bd7vofH8.

58. Judge Jones's decision, 66.

59. Pennock, Expert Report, 29.

60. Pennock, Expert Report, 11; Pennock, Testimony of 28 September 2005, morning session, 28-29, http://www.discovery.org/scripts/viewDB/filesDB-download.php?command=download&id=552, archived at http://www.webcitation.org/5bd8lMFvD.

61. Pennock, Testimony of 28 September 2005, morning session, 29.

62. Mark Perakh, *Unintelligent Design* (Amherst, NY: Prometheus, 2004), 358.

63. Pennock, Testimony of 28 September 2005, morning session, 84.

64. Pennock, Testimony of 28 September 2005, morning session, 104–05.

65. Pennock, Testimony of 28 September 2005, morning session, p. 105.

66. Niall Shanks, *God, the Devil, and Darwin* (New York: Oxford University Press, 2004), 141–42.

67. Steve Fuller, as quoted in Judge Jones's decision, 67.

68. Pennock, Expert Report, 25.

69. Barbara Forrest, Expert Report, 1, http://www.creationismstrojanhorse.com/FORREST_EXPERT_REPORT.pdf, archived at http://www.webcitation.org/5bd9oKjIC.

70. For simplicity I will focus on the positive part of their doctrine, ignoring the "not an undirected process such as natural selection" part.

71. When I originally posted this paper online, I called "shintelligent shesign" "ID*," but it's been pointed out to me that while use of this "*" modifier is something that academic philosophers are familiar with, it's something that might be confusing to other readers.

72. For more information on the Raelians, see for example http://web.archive.org/web/20060829194959/religiousmovements.lib.virginia.edu/nrms/rael.html, archived at http://www.webcitation.org/5bd5DlHpp.

73. Nick Bostrom, "Are You Living in a Computer Simulation?" *Philosophical Quarterly* 53 (2003): 243–55.

74. A *disjunction* occurs when a claim is formed by joining two claims with an "or" clause. The claim on each side of the "or" clause is a *disjunct*. For example, the claim "grass is green or snow is white" is a disjunction, and in the context of that claim, "grass is green" is a disjunct, as is "snow is white."

75. Judge Jones's decision, 64.

76. Note that I'm not the only one to see a tension between what Pennock says in his testimony and what he says in his book. As intelligent design opponent Sahotra Sarkar writes, "Pennock's testimony … goes against the more nuanced discussion of Pennock (1999)." See Sahotra Sarkar, "The Science Question in Intelligent Design," *Synthese*, forthcoming, footnote 2.

77. To be clear, though, I endorse a stronger view—I don't want to just say that it's possible that future developments in science will lead to a situation where intelligent design counts as science; I want to say that it's now legitimate to count intelligent design as science. (I hold that trying to argue that intelligent design isn't science just does emotive work.)

78. *Tower of Babel*, 196.

79. To be more precise—they could give a particular account of what happened in the atom during the decay process, but as for why that process happened when it did, there's no answer.

80. *Tower of Babel*, 205.

81. Isaac Newton, *Opticks* (1704), Book 3, Part I.

82. "Lebnitz's First Paper," November 1715, in Samuel Clarke, *A Collection of Papers which passed between the late learned Mr. Leibnitz and Dr. Clarke in the years 1715 and 1716 relating to the Principles of Natural Philosophy and Religion* (1717).

83. *Tower of Babel*, 294.

84. This should go without saying, but given the criticisms I've gotten for pointing out that Newton doesn't endorse methodological naturalism, perhaps I should say it: in claiming that Newton doesn't endorse methodological naturalism, I am not claiming that Newton's postulation of supernatural involvement was the ideal scientific postulation to make in the circumstances that he was in. Perhaps it's even the case that Newton's postulation of supernatural involvement impeded the progress of science; I don't know enough history to say. (Perhaps it's the case that Newton's postulation of supernatural involvement advanced the progress of science, by encouraging future scientists to investigate the stability of orbits; again, I don't know enough history to say.) All I am claiming is that (a) Newton was a great scientist; (b) Newton did not follow the rule of methodological naturalism; (c) Newton's postulation of supernatural involvement did not stop the progress of science; and (d) Newton's postulation of supernatural involvement did not lead to absolute chaos in the scientific worldview.

85. *Tower of Babel*, 202–03.

86. *Tower of Babel*, 289–90.

87. *Tower of Babel*, 290.

88. *Tower of Babel*, 292.

89. See for example Carol Cleland, "Methodological and Epistemic Differences between Historical Science and Experimental Science," *Philosophy of Science* 69 (2002): 474–96.

90. See, for example, Harvard Medical School News Release, "Largest Study of Third-Party Prayer Suggests Such Prayer Not Effective In Reducing Complications Following Heart Surgery" (2006), http://web.med.harvard.edu/sites/RELEASES/html/3_31STEP.html, archived at http://www.webcitation.org/5bjyHkZAf.

91. *Tower of Babel*, 194.

92. *Tower of Babel*, 195.

93. *Tower of Babel*, 304.

94. *Tower of Babel*, 302.

95. *Tower of Babel*, 303.

96. *Tower of Babel*, 308.

97. *Tower of Babel*, 307.

98. Philip Johnson, *Reason in the Balance: The Case Against Naturalism in Science, Law, and Education* (Downers Grove, IL: InterVarsity Press, 1995), 110; quoted in *Tower of Babel*, 306.

99. *Tower of Babel*, 306.

100. Young and Edis, *Why Intelligent Design Fails*, 8.

Chapter Three

101. While some proponents of the fine-tuning argument cap the possible range of forces at $10^{40}G$, that cap doesn't seem justified. In fact, it seems possible that the value of the gravitational constant could be arbitrarily large. This point is made by for example, Tim McGrew, Lydia McGrew, and Eric Vestrup, who argue that it leads to the downfall of the fine-tuning argument. See McGrew, McGrew, and Vestrup, "Probabilities and the Fine-Tuning Argument: A Sceptical View," *Mind* 110 (2001): 1027–37.

    For a reply to their argument see my 2006 paper "God, Fine-Tuning, and the Problem of Old Evidence," *British Journal for the Philosophy of Science* 57: 405–24, http://spot.colorado.edu/~monton/BradleyMonton/Articles_files/FT%20paper%20BJPS.pdf, archived at http://www.webcitation.org/5box77RZV.

102. Stephen Barr, *Modern Physics and Ancient Faith* (Notre Dame, IN: Notre Dame University Press, 2003), 118–37.

103. Steven Weinberg, "A Designer Universe?" *New York Review of Books*, 21 October 1999, http://www.physlink.com/Education/essay_weinberg.cfm, archived at http://www.webcitation.org/5boy20ErD.

104. See Robin Collins, "Evidence for Fine-Tuning," in *God and Design: The Teleological Argument and Modern Science*, ed. Neil Manson (New York: Routledge, 2003), 178–99.

105. For more related to the line of reasoning I'm pushing here, see Michael Huemer, "Is Critical Thinking Epistemically Responsible?" *Metaphilosophy* 36 (2005): 522–31.

106. The reason I think it's lower is that I think there's a non-zero probability that God would want life, but would not care whether the life was embodied. In fact, I think it would be rather strange for someone to feel absolutely certain that, in a situation where God wants life, God wants embodied life.

    Here and elsewhere, when I talk about God wanting life, I'm talking about God wanting *created* life—at least some theists would say that God himself is alive, but that's not the sort of life I'm talking about God wanting.

107. Richard Dawkins, *The God Delusion* (Boston: Houghton Mifflin, 2006), 146–47.

108. Bas van Fraassen, *The Scientific Image* (New York: Oxford University Press, 1980), 90.

109. I have a lot more to say about the fine-tuning argument, beyond what I've said here. See for example my 2006 paper "God, Fine-Tuning, and the Problem of Old Evidence," *British Journal for the Philosophy of Science* 57: 405–24, http://spot.colorado.edu/~monton/BradleyMonton/Articles_files/FT%20paper%20BJPS.pdf, archived at http://www.webcitation.org/5box77RZV. I've been working on a book that's all about physics-based arguments for the existence of God; I've currently written over 30,000 words on the fine-tuning argument alone.

110. For more on the hypothesis that the universe caused itself to exist, see J. Richard Gott, *Time Travel in Einstein's Universe: The Physical Possibilities of Travel Through Time* (Boston: Houghton Mifflin, 2001), Chapter 4.

111. William Lane Craig, *The Kalam Cosmological Argument* (Eugene, OR: Wipf and Stock, 1979), 141.

112. John Norton, "Causation as Folk Science," *Philosophers' Imprint* 3,4 (2003), http://www.philosophersimprint.org/003004/.

113. William Rowe, "Cosmological Arguments," in *The Blackwell Guide to the Philosophy of Religion*, ed. William Mann (Oxford: Blackwell, 2005), 115.

114. See C.L. Bennett, et al., "First-year Wilkinson Microwave Anisotropy Probe (WMAP) Observations: Preliminary Maps and Basic Results," *Astrophysical Journal Supplement Series* 148 (2003): 1–27, and D.N. Spergel, et al., "First-year Wilkinson Microwave Anisotropy Probe (WMAP) Observations: Determination of Cosmological Parameters," *Astrophysical Journal Supplement Series* 148 (2003): 175–94. See also "Is the Universe Infinite?" at http://map.gsfc.nasa.gov/universe/uni_shape.html, archived at http://www.webcitation.org/5bnkjQefh.

115. See for example J. Brian Pitts, "Why the Big Bang Singularity does not Help the Kalam Cosmological Argument for Theism," *British Journal for the Philosophy of Science*, forthcoming, preprint available at http://philsci-archive.pitt.edu/archive/00003496/. For an informal reply by William Lane Craig see his "Question 80: J. Brian Pitts on the *Kalam* Cosmological Argument," http://www.reasonablefaith.org/site/PageServer?pagename=q_and_a, archived at http://www.webcitation.org/5c2ipqamO. I wrote this paragraph before seeing Craig's reply, but the reader of both will see that our replies are consistent.

116. William Lane Craig, *The Kalam Cosmological Argument* (New York: Macmillan, 1979), 130.

117. J. Richard Gott, James Gunn, David Schramm, and Beatrice Tinsley, "Will the Universe Expand Forever?" *Scientific American* (March 1976): 65.

118. Bas van Fraassen, *The Scientific Image* (New York: Oxford University Press, 1980).

119. Gott et al., 65.

120. For discussion of the idea that string theory has many models, see for example Leonard Susskind, *The Cosmic Landscape: String Theory and the Illusion of Intelligent Design* (New York: Back Bay Books, 2005).

121. This isn't just an outré worry—there are models of the universe, informed by general relativity and quantum physics, that are compatible with the universe having been in existence forever. See for example the discussion of the cyclic model in Paul Steinhardt and Neil Turok, *Endless Universe: Beyond the Big Bang* (New York: Doubleday, 2007). See also "The Cyclic Model Simplified," http://www.physics.princeton.edu/~steinh/dm2004.pdf, archived at http://www.webcitation.org/5c2naW8EI.

122. William Lane Craig, "The Finitude of the Past and the Existence of God," in *Theism, Atheism, and Big Bang Cosmology*, ed. William Lane Craig and Quentin Smith (New York: Oxford University Press, 1993), 67–69.

123. For some related discussion regarding the kalam cosmological argument, see my manuscript "Prolegomena to Any Future Physics-Based Metaphysics," http://philsci-archive.pitt.edu/archive/00004094/.

124. Francis Crick, *Life Itself: Its Origin and Nature* (New York: Simon and Schuster, 1981), 88.

125. Robert Shapiro, *Origins: A Skeptic's Guide to the Creation of Life on Earth* (New York: Bantam, 1986), 127.

126. See, for example, the discussion of the problem of old evidence in my 2006 paper "God, Fine-Tuning, and the Problem of Old Evidence," *British Journal for the Philosophy of Science* 57: 405–24, http://spot.colorado.edu/~monton/BradleyMonton/Articles_files/FT%20paper%20BJPS.pdf, archived at http://www.webcitation.org/5box77RZV.

127. For pre-WMAP evidence that the universe is spatially infinite, see Neta Bahcall, Jeremiah Ostriker, Saul Perlmutter, and Paul Steinhardt, "The Cosmic Triangle: Revealing the State of the Universe," *Science* 284 (1999): 1481–88. For the WMAP evidence, see Spergel et al. and Bennett et al., cited

above. See also "Is the Universe Infinite?" at http://map.gsfc.nasa.gov/universe/uni_shape.html, archived at http://www.webcitation.org/5bnkjQefh. To be precise, the WMAP evidence is that, on a large scale, the universe is spatially flat. It is mathematically possible for the universe to be spatially flat and yet finite, but such non-standard topologies are usually rejected by physicists. In addition to the empirical evidence, there is theoretical support for the hypothesis that the universe is spatially infinite. Most versions of inflationary cosmology make this prediction, as explained by Andrei Linde, "Inflationary Cosmology," *Physics Reports* 333/34 (2000): 584–86.

    For information on how the universe could be flat and yet finite, see for example O. Heckmann and E. Schücking, "Relativistic Cosmology," in *Gravitation: An Introduction to Current Research*, ed. Louis Witten (New York: Wiley, 1962), 438–69. For an accessible discussion of one (highly contentious) proposal for how space could be flat and yet finite, consistent with the WMAP data, see Dennis Overbye, "Cosmic Soccer Ball? Theory Already Takes Sharp Kicks," *New York Times*, 9 October 2003, http://www2.math.uic.edu/~agol/blog/Soccer.htm, archived at http://www.webcitation.org/5bp2ikJtB. For more general discussion, see European Space Agency, "Is the Universe Finite or Infinite? An Interview with Joseph Silk" (2001), http://www.esa.int/esaSC/SEMR53T1VED_index_0_iv.html, archived at http://www.webcitation.org/5bp3IOlZ2. Note that that interview was conducted before the WMAP data came out; the majority view is that the WMAP data do not provide evidence for the flat but finite universe possibility that Silk discusses.

128. For a more technical discussion of these further conditions, see G.F.R. Ellis and G.B. Brundrit, "Life in the Infinite Universe," *Quarterly Journal of the Royal Astronomical Society* 20 (1979): 37–38. For some evidence that these conditions hold, see Max Tegmark, "Parallel Universes," in *Science and Ultimate Reality: Quantum Theory, Cosmology, and Complexity*, ed. John Barrow, Paul Davies, and Charles Harper (Cambridge: Cambridge University Press, 2003), 463.

129. If this last sentence confuses you, here's an analogy that might help. I believe that God doesn't exist, just as I believe that there's not going to be a tornado in Boulder tomorrow, even though I think there's a non-zero probability that God exists, just as I think there's a non-zero probability that there will be a tornado in Boulder tomorrow.

    For more on these infinite universe issues, see my paper "Design Inferences in an Infinite Universe," forthcoming in *Oxford Studies in Philosophy of Religion Volume II*, Oxford University Press. A draft is available at http://philsci-archive.pitt.edu/archive/00003997/.

130. Antony Flew and Gary Habermas, "My Pilgrimage from Atheism to Theism: An Exclusive Interview with Former British Atheist Professor Antony Flew," *Philosophia Christi* (2004), published online at http://www.biola.edu/antonyflew/flew-interview.pdf, archived at http://www.webcitation.org/5bp4I07oX. This portion of the interview is interesting, for a couple of reasons. Here's the full text:

> *Flew*: I think that the most impressive arguments for God's existence are those that are supported by recent scientific discoveries. I've never been much impressed by the *kalam* cosmological argument, and I don't think it has gotten any stronger recently. However, I think the argument to Intelligent Design is enormously stronger than it was when I first met it.
>
> *Habermas*: So you like arguments such as those that proceed from big bang cosmology and fine tuning arguments?
>
> *Flew*: Yes.

One of the interesting things about this is that, while normally the first thing that comes to mind when one talks about intelligent design arguments are biology-based arguments, Habermas immediately makes the connection to physics-based arguments. Another interesting thing about this is that, while Flew has just said that he's unimpressed with the kalam cosmological argument, Habermas gets him to agree that a design argument proceeding from big bang cosmology is promising. The only design argument I know of that proceeds from big bang cosmology is the kalam cosmological argument.

131. "Letter from Antony Flew on Darwinism and Theology," *Philosophy Now* 47 (August/September 2004): 22.

132. Letter to Roy Varghese, http://www.thewonderoftheworld.com/Sections1-article227-page1.html, archived at http://www.webcitation.org/5bp5SW6tq. For further developments of Flew's position, see Antony Flew, *God and Philosophy* (Amherst, NY: Prometheus Books, 2005), 11.

133. See Michael Behe, *Darwin's Black Box: the Biochemical Challenge to Evolution* (New York: Free Press, 1996) and Michael Behe, *The Edge of Evolution: The Search for the Limits of Darwinism* (New York: Free Press, 2007).

134. *Darwin's Black Box*, 39.

135. For the bacterial flagellum, for example, see N.J. Matzke, "Evolution in (Brownian) Space: A Model for the Origin of the Bacterial Flagellum," (2003), http://www.talkdesign.org/faqs/flagellum.html, archived at http://www.webcitation.org/5dpR2iQaZ. Also see the partial guide to the literature provided by N.J. Matzke, "Background to 'Evolution in (Brownian) Space: A Model for the Origin of the Bacterial Flagellum,'" (2006), http://www.talkdesign.org/faqs/flagellum_background.html, archived at http://www.webcitation.org/5dpR6HTSN. Matzke writes in the latter piece: "As no one has ever really given the topic of flagellar origins the serious treatment it deserves, there is currently no such thing as an expert." Biologists don't have a definite account for how the bacterial flagellum actually evolved, though they do have plausible hypotheses.

136. For just one set of examples, see many of the essays in Matt Young and Taner Edis, eds., *Why Intelligent Design Fails: A Scientific Critique of the New Creationism* (Piscataway, NJ: Rutgers University Press, 2004).

137. Kenneth Miller, "Answering the Biochemical Argument from Design," in N. Manson (ed.), *God and Design: The Teleological Argument and Modern Science* (New York: Routledge, 2003), 293. Preprint available at http://www.millerandlevine.com/km/evol/design1/article.html, archived at http://www.webcitation.org/5dpTVpNsn.

138. *Darwin's Black Box*, 73.

139. Michael Behe, *The Edge of Evolution: The Search for the Limits of Darwinism* (New York: Free Press, 2007), 222.

140. *The Edge of Evolution*, 222.

141. *The Edge of Evolution*, 222.

142. *The Edge of Evolution*, 223.

143. *The Edge of Evolution*, 225.

144. *The Edge of Evolution*, 227.

145. While I think this account is right, I recognize that more would need to be said here to fully defend this account. I don't think anyone has given an adequate defense of this account, so I'm currently working on a paper on this topic, tentatively entitled "Probabilistic Inferences in an Infinite Universe."

146. Ken Miller, *Only A Theory: Evolution and the Battle for America's Soul* (New York: Viking, 2008), 183.

147. William Dembski, *Intelligent Design: The Bridge Between Science & Theology* (Downers Grove, IL: InterVarsity Press, 1999), 14–15; quoted in *Only A Theory*, 190. In addition to discussing this passage from Dembski, Miller also discusses the 1998 Wedge Document and the opinions of the 2005 Kansas Board of Education, but it's unfair to take either of these as providing the current opinions of the most intellectually sophisticated proponents of intelligent design, such as Dembski and Behe.

148. *Only a Theory*, 190.

149. Note that saying that Dembski is pro-science doesn't imply that he always does good science; one can be pro-science and also make a lot of false claims about science.

150. *Intelligent Design: The Bridge Between Science & Theology*, 13.

151. William Dembski, "Skepticism's Prospects for Unseating Intelligent Design" (2002), http://www.discovery.org/a/1185, archived at http://www.webcitation.org/5dsVoaUwo.

152. *Only A Theory*, 198.

153. *Only a Theory*, 217.

154. Denis Alexander, *Creation or Evolution: Do We Have to Choose?* (Toronto: Monarch Books, 2008), 314.

155. *Creation or Evolution*, 306.

156. For a nice article on this topic of how the designer could intervene, see Al Plantinga, "What is 'Intervention'?" *Theology and Science* 6 (2008): 369–401.

157. And indeed, we don't know where ultra-high-energy cosmic rays come from. "The origin of ultra-high-energy cosmic rays is one of the great mysteries of cosmology.... No one understands how ... any known phenomena ... makes these rays." Katharine Sanderson, "Cosmic-Ray Source Still in Doubt," *Nature* (2007), doi:10.1038/news.2007.266. This should go without saying, but just to be absolutely clear: I personally do not think that cosmic rays will turn out to be the product of an intelligent cause.

158. Nick Bostrom, "Are You Living in a Computer Simulation?" *Philosophical Quarterly* 53 (2003): 243–55, preprint available at http://www.simulation-argument.com/simulation.pdf, archived at http://www.webcitation.org/5bp6Hb7Iu.

159. To be precise: the simulation argument has the consequence that your mind, and indeed the whole universe that you experience yourself living in, is the product of a computer simulation. In this sense, the simulation argument is an intelligent design argument—your mind, and the universe as you experience it, is the product of an intelligent designer. In response to this section of my book, some have objected that the simulation argument doesn't really count as an intelligent design argument, because it doesn't show that the *real* universe—the one that the beings running the computer simulation are living in—is designed. (It could be the case that the beings simulating our universe are also living in a computer simulation, but (presumably?) the chain of simulations would have an end somewhere.) I take the simulation argument to be an intelligent design argument, because it has the consequence that our minds, and the universe that we take ourselves to be living in, are all the product of a designer. But if someone wanted to put their foot down and say that the simulation argument isn't an intelligent design argument, I don't have any knock-down way to show that I'm right; at this point it just becomes a matter of terminology.

160. Adam Elga, "Defeating Dr. Evil with Self-Locating Belief," *Philosophy and Phenomenological Research* 69 (2004): 383–96, preprint available at http://www.princeton.edu/~adame/papers/drevil/drevil.pdf, archived at http://www.webcitation.org/5bp6qw52V.

161. We don't have much reason to think that the real, physical universe is spatially infinite, because if we're living in a computer simulation, all the empirical reasons we thought we had, like the reasons provided by the WMAP data, actually don't apply to the real, physical universe. But we might have *some* reason to think that the real, physical universe is spatially infinite. For example, we could think it more likely that there would be civilizations running computer simulations in an infinite universe than in a finite universe.

    I don't have a definite account of what we should think here, and the reason I don't is that a full discussion of this point would get into the tricky question of whether the Self-Indication Assumption is true. The Self-Indication Assumption basically holds that finding that you exist gives you reason to think that there are many observers (since the more observers there are, the more likely it is that you would exist). Nick Bostrom argues against the Self-Indication Assumption in his 2001 paper "The Doomsday Argument, Adam and Eve, UN++, and Quantum Joe," *Synthese*

127: 359–87. I give a partial defense of the Self-Indication Assumption in my 2003 paper "The Doomsday Argument Without Knowledge of Birth Rank," *Philosophical Quarterly* 53: 79–82, http://spot.colorado.edu/~monton/BradleyMonton/Articles_files/Monton%20Doomsday%20Birth%20Rank.pdf, archived at http://www.webcitation.org/5bzqlSrD2. I'm still not completely sure whether or not the Self-Indication Assumption is true.

162. Or at least, any other *non-extremal* probability assignment does. By "non-extremal," I mean non-0 and non-1. Assigning 0 to both the premise and the conclusion, and assigning 1 to both the premise and conclusion, are stable assignments, simply because, according to standard probability at least, those assignments can't be revised in light of new evidence. Also, regarding the "as far as I can tell" qualifier, that's put in there because I'm not that confident about what I'm saying here; I (and hopefully other people too) will think about this more.

163. It would be hard for us to get conclusive evidence that that is the case. But suppose we were able to measure every constant out to hundreds of decimal places, and we got "0" for every number after the sixteenth decimal place; that would provide significant evidence that the decimal representations stop after 16 digits.

164. To do the math takes some knowledge of probability theory, and I'm not going to try to explain probability theory here. But in case you're interested here's the calculation: Bayes' rule holds that the probability of the explosion, given that one didn't hear anything, $P(E|{\sim}H)$, is equal to $P({\sim}H|E)$ $P(E)$ / $[P({\sim}H|E)$ $P(E)$ + $P({\sim}H|{\sim}E)$ $P({\sim}E)]$, which equals 0.9×0.2 / $(0.9 \times 0.2 + 1 \times 0.8)$, which equals $0.18/0.98$, which is about 0.184.

165. I am assuming for simplicity that there's no chance that the decimal representations would all stop at 16 digits if we weren't living in a simulation. Taking that possibility into account would lead to a probability higher than 18.4 per cent (but still less than 20 per cent).

Chapter Four

166. From http://www.mbhs.edu/departments/socialstudies/, archived at http://www.webcitation.org/5cHOhHxpF.

167. From http://www.discovery.org/csc/topQuestions.php#questionsAboutScienceEducationPolicy, archived at http://www.webcitation.org/5cHOqqThu.

168. I wouldn't necessarily want to go with just whichever approach would benefit the majority of the students, since it could be that the majority of students would receive a minor benefit from the approach, while a small number of students would suffer significant pedagogical harm. If the alternative approach would only cause minor pedagogical harm to a majority of the students, and significant pedagogical benefit to a minority, the alternative approach could well be preferable.

169. See for example J.A. Shymansky, W.C. Kyle, and J.M. Alport, "The Effects of New Science Curricula on Student Performance," *Journal of Research in Science Teaching* 24 (1983): 39–51.

170. From Carl Weiman, "Reinventing Science Education," *Korea Times*, 25 February 2008, http://www.koreatimes.co.kr/www/news/opinon/2008/02/137_19559.html, archived at http://www.webcitation.org/5cI10Maic. In the passage I quoted, Weiman is talking about university education, but the research that he is talking about applies to pre-college education as well. For more by Weiman see his 2006 testimony before Congress, available at http://science.house.gov/commdocs/hearings/research06/march%2015/weiman.pdf, archived at http://www.webcitation.org/5cI19Z9lo. An example of the sort of study Weiman is talking about is Song-Ling Mao, Chun-Yen Chang, and James Barufaldi, "Inquiry Teaching and Its Effects on Secondary-School Students' Learning of Earth Science Concepts," *Journal of Geoscience Education* 46 (1998): 363–68, http://www.nagt.org/files/nagt/jge/abstracts/mao-chang-baruf.pdf, archived at http://www.webcitation.org/5cI1PF6uK.

171. In a 2005 Pew survey, just 26 per cent of respondents held that living things evolved through natural selection, not guided by a supreme being. The survey also reports that 18 per cent believed in guided evolution, while 42 per cent believed that living things have existed in their present form only. See The Pew Forum on Religion & Public Life, "Public Divided on Origins of Life" (2005), http://pewforum.org/surveys/origins/#3, archived at http://www.webcitation.org/5cI3ZQyzn.

172. Louisiana Science Education Act (2008), http://www.legis.state.la.us/billdata/streamdocument.asp?did=482728, archived at http://www.webcitation.org/5cI4bd0A2.

173. Though, as David Boonin has pointed out to me, it's easier to enforce a rule that says "don't teach intelligent design at all" than to enforce one that says "don't teach it in a bad or proselytizing way." So it could be that if one allows intelligent design to be taught, it will largely be taught in an objectionable manner and that if one forbids it to be taught, it will largely not be taught at all. This would provide a pragmatic argument for banning the teaching of intelligent design—even though, if it were taught in the right way, it would overall be pedagogically beneficial to the students.

174. Michael B. Berkman, Julianna Sandell Pacheco, and Eric Plutze, "Evolution and Creationism in America's Classrooms: A National Portrait," *PLoS Biology* (2008), available at http://biology.plosjournals.org/perlserv/?request=get-document&doi=10.1371%2Fjournal.pbio.0060124&ct=1, archived at http://www.webcitation.org/5cI4bd0A2.

175. General Conference 2008, Petition 80839, "Evolution and Intelligent Design," http://calms.umc.org/2008/Menu.aspx?type=Petition&mode=Single&Number=80839, archived at http://www.webcitation.org/5cIx1Adv2.

176. Eugenie Scott, "Creation Science Lite: 'Intelligent Design' as the New Anti-Evolutionism," in *Scientists Confront Intelligent Design and Creationism*, ed. Andrew Petto and Laurie Godfrey (New York: W.W. Norton, 2007), 101.

177. "Intelligent Design is Not Science" (2005), http://web.archive.org/web/20060115091707/http://www.science.unsw.edu.au/news/2005/intelligent.html, archived at http://www.webcitation.org/5cIxZtBrf.

178. Francis Crick, *Life Itself: Its Origin and Nature* (New York: Simon and Schuster, 1981).

179. Scott, 92.

180. Andrew Petto and Laurie Godfrey, "Why Teach Evolution?" in *Scientists Confront Intelligent Design and Creationism*, ed. Petto and Godfrey (New York: W.W. Norton, 2007), 409.

181. John Cole, "Wielding the Wedge: Keeping Anti-Evolutionism Alive," in *Scientists Confront Intelligent Design and Creationism*, ed. Andrew Petto and Laurie Godfrey (New York: W.W. Norton, 2007), 123.

182. See *Science Framework for California Public Schools*, adopted by the California State Board of Education in 2004, p. ix, available at http://www.cde.ca.gov/ci/cr/cf/documents/scienceframework.pdf, archived at http://www.webcitation.org/5cJShNG5k.

183. For this sort of reason, Robert Pennock expresses some sympathies with the idea that creationism should be taught in science classes. He writes:

> As John Dewey pointed out, science education is a failure if it consists of nothing more than the recitation and memorization of scientific facts. To teach science well is to teach the methods of scientific reasoning, and a critical examination of creationism could serve very well for this purpose. It is because of the possible pedagogic utility of this approach that I actually find myself of two minds about whether teachers should introduce creationism into their science lesson plans.

Ultimately, though, he comes down against teaching creationism:

> [I]ntroducing creationism in the science classroom would necessarily place [students'] religious beliefs under critical scrutiny.... Given that we expect the government to

neither help nor hinder religion, it does not seem wise policy to open the door to having children's religious beliefs explicitly analyzed and rebutted in the public schools in this way.

I have three thoughts about this. First, I think I might be more willing to have science teachers explicitly present evidence against students' religious beliefs than Pennock is. But second, teachers can present evidence against students' religious beliefs without *rebutting* those beliefs—if students are used to teachers presenting arguments for and against various doctrines, then the students would recognize that they have to evaluate the evidence to decide whether it constituted a rebuttal. Third and finally, I think it's unfortunate that Pennock focuses on creationism instead of intelligent design. It's true that creationist doctrines are typically closely linked to religious views, but intelligent design doctrines (as I've argued) are not so closely linked. Thus, it could be easier for teachers to take up intelligent design issues without getting into battles over students' religious beliefs.

The Pennock quotations come from his 2001 paper "Why Creationism Should Not Be Taught in the Public Schools," in *Intelligent Design Creationism and its Critics*, ed. Robert Pennock (Cambridge, MA: MIT Press, 2001), 763, 771–72.

184. As quoted in Lewis Smith and Mark Henderson, "Royal Society's Michael Reiss Resigns Over Creationism Row," *The Times*, 17 September 2008, http://www.timesonline.co.uk/tol/news/uk/science/article4768820.ece, archived at http://www.webcitation.org/5cJUhDU4u.

185. Petto and Godfrey, 408.

186. Petto and Godfrey, 422.

187. Petto and Godfrey, 423.

188. Moreover, there is empirical evidence that pre-college students in the United States aren't learning science as well as students in other countries. See for example the research by William Schmidt discussed in "Researchers Find Systemic Problem in U.S. Mathematics and Science Education," *New Educator* (Fall 2000), http://www.educ.msu.edu/neweducator/Fall00/Timss.htm, archived at http://www.webcitation.org/5cJWQuk9D.

INDEX

ACLU (American Civil Liberties Union), 48
Alexander, Denis, 114–16
    Creation or Evolution, 114
alien minds, 18, 41, 44–45, 52, 57, 149
atheism, 7–8, 13, 18, 20, 39, 133
Australian Academy of Science, 150

backwards causation, 90. *See also* time travel
bad people/good arguments, 13
Barr, Stephen, 81
    Modern Physics and Ancient Faith, 80
Behe, Michael, 43–44, 50–51, 54, 105–08
    Darwin's Black Box, 107, 154
    The Edge of Evolution, 107
    freak observers, 110
    irreducible complexity argument, 111,
        114–16, 142, 150–51
    science-based arguments, 154
big bang, 45, 95-96, 98–99, 167n130
    quantum theory and, 97
big crunch, 45
biology-based arguments for intelligent design,
    30, 32, 51, 142. *See also* irreducible
    complexity
Bostrom, Nick, 57, 118, 127
brain in a vat, 110, 120, 146
Broad, C.D., 94–95

category mistakes, 162n36
    mind/brain category mistake, 44
causation
    backwards, 90
    counterfactual analysis of, 89–90

simultaneous, 90–91
supernatural, 51
universe as cause of its own existence, 21
causation is just folk science, 91–92
causes precede effects assumption, 46
church and state, 11, 48, 149
classical electromagnetism, 144
Cleland, Carol, 164n89
Cole, John, 153
common descent belief, 24, 112, 154
comparative religion, 134–35, 150
computer simulation scenario, 41, 57. *See also*
    simulation argument
consensus by scientists, 53–56, 151–52, 156
cosmological argument. *See* kalam cosmologi-
    cal argument
counterfactual analysis of causation, 89–90
Craig, William Lane, 87–88, 94–95, 97
    The Kalam Cosmological Argument, 96
    *Theism, Atheism, and Big Bang Cosmol-
        ogy*, 98
Creation or Evolution (Alexander), 114
creationism, 16, 31–32, 49, 55, 59, 112
    "equal time" in science classes, 11, 14, 132,
        136, 151
Crick, Francis, 99, 151
"cultural renewal" focus of intelligent design,
    14
culture war, 9, 12, 59, 157
cyclic model of the universe, 45

dart-throwing analogies, 77–78, 103

173